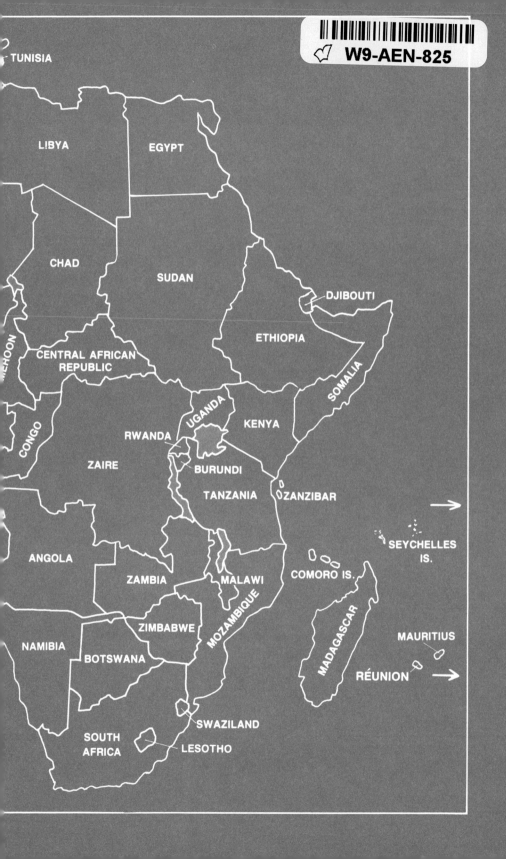

Photo: Steven Bushell

Robert I. Rotberg is Academic Vice-President for Arts, Sciences, and Technology, Tufts University, and formerly was professor of history and political science at M.I.T. He is a trustee of Oberlin College and the World Peace Foundation.

Robert I. Rotberg is the author and editor of a number of books on southern Africa, including: *Suffer the Future: Policy Choices in Southern Africa* (1980), *South Africa and its Neighbors: Regional Security and Self-Interest* (1985), *Namibia: Political and Economic Prospects* (1983), *Conflict and Compromise in South Africa* (1980). He also writes regularly for the *New York Times* and the *Christian Science Monitor*.

Africa
in the 1990s
—and beyond

Africa

Tunis
TUNISIA
Algiers
Rabat
Tripoli
MOROCCO
Benghazi
Cairo
El-Ayoun
ALGERIA
LIBYA
EGYPT

CAPE VERDE
MAURITANIA
Praia
Nouakchott
MALI
Khartoum
SENEGAL
Dakar
Bamako
NIGER
CHAD
DJIBOUTI
GAMBIA
Banjul
BURKINA FASO
Niamey
SUDAN
Djibouti
Conakry
Ouagadougou
GUINEA
Ndjamena
GUINEA-BISSAU
Bissau
BENIN
NIGERIA
ETHIOPIA
SIERRA LEONE
IVORY COAST
GHANA
Porto Novo
Addis Ababa
Freetown
Monrovia
Abidjan
Accra
Lagos
CENTRAL AFRICAN REPUBLIC
SOMALIA
LIBERIA
TOGO
Lomé
Malabo
CAMEROON
Yaoundé
Bangui
EQUATORIAL GUINEA
Libreville
UGANDA
KENYA
Mogadishu
SÃO TOMÉ E
GABON
CONGO
RWANDA
Kampala
Nairobi
SEYCHELLES IS.
PRÍNCIPE
ZAIRE
Kigali
Brazzaville
Bujumbura
Victoria
Kinshasa
BURUNDI
ZANZIBAR
TANZANIA
Dar es Salaam
Luanda
COMORO IS.
Lilongwe
Moroni
ANGOLA
ZAMBIA
MALAWI
Lusaka
MAURITIUS
Harare
Antananarivo
Port Louis
NAMIBIA
ZIMBABWE
RÉUNION
Windhoek
MADAGASCAR
BOTSWANA
Gaborone
Pretoria
Maputo
Mbabane
SWAZILAND
Maseru
SOUTH AFRICA
LESOTHO

AFRICA

in the 1990s and Beyond

U.S. Policy Opportunities and Choices

Edited by

ROBERT I. ROTBERG

A World Peace Foundation Study

REFERENCE PUBLICATIONS, INC.

Published 1988

Copyright © World Peace Foundation

Printed in the United States of America

Library of Congress Cataloging-in-Publication Data

Africa in the 1990s—and beyond : U.S. policy opportunities and
choices / edited by Robert I. Rotberg.
    p. cm. — (A World Peace Foundation Study)
    Includes index.
    ISBN 0-917256-43-3 : $24.95. ISBN 0-917256-44-1 (pbk.) : $12.95
    1. Africa—Relations—United States. 2. United States—Relations—
—Africa. 3. Africa—Forecasting. I. Rotberg, Robert I.
II. Series.
DT38.A44 1988
303.4'8273'06—dc19   88-6724
                                  CIP

Library of Congress Catalog Card Number: 88-6724
International Standard Book Number: 0-917256-43-3 (hardcover)
                          0-917256-44-1 (paperback)

Reference Publications, Inc.
218 St. Clair River Drive, Box 344
Algonac, Michigan 48001

Preface

Under the auspices of the World Peace Foundation of Boston, in October 1987 I convened a conference with the same title as has this book. The conference was held in idyllic surroundings at the Bald Peak Colony Club on Lake Winnipesaukee in New Hampshire. For their shared wisdom and good companionship, I am grateful to the participants: Henry S. Bienen, Mohamed T. El-Ashry, William J. Foltz, Kenneth W. Grundy, Mark N. Katz, Helen Kitchen, David Laitin, E. Gibson Lanpher, G. Andrew Maguire, Charles N. Myers, Donald S. Rothchild, Jeswald W. Salacuse, Newell Stultz, and John Underwood. Rhoda Fischer and Prunella Fiddian-Green organized us all with great flair.

On behalf of all of us, I also thank the other trustees of the World Peace Foundation and Ambassador Richard Bloomfield, its executive director, and Margaret Kourbetis, his assistant, for their enduring support.

— R.I.R.

3 March 1988

Contents

List of Tables, Figures, and Charts

TABLES

FIGURES

CHART

1: A New U.S. Policy For Africa

by ROBERT I. ROTBERG

Africa—its 53 nations, 600 million people, and 12 million square miles astride crucial trade routes and at least one war zone—presents fresh opportunities for the next president of the United States, his secretary of state, and the entire policy making community. After eight years characterized by few successful initiatives and a largely reactive overall policy posture, a new administration will be obliged to address the futures of Libya and North Africa, Somalia and Ethiopia, and South Africa. It will need to concentrate its attention on the economic rebuilding and a resolution of the debt crisis of black Africa, the arms race in the continent and the drift toward small wars, Africa's massive public health menace, its recurrent food shortages, the degradation of its environment, and the increasing pressure of its multiplying population. It will want to be certain of Africa's real place in global politics. The agenda is daunting, but inescapable.

The United States has critical interests in Africa: the search for a solution to the growing conflict between black and white in South Africa, the prevention of the further ascendancy of the Soviet Union in sections of Africa like Ethiopia and Angola, and ending, avoiding, or diminishing the heat of those regional conflicts which could help disseminate Soviet influence across the continent. The United States will be faced with the need to halt the spread of AIDS within Africa and to help relieve famine and break the cycles of recurrent hunger that have beset much of the continent. We should have a profound interest in reducing rampant population growth, preserving Africa's fragile national resource base, helping Africa to return to agricultural self-sufficiency, lessening or eliminating Africa's heavy burden of debt, and—overall—in transforming Africa from a collection of largely failing economies into an array of promising if not yet prosperous states capable of feeding themselves and sponsoring improvements in real income generation capabilities.

The United States has almost always sought to promote peace (not always by peaceful means) and economic growth, but it has not invariably done so responsibly or effectively. Its macroeconomic policies have undercut even generous examples of targeted economic assistance. Likewise, the United States espouses human rights in Africa, but has supported repressive regimes and pursued policies which have placed considerations of global strategy and mineral availability before any detailed attention to the participatory character of local governments.

Stability—a sound administration, and the absence of internal tumult—has been a prime interest, as has a country's ideological bent. But there is a growing realization that Africa has value for the United States beyond its geographical proximity to the Middle East, beyond its trade opportunities, beyond its oil, beyond its shipping lanes, beyond its manganese, chrome, vanadium, cobalt, copper, diamonds, and other minerals, and beyond its many votes in the United Nations. What happens in Africa—ethnic battles, color conflicts, deepening poverty, drought and death, epidemics, the apocalypse of AIDS, joblessness, illiteracy, and intolerance—impinges on Americans and is therefore intrinsically of concern to policy makers in Washington. Africa ought no longer remain a distant and dark continent of only episodic and reactive interest to the United States. So long as so many of its rulers disappoint their own subjects and the West and so long as much of Africa and its peoples fail to thrive, so the United States is obliged to concern itself even more intimately than it usually has with the affairs of those countries, like Botswana, which have grasped the nettle of tolerance and democratic practice and, equally, with those states which still endure authoritarian or predatory domination.

Washington cannot solve the problems of Africa alone, and usually accomplishes more in cooperation with host countries, European and Asian allies, and multilateral agencies like the World Bank. Both what the United States can try to do, and the beneficial effects of such actions, are bound to be limited. Nevertheless, United States policy makers in the years from 1989 onward will inescapably confront both crucial and profound choices.

The chapters of this book provide an implicit agenda for a new administration and its successors to the end of the century. Its chapters explain how American policy is being made in the 1980s. They provide an analytical framework for the understanding of issues as diverse as the AIDS crisis and the South African dilemma. They examine the structure of Africa's economic and social malaise (and discuss successes, too). They focus on external debt, on the spread of arms, on Soviet interests and objectives, on ethnic rivalries, on agriculture, on Muslim fundamentalism and Islamic radicalism, and—in general—on the critical problems that will face policy makers immediately and for much of the coming decade. The chapters are not intended to be encyclopedic; nor does the book as a whole cover all of the problems of Africa. But it does dissect most of the issues which are central to the future functioning of the peoples and nations of the continent, and which are therefore of considerable concern to the United States. Each chapter explores policy options and offers recommendations.

Together, at a meeting in New Hampshire in late 1987, the authors of the chapters and an invited group of foreign policy officials, politicians, journalists, and American academic specialists discussed drafts of the chapters in this book and examined the various individual recommendations.[1] Concerned that United States foreign policy should be founded on a clear appreciation of our national interest and a genuine understanding of the dynamic realities of Africa, they also advanced a range of policy options for consideration by the next American administration. Those recommendaions (the editor was asked to draw upon the views of his collaborators, but to present the results in his own prose and on his own authority) go beyond (but partially incorporate) the individual chapter conclusions.

Recommendations:

It is incumbent upon American policy makers to respect the traditions and political, social, and economic varieties of Africa. But the United States cannot ignore a lack of indigenous public participation. While dealing diplomatically and correctly with the states in Africa, it ought to remember its own noble heritage and give less rather than more support to dictatorial predators, one party autocrats, or minority oligarchs.

There will always be a temptation to join hands with governments that oppose the Soviets and espouse capitalism. Yet it may be more important to encourage those governments, whatever their ideological bent, that treat their people well and are attempting honestly to develop their nations instead of gaining personal reward, are combating famine and illiteracy, and are tackling questions of overpopulation. The United States no longer should prop up corrupt, mendacious, and single-minded regimes simply because they oppose the Soviet Union. Washington should favor intellectually honest governments, and assist them economically. We should no longer seek surrogates, create or help support proxy rulers or insurgencies, or place our emphasis solely on favored nations. The results of our well-intended political assistance, as in Zaire and Somalia, have often been disappointing. Our history of picking ultimate victors in local contests has been limited. Too often previous American administrations have been surprised by unexpected reverses, as in the Horn of Africa. Overall, Washington ought to choose a set of enduring principles and hew to them. Africa is a very poor place to pursue short-term advantages or to campaign for ideological purity.

On the economic front, although it will be essential to distribute food in times of famine, the import of free food undercuts the development of proper incentive structures in African agriculture. Our AID officials could devise mechanisms to promote productive pricing structures, as have the governments of Zimbabwe and Cameroun. We should offer to continue to help those African countries which are beating a retreat from a dependence upon state-owned enterprises, centralized control of food production, and fully administered wages and prices. As African states move (following Nigeria and Ghana) toward more open economies, the United States must explore macroeconomic ways to help those who are helping themselves. We cannot again afford, for example, to depress the world price of cotton and thus cripple the Sudan and Chad (both of which we assist militarily and with food). It is much less expensive for us to provide steady markets than to appropriate aid.

We will want to forgive the comparatively limited but economically crippling official debts of the sixteen poorest African countries. Yet we cannot and should not do so before procedures have been implanted to put the economies of those countries on a sound footing. It is in the interest of the

United States to take the lead internationally in inventing a workable and flexible economic response which will, like the Marshall plan, encourage the recovery of the poorest countries of the continent. If we limit subsidies to American farmers just a little, Africa will benefit. Finding an enduring means to improve the terms of trade for African and Africans with the world would help immensely.

There are many fundamental reasons for Africa's failure to follow India and sponsor a green revolution. Most significantly, the starting conditions for the green revolution in much of Asia and Mexico, which include fertile soils, substantial irrigation, large infusions of fertilizers and pesticides, and strong national research programs, are absent in Africa. For example, rain gauges are non-existent or unread. Population statistics are poorly collected or politically controversial. Knowledge about soils has deteriorated. The extent of deforestation and ecological decay is guessed at, but known imperfectly. Easy transport and communication are still wanting. The spread and virulence of diseases are imperfectly understood and mapped.

Comparatively inexpensively, the United States could help Africa learn more about itself and its underlying problems. Real growth and development depends on a fuller appreciation of the transformation and the obstacles to growth of rural and urban Africa since colonial times. The future of Africa may well depend upon its small farmers; we should focus more of our effort and attention on the techniques and materials which could help them.

For domestic political reasons, the Reagan administration vitiated burgeoning attempts to limit the rapid rise of populations in Africa. Episodes of famine, moreover, reflect high birth and survival rates as much as they do unexpected droughts, environmental disappointments, and poor logistical planning. Kenya's population is doubling every seventeen years, for instance, and Zimbabwe and others are not far behind. The next American administration needs to give energetic support to the efforts of those countries, including Kenya and Zimbabwe, that have recognized how excessive population increases dramatically undermine limited efforts at achieving economic self-sufficiency and growth. There is no less expensive or more effective economic assistance than American monies devoted to education about family size and spacing.

The United States and tropical Africa are the regions of the world most afflicted by AIDS. Data gathering is crucial in the struggle to halt its spread. Funds devoted to AIDS research in Africa will, it is to be hoped, assist in halting the spread of AIDS throughout Africa and the world. Zambia, Zaire, Uganda,

Kenya, and the Central African Republic deserve special attention by devoted American epidemiologists and forensic pathologists.

The most effective way of limiting Soviet incursions into Africa is to strengthen the way African governments function and take decisions, and to help upgrade the quality of the continent's infrastructure. Devising a workable tax collection office or dredging a harbor should mean more to Africa than selling military hardware to potential satraps. Soviet military incursions must be countered, but not necessarily by arming an opposing group and thus adding to the escalation of warfare and of wasteful expenditures by African governments. We can more effectively remove Cuban troops from Angola and do more for peace and development of that country by joining the rest of the international community in recognizing its thirteen-year old government than by arming its domestic opponent. Similarly, in Mozambique, we ought to help the trains run rather than argue about recognizing or otherwise befriending the South African backed anti-government guerrilla force called Renamo. Britain's positive approach to Mozambique could well be emulated.

What to do about South Africa is discussed at length in Chapter 10. Only a far-seeing and wise new American president will have the prestige and authority to do what Congressionally mandated sanctions, massive and continuing disinvestment, and widespread black protest have not—to help bring a stubborn minority government and a weak exiled force of militant representatives of the majority (and others) to a bargaining table. Sponsoring, or helping with our European and African allies to sponsor, a negotiating session can provide no guarantee of success, but there is no earlier or surer way of avoiding decades of upwardly escalating equilibria of violence.

The majority in this instance has numbers and ultimate legitimacy, but the minority has almost all the guns, authority, determination, and nowhere to run. The road to peace may in the end prove the road to civil war and partition, but it is incumbent upon an American president, with but limited direct influence on the policies of the Republic of South Africa, and much to lose, to inject himself and his administration (along with allies) directly into the middle of the problem. He will not want to prescribe the answer that only South Africans can provide, but he will want to persuade blacks and whites to bridge a chasm of color that grows wider by the month and for which no purely local construction appears satisfactory.

Helping defend South Africa's immediate neighborhood against the expansive military might of South Africa could mean assisting in the active defense of some of the imperiled countries of the region, the cutting off of support for UNITA, the expenditure of developmental funds, and an active diplomacy. It may also assume tacit co-operation with the Soviet Union, which also opposes the kind of regime now ruling South Africa.

For eight years our regional initiatives have been hostage to global concerns. The Soviets have not been hindered by those anti-Soviet strategies. Yet our initiatives in Africa and our relations with Africans have suffered as a result of linking our policies too tightly to an anti-Soviet crusade. Some of that same approach may continue to be necessary and inevitable, but we can do more for Africa, and more for our own interests, by understanding and countering the regional disadvantages that flow from a strict global interpretation of all these questions. No globalist action has been more counterproductive regionally than the provision of missiles to UNITA, an initiative which broader policy considerations and common sense should end.

The arena of the United Nations is and will continue to be a great source of frustration for American policy makers. Many Africans will continue to vote along Third World lines and thus against the United States, even though not all votes registered "against" have in fact been hostile to real United States' interests. It will be wise to bring more African questions to that great world forum, to ignore the United Nations less in general and for the sake of Africa and its dignity as much as for the great institution itself. When we use the United Nations for domestic political advantage we sow trouble for the future and make our overall policy stance toward Africa increasingly tendentious.

The nations of Africa still look anxiously to the United States. However they vote in the United Nations, they respect and favor the United States. We have much more than goodwill to gain and much more to do—for them and with them, and hence for ourselves. When we help Africans help themselves, we follow Presidents Woodrow Wilson and Franklin D. Roosevelt and make the world a better place—for them, and for us.

Notes

1. An earlier version of this introduction was improved after readings and critiques by several of my colleagues and collaborators: I particularly thank Henry S. Bienen, Mohamed T. El-Ashry, William Foltz, Kenneth W. Grundy, Helen Kitchen, David Laitin, G. Andrew Maguire, and Newell Stultz.

2: The Making of U.S. Policy Toward Africa

BY HELEN KITCHEN

In May 1978, at a time when leading personalities of the Carter administration, the intelligence community, and Congress were engaged in a public squabble over how much blame should be placed on the Soviet Union and Cuba for an invasion launched by Angola-based Zairian exiles into their home province of Shaba, British Prime Minister James Callaghan observed during a Washington press conference: "There seem to be a number of Christopher Columbuses setting out from the United States to discover Africa... It's been there a long time." In effect, Prime Minister Callaghan was saying that one of the positive heritages of the colonial era relationship between Europe and Africa is a more ecumenical and measured view of developments on the continent than one finds among newcomers.[1]

We sometimes forget that (in contrast to Britain, France, Belgium, Portugal, Spain, and Germany) United States interaction with Africa was largely limited before World War II to episodic links with Liberia, Morocco, Ethiopia, and Zanzibar, and to the distortions inherent in the slave trade. It was not until 1958 that the Department of State created a Bureau of African Affairs. Even this action was amended in 1974, when the Nixon administration had second thoughts about what constituted Africa and shifted four of the key members of the Organization of African Unity since 1963—Tunisia, Morocco, Algeria, and Libya—back into the bureau of Near Eastern and South Asian Affairs.

The continuing significance of the historical lag factor is illustrated by the contrast between the circumstances and substantive content of Secretary of State George Shultz's first visit to Africa in January 1987 and the November 1986 trek to the continent by France's President François Mitterrand and Prime Minister Jacques Chirac.

Senior officials of more than two-thirds of the member states of the Organization of African Unity (including nine whose colonial-era links were with European countries other than France) joined Mitterrand and Chirac in Lomé, Togo, to participate in the thirteenth French-African summit since 1973—a meeting deliberately planned with no fixed agenda "to allow ample time for free-flowing discussion and informal bilateral meetings." During their time on the continent, each of the French leaders also made stops to mend fences, cement old friendships, and (as in the case of Mitterrand's visit with Burkina Faso's President Thomas Sankara) engage in a spirited public match of wits on the issue of "neocolonialism." [2]

Secretary Shultz's long-awaited trip, in contrast, was carefully confined to six predictable hosts stretching across the middle of the continent (Kenya, Senegal, Cameroon, Nigeria, Ivory Coast, and Liberia), where both his message and reception made few headlines. Commenting on his visit, the *New York Times* observed that what the secretary prescribed for the continent (more private enterprise and more local initiative) was good advice, but Africa's troubles and United States interests there require more—beginning with joint United States-African practical efforts in one or two key areas such as debt management and food aid.[3]

Institutional Memory Discontinuities
The gaps in our knowledge and understanding of Africa's political history that derive from the lack of a colonial-era presence on the continent are understandable. Less defensible is the low priority given to present-day continuity in the "clean slate" approach that, more often than not, characterizes the changes that take place in the policy-making apparatus and hierarchy with each White House turnover. Every presidential transition and each biennial congressional election brings into central policy-making and policy-vetting roles a new wave of officials and legislators who may have only a nodding

or narrowly focused acquaintance with African issues. Even in the career Foreign Service, area specialization has become a risky course for the officer who aspires to rise to senior (i.e. ambassadorial) rank.[4]

Many specific examples can be cited of discontinuities of institutional memory in critical positions or at critical junctures. As late as the third year of the Carter administration, for instance, no officer serving in the Department of State's Office of Southern African Affairs had had prior experience in the country or countries for which he was responsible. No substantive consultation took place between Assistant Secretary for African Affairs Chester Crocker and his predecessor, Richard Moose, during the Carter-to-Reagan transition or in the year thereafter. When Crocker's experienced senior deputy, Frank Wisner, was appointed ambassador to Egypt in 1986, the No. 2 post in the Africa Bureau went to a career officer with no previous African experience.

Congress also contributes to the disruption in institutional memory continuity by dragging out the questioning and confirmation of presidential appointees perceived as controversial by some key member or members of the Senate Foreign Relations Committee. Almost a half year elapsed in 1981 between the White House announcement of the appointment of academician Crocker as head of the Bureau of African Affairs and final Senate confirmation. The all-time record is claimed by Melissa Wells, a career Foreign Service Officer fluent in Portuguese and with previous experience at ambassadorial rank in lusophone Africa. Her September 1987 confirmation as ambassador to Mozambique came through 11 months after announcement of her appointment was made. In both the Crocker and Wells cases, the blockage was orchestrated by Senator Jesse Helms (R-NC), a master parliamentary tactician whose emphasis on rigid anti-Communist, pro-"freedom fighters" credentials has never coincided with the more flexible regional guidelines of "constructive engagement."

Who's in Charge?

Although Africa is a special case in the sense that it became an integral part of the United States foreign policy agenda only in the 1950s, the problem of institutional memory gaps and divided authority is one that spreads across the full spectrum of our relations with the international community. In the years following World War II, dozens of new fiefdoms were established, largely outside the Department of State, to deal with specific aspects of the vastly expanded role that the United States was assuming in world affairs. By 1970, in contrast to the few thousand Americans posted abroad before the war, official United States civilian personnel overseas numbered 56,488. Domestic foreign affairs agencies (not including the Central Intelligence Agency or those in the Department of Defense having international policy functions) numbered 65,166. In larger African countries, as elsewhere around the globe, the United States embassy complex of the 1980s may shelter missions or attachés from up to 20 federal departments or agencies, of which at least four (Agency for International Development, USIA, the Department of Commerce, and the Department of Agriculture) have their own "foreign service" bureaucracies. In some cases, as few as 30 percent of the total embassy roster represent the Department of State per se.[5]

Congress, confronted with the increasing complexity of the foreign policy conglomerate in the postwar years, followed suit and gradually created a bureaucracy of its own to gather and filter information deemed necessary to assess judgments and requests coming from the executive branch, and also (increasingly) to make action recommendations that by the late 1980s amounted to micromanagement of some aspects of foreign policy. In the period between 1940 and 1970, the congressional staff roster grew from 17,099 to 30,869; by 1987, it had risen to over 37,000.

One of the most controversial episodes of congressional micromanagement affecting Africa occurred in October 1987, when the Senate took up the Foreign Relations Authorization Act of 1988. In the course of four days, the upper house not only voted to slash $84 million from the president's requested 1988 fiscal year operating budget for the State Department (including USIA and the Voice of America), but also passed 86 of 98 proposed amendments having to do with specific operational aspects of United States foreign relations. Several of the Senate amendments would have involved added costs—for example, creation of a new position of under secretary for security, construction, and foreign missions; designation of an "ambassador-at-large" for Afghanistan; extensive new reporting requirements; and daily Voice of America broadcasts in Slovenian.

Although the Senate action on the authorization bill was only one part of a complicated multistep process, Secretary of State Shultz elected to take it as a given that his department's budget would be "brutalized" and promptly went on the counterattack with a well-publicized cutback strategy calculated to set in motion some consciousness-raising in Congress via the media.

Since the FY [fiscal year] 1988 budgetary squeeze came on the heels of earlier congressional slashes of executive branch funding requests for the State Department ($60 million below the requested figure in 1986 and $125 million below the requested figure in 1987), the secretary emphasized that further axing in 1988 would cut sharply into infrastructure, employee rosters, and functions. In a speech to departmental personnel shortly before the anticipated Senate action, he enumerated some of the steps that probably would have to be taken. The list included (1) the closing of two embassies, both in Africa (Equatorial Guinea and the Comoro Islands); (2) reduction in the functions of several other embassies; (3) elimination of as many as 13 consulates or consulates-general worldwide, in addition to several scrubbed in FY 1987; (4) a substantial reduction of senior- and middle-level positions within the department (including a total of 21 from the secretary's, the deputy secretary's, and the under secretaries' "seventh floor" staffs).

Subsequent elaborations of these general guidelines by other State Department officials specified elimination of up to 1,300 Foreign Service and civil service jobs (mostly in Washington and hopefully largely by attrition and early retirement incentives with a minimal reduction in force), trimming of the number of deputy assistant secretaries to no more than three for any of the 14 bureaus within the State Department, and a 25 percent cut in the personnel roster of bureaus concerned with press and public information, economic affairs, political-military affairs, and congressional relations. Attention was called to the fact that cutbacks in India, the world's second most populous nation, had by late 1987 left the United States with only 96 professional diplomats and 260 support officials, while the Soviet diplomatic staff had grown to about 600.

The counteroffensive spearheaded by Secretary Shultz achieved at least a fiscal year 1988 reprieve. An omnibus appropriations bill (lumping 13 separate pieces of legislation) passed by Congress and signed into law by President Reagan in late December 1987 gave the State Department some $60 million more than was signaled earlier and omitted the unrequested personnel add-ons included in the Senate version. As a result, the closing of embassies and consulates was put on hold and plans to eliminate 27 deputy assistant secretary positions were also set aside. But as Under Secretary for Management Ronald I. Spiers phrased it, the revised appropriations legislation only shifted the situation "from the catastrophic to the difficult." The higher rate of inflation abroad and the dramatic decline of the dollar would require, he said, a budget increase of 10.5 percent for fiscal year 1989 just to maintain the current level of programs. All plans for construction of new facilities, including a permanent School of Foreign Service building in Washington, were being shelved and the "near-total hiring freeze" probably would have to remain in place indefinitely.

Unless a sea change takes place in relations between "the Hill" and "Foggy Bottom" [i.e. between Congress and the State Department], there is every reason to expect that the maintenance of 48 United States embassies and 11 consulates-general and consulates in 59 different African cities will continue to be questioned by congressional committees on budgetary, security, and relevance grounds. There is an answer to the question of relevance, but it is not a simple one. Given the fluidity of African politics (e.g., more than 75 changes of government by coup d'etat since 1957), who is to decide which states are not relevant? Would Chad have any significance for United States interests if Libya's Muammar al-Qaddafi had not undertaken to bring it under his tent? How much has our intelligence suffered because we have not join-ed the rest of Africa and Western Europe in establishing diplomatic rela-tions with the government that has ruled Angola for the past dozen years? Conducting foreign relations is never a static process, but nowhere are day-to-day human contacts more relevant than in a continent where personalities are in so many cases more important than institutions.

Reactions to the 1987 Congress-State micromanagement imbroglio were varied and crossed party lines. Senator John C. Danforth (R-MO), referring to the flood of hasty Senate amendments to the authorization bill, said: "We are in a cacophony of confusion. I submit that no reasonable person anywhere in the world can predict how the United States stands on any foreign policy issue." Assistant Secretary of State for Inter-American Affairs Elliot Abrams went further: "When the next crisis strikes, let no one go to the House or Senate floor and ask, how did this happen? Why couldn't we avoid this? Why didn't we know sooner? The answer, in part, will be that in the 1980s Congress decided that having a foreign ministry was an Old World practice too dangerous for us... [I]n the end, we are making the world a more dangerous place for ourselves and our allies, and in the end we will regret it." [6]

The overlapping lines of authority on foreign policy matters have complicated the roles of diplomatic missions in Washington and spawned a new growth industry. More and more governments (including those of some African states as small as Togo) employ professional lobbyists whose services may include monitoring (and appraising) the roles of various fiefdoms involved in policy decisions affecting the client state directly or indirectly; making the "educational" rounds of the offices of committees and members of Congress; and, in some cases, producing newsletters or cultivating media contacts.

When a delegation of ambassadors called on Deputy Secretary of State John Whitehead in November 1987 to protest the failure of the United States to pay its share of the costs of maintaining the United Nations peacekeeping force in southern Lebanon, some of the envoys were said to have been astonished at Whitehead's response. He made it clear that he personally, the Department of State, and the administration were in full agreement with the case presented. But given the limited leverage the administration had over fiscal aspects of foreign policy, the best counsel he could offer was to suggest that the ambassadors petition Congress directly. "It seems to me highly unusual," one ambassador told the *New York Times,* "that representatives of foreign countries are required by responsible officials to interfere in the internal affairs of a sovereign state." Another envoy, referring to lobbying Capitol Hill as a "humiliating experience," observed: "It's easier for me to see the president of the United States than to get an appointment with a congressional aide." [7]

Not all Washington sources blame Congress for the increasingly adversarial character of State-Capitol Hill interaction. Senior congressional staffers attribute much of the discord to the level, caliber, and commitment of those in today's foreign policy establishment whose responsibility or interest it should be to keep lines of communication open with Senate and House principals, and draw negative comparisons with the careful attention given to this aspect of policy-making in earlier decades. The Acheson era is often cited as a model for State relations with the Hill. The Bureau of African Affairs, in particular, receives low marks from congressional critics for its perceived failure during the 1980s to devote appropriate attention to friends and potential friends on Capitol Hill.

Three Operational Case Studies
The delays and incoherence that result from scattered responsibility for defining and implementing elements of policy in various functions can be illustrated by three African examples:

(1) *Strategic Minerals*. One case in point is the lack of a unified United States policy on strategic minerals. Decision making about strategic minerals is the shared responsibility of a complex assortment of government agencies with differing jurisdictions and priorities. While the Federal Emergency Management Agency (FEMA) is the lead agency responsible for coordinating a mineral stockpile policy, the General Services Administration (GSA) administers the stockpile and Congress funds it. The Departments of Defense, Interior, Energy, and Commerce, along with the National Aeronautics and Space Administration (NASA), have important research responsibilities. Other federal departments and regulatory agencies also are involved indirectly through taxation policies, regulation of commerce, environmental protection, federal lands management, antitrust enforcement, patent policy, foreign affairs and trade policy, and in other ways. In the Congress, at least six key committees and fifteen or more subcommittees have statutory authority over some aspect of minerals policy.[8]

(2) *Aid*. Similarly, United States aid to Africa falls into a range of categories involving a labyrinth of players in both the executive and legislative branches of government—players whose differing responsibilities, processes, and priorities introduce complications, contradictions, and delays into every decision taken.

As Carol Lancaster has noted (in a 1984 overview of "U.S. Aid to Africa: Who Gets What, When, and How?"), the turf problems in the executive branch primarily involve the Departments of State, Treasury, and Agriculture; the Agency for International Development (which reports directly to the president, though remaining on organizational charts as an entity of the State Department); the Office of Management and Budget (OMB); and the National Security Council. Members, staffers, and a range of committees of Congress also influence aid policy and amounts through the formal authorization and appropriations processes, through executive branch consultations with Congress on reprogramming aid from originally proposed purposes or countries or on the undertaking of any new initiatives, and through a network of relationships between individuals and agencies in the executive branch and their contacts and, often, former colleagues on the Hill.[9]

An example of the circuitous path a given aid agreement must navigate between conception and the actual obligation of funds is highlighted in a recent study of United States security (i.e. military) assistance to Africa. Once negotiations are concluded with a prospective recipient (a process that addresses such issues as threat analysis, the country's economic and financial problems, life-cycle costs of proposed equipment acquisitions, the structure and professional capabilities of the recipient's military establishment, and logistics support facilities), a new sequence begins. The following flow chart outlines the more significant steps in the security assistance budget cycle for a given year's appropriation:

Year 1   U.S. country teams in the field (spring)
            Executive branch review (spring-summer)
            State Department recommendation to Office of
                Management and Budget (fall)
            OMB passback to State Department (late fall)
            State Department justification ("reclama") of request to
                administration (late fall)
            Presidential approval (Christmas)
            To Congress (late winter)

Year 2   Congressional hearings (spring)
            Congressional committee markups (summer)
            Bill passage (fall)
            President's signature (late fall)
            Allocation of funds (late fall)
            Notify country (winter)

Year 3   Apportion funds (winter)
            Obligate funds (spring).[10]

(3) *Diplomatic Strategy*. The relatively low priority accorded Africa as a region at the higher levels of Washington's policy-making and policy-monitoring institutions helps to explain the episodic and erratic focus on specific issues or countries.

One bizarre zig-zag that occurred in 1987, when the Department of State came under heavy attack for its success in becoming "constructively engaged" with a Mozambican government once written off as firmly in the Soviet orbit. A further irony, reminiscent of the differences between Secretary of State Cyrus Vance and Assistant to the President for National Security Affairs Zbigniew Brzezinski over Angolan policy during the Carter administration, was that the principals in this 1987 confrontation over relations with Mozambique were all officials or nominal supporters of the Reagan administration.

As of late 1987, defense of the carefully developed policy of full recognition of and supportive economic ties with the FRELIMO government of President Joaquim Chissano was centered in the Department of State and extended to significant personalities within the revamped National Security Council, the Agency for International Development, and some elements (but by no means all) of the Department of Defense and the CIA. Leading the attack against administration policy and for recognition of the Resistência Nacional Moçambicana (known as Renamo or the MNR) as "anti-Communist freedom fighters" worthy of U.S. recognition and military support were several powerful Republican members of Congress, backstopped by an anti-State media blitz from a range of political action groups, newspapers and journals, and other fora on the right of the political spectrum.[11]

What Can We Learn from Europe?

While Americans have neither reason nor the remotest inclination to remodel our government on the pattern of either Britain or France, there are attitudinal and structural aspects of the way these allies deal with Africa that warrant comparative study. As previously noted, European governments are more comfortable with Africa and Africans and less inclined to think in terms of localized "quick fixes" or East-West chess than is much of the U.S. policy establishment.

When France intervenes in Chad, it does not focus narrowly on bashing Libya's Qaddafi but looks through a broader lens that views the Chad issue in a context of a range of long-term regional rapprochement possibilities and of French interests in Africa overall. It may or may not have been a coincidence that the *New York Times* chose November 1987 to feature a report from Equatorial Guinea (the former Spanish colony in West Africa likely soon to be without a U.S. diplomatic presence), describing how the growth of low-key French economic, fiscal, cultural, and political links had led, over time, to Equatorial Guinea becoming in 1985 the first non-French-speaking member of the 13-country African franc zone.[12]

Among the differences between British and U.S. policy approaches to Africa is that, while both naturally like to be liked, the British do not *expect* to be liked. As a veteran British diplomat phrased it in a recent exchange with the author, Britain is "well used to a uniquely intimate love-hate relationship with [its] former colonies, a political Oedipus complex with Britain as both parents," and "better able than the United States to accept hostile African rhetoric as an inevitable fact of life." [13]

There are also several fundamental differences between the policy-making structures, processes, and assumptions of Britain and the United States:

(1) There is no executive-legislative separation of powers in the British parliamentary system. The prime minister and all other ministerial-level officials are elected members of parliament and directly accountable to that body. The ruling majority, if reasonably well-disciplined, can drive policy through the House of Commons. (The House of Lords, whose members are appointed rather than elected, can debate and delay parliamentary action, but cannot act.)

(2) In practice, British foreign policy is largely made by permanent officials of the diplomatic service, on home posting in the Foreign and Commonwealth Office (the equivalent of the U.S. Department of State). The only political appointees in the FCO are a half-dozen junior- and senior-level ministers (all elected members of parliament, except for one from the nonelected House of Lords). Assistant Secretary Crocker's counterpart (the deputy under secretary for African and Middle Eastern Affairs) is a career diplomat whose tenure in office is not affected by a change in government.

(3) British policymakers do not see their prime function as shaping events in Africa, but as defending British interests on the continent. This relative predictability of British (and also French, German, and Belgian) priorities contrasts with what Africans perceive as United States ambiguity (or worse, a loose cannon on the deck) in our dealings with the continent.

(4) British policy, like that of France, has a low ideological component. The perception of the strategic importance of Africa has declined steadily as European diplomats have found it increasingly hard to visualize major concrete threats to Western interests, even in the event of the entire continent going notionally "Communist." "Notionally," as Britain's former deputy high commissioner in Zimbabwe has observed, is an appropriate modifier, because most diplomats with African experience see the continent's inherent "African-ness" as transcending any ideological label. While remaining a reliable friend to consistently "friendly governments" is the rule, a modus vivendi based on continuing mutual interests is normally soon established with a successor regime.

The only new "ideological" criterion introduced by the Thatcher government in assessing British interests is in the area of economic policy. The aim of the 1980s has been to reinforce the continent-wide tide now flowing strongly against previous excessive centralization (e.g., in Ghana), irrespective of any other considerations.[14]

Paradoxically, some of the most European-like arguments against an imperial United States response to the Soviet presence in Africa have come in recent years from a seemingly unlikely source—the military. While serving as principal deputy assistant secretary of defense for international security affairs in 1985, for example, Noel C. Koch offered some observations on United States interests in Africa that included this counsel: "Africa is fundamentally unengaged as regards great power conflicts. She has made no choices of irrevocable, long-term consequence... Some form of socialism is endemic to most African cultures—but as a cultural rather than a political and economic predilection... Over the long run, neither of the great powers, with their alliances and their conflicting values, will exert absolute influence over Africa, or have an absolute hegemonic position there. Over the long run, Africa will either manifest a receptive, friendly, and trusting attitude toward the industrialized democracies—which is the most desirable outcome for the United States—or she will say a plague on the house of democratic capitalism, as well as that of totalitarian communism, and, in a reactionary fashion, pursue some other destiny... In the end, without ever confronting the Soviets directly in Africa, the Western democracies will prevail there by the force of our values, by helping where help is needed and asked for, and by otherwise stepping back and letting Africa find her own destiny. Which she will surely do, anyway, whatever policy we here may set, and however we may construe our interests there."[15]

Is Consensus Possible?

The achievement of anything approaching consensus on the extent, nature, and management of United States interests in Africa will remain blocked as long as there is no clear resolution of one basic set of questions: Is this 12 million-square-mile continent of 53 entities primarily an East-West chessboard—as perceived by the right flank of the Republican party and a mushrooming list of allied political action groups and publications pressing the case for United States military support of a range of movements presenting themselves as "anti-Communist freedom fighters"? Or are we manufacturing self-fulfilling prophecies when we box and label any government or movement that uses quasi-Marxist terminology and/or has access to Soviet arms or the services of Cuban support personnel as irretrievably "Communist"? Can we, or can we not, agree with the Soviet position of recent years that both major powers have "legitimate" interests in Africa, but neither the continent as a whole nor any specific region or entity therein is of "vital" geostrategic importance to either Moscow or Washington?

It is becoming increasingly clear, as we move toward the 1990s, that this set of questions is critically linked to the vastly larger issue of the overall state of the United States polity. Is there an electable potential presidential candidate in either political party with the vision and leadership capabilities to orchestrate a restoration of order and credibility to our overgrown, overlapping, and multivoiced foreign policy apparatus?

Notes

1. For a revealing chronological account of the U.S. policy-making process, see "Evolution of a Policy: A Chronicle of Developments in U.S. Relations with Africa, May 1-July 10, 1978." in *African Index*, I (1978), 1-5.

2. J. Coleman Kitchen, Jr., "The Enduring French Connection," in *CSIS Africa Notes*, 68 (January 26, 1987).

3. *New York Times*, January 19, 1987.

4. Helen Kitchen, *U.S. Interests in Africa*. (New York, 1983) 30-33.

5. David D. Newsom, "The U.S. Foreign Affairs Structure in a Changing World," *Washington Quarterly*, (Summer 1987), 205, 210.

6. See the *Washington Post,* October 11, October 19, 1987; *Washington Post,* October 18, 1987; Elaine Sciolino, "Austerity at State Dept. And Fear For Diplomacy," *New York Times,* November 15, 1987.

7. *New York Times,* November 17, 1987.

8. For elaboration of these and related points, see Charles Ebinger, "The Strategic Minerals Maze," in *CSIS Africa Notes*, 57 (April 4, 1986).

9. Carol Lancaster, "U.S. Aid to Africa: Who Gets What, When, and How?" in *CSIS Africa Notes*, 25 (March 31, 1984).

10. William H. Lewis, "U.S. Military Assistance to Africa" in *CSIS Africa Notes*, 75 (August 6, 1987).

11. Helen Kitchen, "Introduction," in Helen Kitchen (ed.), *Angola, Mozambique, and the West*, (New York, 1987), vii-ix.

12. James Brooke in the *New York Times,* November 1, 1987.

13. From an extensive exchange in October 1987 between the author and Roger Martin, Britain's former deputy high commissioner in Zimbabwe.

14. Roger Martin, John de St. Jorre, and CSIS Visiting Fellow Gillian Gunn provided valuable counsel on British priorities.

15. Noel C. Koch, "Some Observations on U.S. Security Interests in Africa," in *CSIS Africa Notes*, 49 (November 19, 1985).

3: Sub-Saharan Africa:

Is It To Be Further Economic Deterioration or Rehabilitation?

BY REGINALD HERBOLD GREEN AND MICHAEL FABER

Where Now?

For the past ten years most of the inhabitants of sub-Saharan Africa (SSA) have experienced deteriorating living standards caused by natural and economic conditions they have been powerless to control. To the political and economic crises associated with these conditions, and to the personal suffering they have so widely caused, no early resolution is in sight.[1]

Tables and Figures 1 and 2 give a picture of the evolution of main macroeconomic and social indicators in selected SSA economies since 1980. While they show significant diversity, the dominant message conveyed is of low levels, fragility, and frequent declines.

Since 1979 few SSA economies have grown as fast as their populations or have been either able to sustain food production per capita or to maintain the value of such simple measures of human welfare as infant mortality, percentage of population with access to pure water, or proportion of children enrolled in primary schools. The record of the 1980s thus contrasts sharply with what was achieved during the 1960s and much of the

1970s—especially 1976-79—when a majority of SSA countries registered positive gains under these headings.[2]

In one sense it is folly to generalize about SSA. To generalize about or to produce averages for some 45 countries ranging in population from under 100,000 (e.g. Seychelles) to nearly 100,000,000 (Nigeria), with gross domestic products (GDPs) per capita ranging from under $200 (e.g. Chad, Mozambique) to over $3,000 (Gabon), and with adult literacy rates ranging from 20 percent or less (e.g. Gabon, Somalia) to over 80 percent (e.g. Mauritius, Tanzania) is to run severe risks of conflation comparable in result to what would be achieved by devising averages from all the economies of the Western Hemisphere south of the Rio Grande or all Asian economies excluding Japan.

Since 1979, however, very few SSA economies have been able to avert major setbacks or to achieve sustained recoveries. Botswana and perhaps Cameroon are the only clear exceptions. Otherwise this lack of success, economically, appears accurate irrespective of the policy orientation of governments prior to 1979 or to their economies' earlier records of achievement—the Ivory Coast has experienced debacles as well as Guinea, and Malawi's economy is almost as dangerously weakened as Tanzania's. More surprisingly, the generalization seems to hold whether or not a formal stabilization and adjustment program endorsed by the International Monetary Fund (IMF) and World Bank was or was not in existence.[3] For example, Zambia and Madagascar have had such programs for most of the past dozen years but have shown little improvement, whereas Tanzania's economy bottomed out in 1983 and reconstruction began some three years before its programs secured Bank and Fund endorsement. By contrast Ghana's progression from a period of policy incoherence in 1973-81, through an unsuccessful 'do-it-yourself' stabilization effort in 1982, to a Bank/Fund 1983-87 guided approach has yielded positive results, whereas the failure of the Sierra Leone government to make any serious effort at policy reform has led to ever-deepening crises.[4]

Despite such diversity there is broad agreement as to what has been happening to most SSA economies since 1979.[5] So, too, would there be agreement on a listing of the main causal elements. But there is strong disagreement as to which causes were primary and which are now most important, and about what SSA states can and should do to alter present trends. These are related but not identical questions, since even if the dominant causes of the crisis are believed to have been external, the practical policy responses may have to be internal if the worsened external

Table 1: Basic Indicators

	Population (millions) mid-1984	Area (thousands of square kilometers)	GNP per capita Dollars 1984	GNP per capita Annual growth rate 1965-84 (percent)	Annual rate of inflation per cent 1965-73	Annual rate of inflation per cent 1973-83	Life expectancy at birth 1983 (years)	Average index of food production per capita 1981-83 (1974=100)
Low-income economies	260.6t	15,694t	220w	(.)w	3.6w	18.5wy	49w	93w
1. Ethiopia	42.0	1,222	110	0.5	1.8	4.4wy	47	106
2. Mali	7.3	1,240	140	1.2	7.6	10.3	45	106
3. Zaire	30.6	2,345	140	-1.3	18.7	48.2	51	93
4. Burkina Faso	6.6	274	160	1.4	2.6	10.8	44	100
5. Guinea-Bissau	0.9	36	180	..	..	6.9	38	84
6. Niger	6.3	1,267	190	-1.2	4.0	11.8	45	122
7. Malawi	6.8	118	210	2.2	4.5	9.8	44	101
8. Tanzania	21.5	945	210	0.9	3.2	11.5	51	103
9. Burundi	4.6	28	220	2.1	2.9	12.4	47	97
10. Uganda	14.3	236	230	-4.4 a	5.6	62.7 b	49	91
11. Togo	2.9	57	250	1.1	3.1	8.3	49	99
12. Gambia	0.7	11	260	1.4	3.0	10.4	36	79
13. Somalia	5.2	638	260	-0.8 a	3.8	20.1	45	72
14. Benin	3.9	113	270	1.0	3.6	10.8	48	95
15. Central African Rep.	2.5	623	270	0.1	3.0	14.4	48	94
16. Madagascar	9.7	587	270	-1.2	4.1	13.9	49	90
17. Rwanda	5.9	26	270	2.3	7.7	11.2	47	114
18. Guinea	5.9	246	300	1.1	3.0	4.0	37	85
19. Kenya	19.7	583	300	2.3	2.3	10.8	57	86
20. Sierra Leone	3.7	72	300	1.1	1.9	14.7	38	98
21. Sudan	21.5	2,506	340	1.3	7.2	18.0	48	94
22. Ghana	13.4	239	350	-2.1	8.1	51.6	59	65
23. Senegal	6.4	196	380	-0.5	3.0	8.9 b	46	71
24. Chad	4.9	1,284	..	..	4.5	8.3	43	101
25. Mozambique	13.4	802	..	..	..	..	46	68

Middle-income oil importers	32.6t	3,257t	620w	1.2w	3.5w	10.8w	53w	89w
26. Mauritania	1.7	1,031	450	0.3	3.9	7.8	46	102
27. Liberia	2.1	111	470	0.8	1.5	7.2	49	92
28. Zambia	6.5	753	470	-1.3	5.2	10.3	51	74
29. Lesotho	1.5	30	530	6.3	4.4	11.9	53	76
30. Ivory Coast	9.9	322	610	1.0	4.1	11.9	52	108
31. Zimbabwe	8.2	391	740	1.5	3.0	9.7	56	79
32. Swaziland	0.7	17	800	2.6	4.3	14.1	55	116
33. Botswana	1.0	600	910	8.5	4.4	9.8	61	68
34. Mauritius	1.0	2	1,100	2.8	5.6	13.1	67	89
Middle-income oil exporters	117.7t	3,256t	800w	3.4w	8.3w	13.2w	49w	95w
35. Nigeria	96.8	924	770	3.2	10.3	13.3	49	98
36. Cameroon	9.9	475	810	2.7	5.8	12.6	54	84
37. Congo, People's Rep.	1.8	342	1,120	3.5	4.6	12.4	63	99
38. Gabon	0.8	268	3,480	3.2	5.8	18.5	50	102
39. Angola	8.4	1,247	..	..	..	..	43	82
Sub-Saharan Africa	410.9t	22,207t	420w	1.8w	4.2w	14.8w	49w	94w
All low-income economies	2,335.4t[c]	31,603t	260w[c]	2.7w[d]	1.4w	5.4w	59w	111w
All lower middle-income economies	665.1t[c]	18,446t	750w[c]	2.9w[d]	5.6w	17.9w	57w	105w
All upper middle-income economies	500.1t[c]	22,079t	2,050w[c]	3.8w[d]	5.3w	34.0w	65w	106w
Industrial market economies	728.9t[c]	30,395t	11,060w[c]	2.5w	5.2w	8.0w	76w	107w

a. Because data for the entire period are not available, figures are for periods other than that specified.
b. Figures are for 1973-82, not 1973-83.   c. Figures are for 1983, not 1984.   d. Figures are for 1965-83, not 1965-84.

Source: World Bank, *Financing Adjustment with Growth in Sub-Saharan Africa, 1986-90*, Washington, 1986.

Table 2a

Selected Quality of Life Indicators: 1960—mid-1980s(a)

	GHANA				Low Income sub-Saharan Africa (1982)
	1960	1970	Late 1970s	1980s	
1 .Average Life Expectancy at Birth	45	49	55	53	48
2. Infant Mortality Rate	132	107	86	107-120	118
3. Child Death Rate	27	21	15	25-30	24
4. Access to Health Facility (b)	-	-	-	30	45
5. Public Health Facility Visits Per Person Per Year	-	-	0.7	0.4	2(f)
6. Health Budget as Percentage of GDP	-	1.2	-	0.26	0.95
7. Access to Pure Water (c)					
Rural	-	14	14	48	14
Urban	-	86	86	75	62
Total	-	35	35	60	22
8. Access to Excreta Disposal (d)					
Rural	-	40	40	30	25
Urban	-	92	95	65	69
Total	-	55	56	44	32
9. Average Calorie Availability as a Percentage of Requirements	92	97	88	68	91
10. Child Malnutrition (Moderate/Severe)	-	-	36	50-55	40
11. Primary Education Enrolment Ratio (e)	38(46)	64(75)	69(80)	-(80)	69(-)
12. Adult Literacy	27	30	-	35-45	44
13. Education Budget as Percentage of GDP	-	3.9	-	0.85	2.81
14. Proportion of Population Below Absolute Poverty Line (f)					
Rural	-	-	60-65	67.5-72.5	65
Urban	-	-	30-35	45-50	35

Notes on Table 2a

(a) 1960 data refer to a year between 1959 and 1961; 1970 between 1969 and 1971; late 1970s between 1975 and 1980; 1980s to 1982, 1984 or 1985.

(b) Defined in terms of location within a 5 kilometre radius. May overstate for urban population when facilities available are small.

(c) 1970 and late 1970s urban figures may be overstated by failing to relate number of water points to population.

(d) 1970 and 1978 figures for urban and possibly rural areas overstate by failing to relate number of drop-holes to supposed user population.

(e) Adjusted for length of primary cycle. ( ) are unadjusted figures. Because of the primary/middle school division Ghana has a shorter primary cycle than most SSA countries.

(f) Estimate made by author based on fragmentary data.

Principal Sources

World Bank, Comparative Analysis and Data Division, Economic Analysis and Projections Department (June 1984), *World Development Report* 1985; UNICEF, *Statistics on Children in UNICEF Assisted Countries* (April 1985); UNICEF Ghana: *Situation Analysis of Women and Children* (July 1984).

economic environment is perceived to be largely irreversible—or is thought likely to worsen further and, *per contra*, even if domestic policy errors played a major role in leading to economic decline, their reversal may be quite inadequate to achieve even stabilization, let alone rehabilitation and recovery, without significant external financial support.

The Road to 1987

A checklist of the key factors[6] that have seriously affected most SSA national economies would include: First, a major worsening of their external terms of trade. This has applied since 1975 to mineral exporters and oil importers; since 1978 for most agricultural product exporters and since

Table 2b: Selected Quality of Life Indicators

		Angola	Botswana	Lesotho	Malawi
Population (millions)		8.5	1.1	1.5	6.9
Under-5 mortality (per 1,000 births)		325-375 [a]	100	145	280
Infant mortality (0-1) (per 1,000 births)		200 [a]	75	110	160
Infant and child malnutrition (percent)		NA	32	NA	31
Average calorie intake relative to requirements (percent)		87	(94)	100	97
Access to health services		(30)	(89)	NA	80
Access to safe water		21	(76)	(14)	(41)
Primary enrolment (percent) (1982) [c]		66	76 [b]	71	46
Adult (over 15) literacy (percentage) (1982)		28	61	70	(36)
One-year-olds fully vaccinated (percent)	TB	40	70	91	72
	DTB	8	82	59	66
	Polio	55	77	64	68
	Measles	62	75	63	64
Life expectancy at birth		(41)	55	50	46
GNP per capita		490	960	530	180

( ) = 1980 (or nearby year). Somalia re-estimated to include unrecorded remittances.

[a] Re-estimated on fragmentary data taking into account impact of war. Standard projections showing 245 under-5 mortality for Angola and 255 for Mozambique assume continuation not reversal of rapid 1975-1980 immediate, post-independence period gains.

[b] 1983

[c] Net ratios except for Tanzania, Zambia and Zimbabwe.

[d] Includes estimates from various unpublished UNICEF studies at various dates 1982 through 1986.

SOURCES: Statistics on Children in UNICEF Assisted Countries, UNICEF, 1986; *The State of The World's Children 1987,* Oxford for UNICEF, 1987; data for GNP per capita taken from World Bank's *World Development Report 1986*, OUP.

- Southern Africa 1984 and Somalia

Mozambique	Swaziland	Tanzania	Zambia	Zimbabwe	Somalia [d]
14.0	0.6	22.0	6.5	8.5	5.5
325-375 [a]	185	185	135	120	174-210
200 [a]	125	110	85	75	146-180
NA	NA	(50)	28	NA	16
79	(108)	101	89	89	(105)
(30)	NA	(70)	75	71	(20)
(13)	48	(47)	46	(52)	33
46 [b]	84 [b]	87 [b]	94	131	15
27	(61)	85 [b]	69	69	16
(46)	95 [b]	(84)	87	88	31
(56)	79 [b]	(58)	49	68	22
(32)	60 [b]	(56)	47	63	22
(32)	51 [b]	(82)	56	55	36
(45)	54	52	52	56	45-49
(230)	790	210	470	760	(350)

about 1983 for petroleum exporters. In 1986 alone, terms of trade falls reduced continental Africa's earned import purchasing power by at least a quarter.

A second factor—partially a consequence of the first—has been the rapid rise in external debt and in debt servicing obligations relative both to export earnings and to gross domestic product. Total SSA external debt (short, medium, and long term, including arrears, commercial credit, and IMF drawings) is of the order of $125-140 billion, with annual debt service obligations nominally payable being of the order of $20 billion. These debt service obligations amount to some 50 percent of total visible and invisible exports from SSA as a whole.[7] In extreme cases—e.g. Somalia—the debt service ratio exceeds 100 percent. The regional average is in fact the highest

Table 2c
Rates of Environmental Degradation

Countries	Sand dune encroachment	Deterioration in rangelands	Forest depletion	Deterioration of irrigation	Rainfed agricultural problems	General assessment
Benin	o	*		o		*
Burkina Faso	o	*			*	*
Cape Verde	*	*	o			*/**
Chad	**	**	*	**	**	**
Djibouti	*	**			NA	*/**
Ethiopia	*	**	**	*	*	*/**
Gambia	*		*	**	*	*
Ghana	o		*	o		*
Guinea	o	o	*	*		*
Guinea Bissau	o	o	**			*
Kenya	o	**	**		**	*/**
Mali	*	**	*	*		**
Mauritania	*	**	**	**		*/**
Niger	o	**	*	o	*	*
Nigeria	*	**	**	*		*
Senegal	*		*	**	*	**
Somalia	**	*	*			*
Sudan	**	*	*	o	*	*
Tanzania	o	*	*	o		*
Uganda	o	**	o	o		*
United Rep. Cameroun	o	*	*	o		*
Zimbabwe	o		*	o	*	*

KEY: o = Stable, * = Some increase, ** = Significant increase, NA = Not applicable.
Source (Adapted): "Desertification Control Bulletin," United Nations Environment Programme, Number 10, May 1984, p. 26 and national data.

Figure 1A

Grain production per capita in 24 African countries affected by drought, 1970-1984

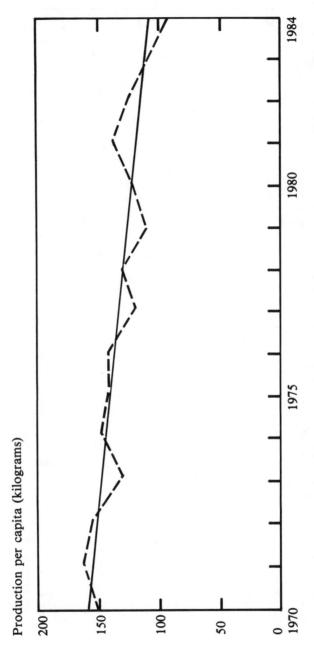

Production per capita (kilograms)

Source World Bank. Toward Sustained Development in Sub-Saharan Africa A Joint Program of Action (Washington, D.C. 1984). p. 14. based on data of the Food and Agriculture Organzation of the United Nations (FAO), except that the 1984 figure is a projection using data from FAO, the United States Agency for International Development and the United States Department of Agriculture.

Figure 1B

Index of food production per capita. 1961-1965—1983

(1961-1965 average = 100)

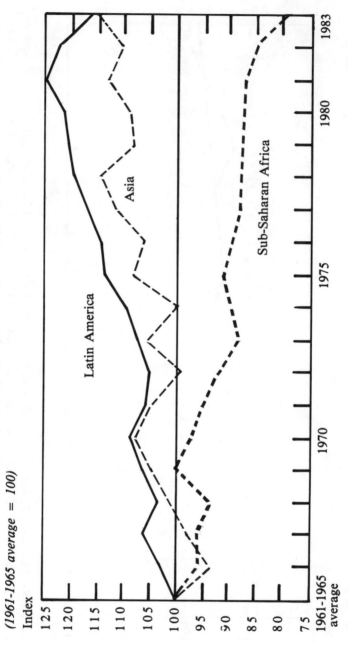

Source: World Bank. Toward Sustained Development in Sub-Saharan Africa A Joint Program of Action (Washington, D.C. 1984). p. 15. based on data provided by the United States Department of Agriculture.

ratio to export earnings in the world. Latin American total debt is of course much larger absolutely but, compared to GDP and foreign exchange earnings, it is less crushing than that of sub-Saharan Africa.

A third exogenous factor has been the weather. Weather changes are not the primary cause of falling agricultural output per capita. It appears, however, that, for a significant proportion of SSA countries, weather since 1965 has been worse than it was in the previous two decades. The Sahel, Eastern/Southern African, and Horn drought cycles since the early 1970s are not unprecedented, but do appear to have been more frequent, severe, and extended than those of the 1940s, 50s, and 60s.

A fourth factor has been the cost of war.[8] This is heaviest for the countries subjected to systematic South African aggression, destabilization, and the stage managing of dissident or proxy forces. For Mozambique and Angola the costs have run to billions of dollars in lost GDP and to hundreds of thousands of direct and indirect deaths. Civil war costs have also been (and remain) immense in several other cases, e.g. the Sudan, Ethiopia/Eritrea, Chad, and Uganda. Even in places where no fighting actually took place, excess defense budgets and/or regional military costs have been very high. For example they represent the largest macroeconomic resource balance difference between Tanzania's successful 1974-76 and failed 1979-81 attempts at economic stabilization and growth restoration.

A fifth factor has been that SSA lacks the infrastructure in terms of physical resources, knowledge, and research to sustain growth of food production safely above the 3-3.5 percent population growth rate. Even in those countries— e.g. Tanzania and Rwanda—which do appear on a trend basis to be able to sustain such rates, severe shortfalls still occur in bad weather years. Indeed even Malawi, which has significant maize surpluses in most years, experienced severe staple food shortages in 1980 and 1987. The contrast with what has been achieved in South and Southeast Asia is again marked. Overall SSA research and extension allocations (in terms of finance and personnel) do not appear to be notably below the developing country average, but the payoff is abysmally low.[9]

A sixth factor derives from what, in retrospect, can be seen to have been an inappropriate response to the oil and interest rate shocks of 1979-80. Most SSA governments duplicated their responses of 1974-75, assuming a parallel Organization for Economic Cooperation and Development (OECD) program of stabilization to be followed by high domestic and import growth over 1981-84, as had happened over 1976-79. While the OECD, IMF, and World

Figure 2

MALNUTRITION AMONG CHILDREN IN BOTSWANA AND GHANA 1980-84

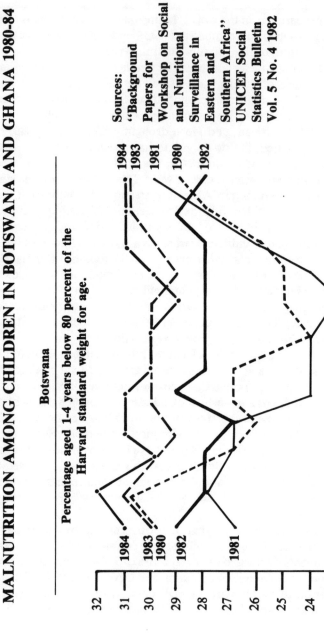

Botswana

Percentage aged 1-4 years below 80 percent of the
Harvard standard weight for age.

Sources:
"Background
Papers for
Workshop on Social
and Nutritional
Surveillance in
Eastern and
Southern Africa"
UNICEF Social
Statistics Bulletin
Vol. 5 No. 4 1982

Ghana

Percentage aged 7-42 months below 80 percent of the Harvard standard weight for age

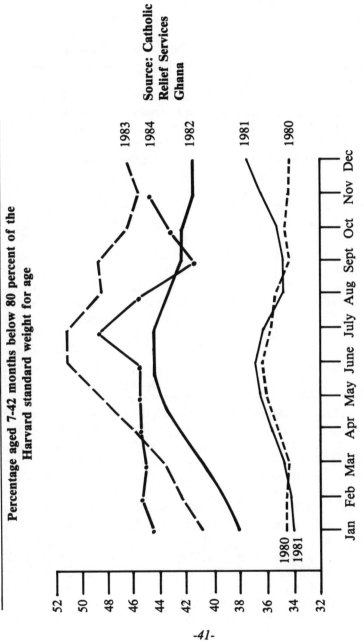

Source: Catholic Relief Services Ghana

Source: UNICEF, *Adjustment With A Human Face*, 1985.

Bank (though not the UN Conference on Trade and Development [UNC-TAD]) projected that outcome, it did not happen. SSA economies were severely damaged by having acted for too long on the assumption that it would.

A seventh factor has been widespread currency overvaluations.[10] This has been evident even in several franc zone countries where the fixed link to the French franc and restrictive access to central bank credit has been shown to be no guarantee against differential price movements, external debt buildup and other fiscal imbalances. But it has been most extreme where collapses in public revenues have been countered by massively expanding the local money supply while rigidly maintaining the official exchange rates, e.g. Guinea (to 1984) and Somalia (since 1979). The adverse impact on visible exports and on the production of import substitutes has been severe, as has been the distortion of price signals and the loss of economic transparency arising from the growth of external and domestic "parallel" markets.

An eighth factor, of earlier origin but particularly troublesome in the 1980s has been the high levels of—and, more particularly, the nature of—state intervention in the economy and the worsening performance of many public sector enterprises. Even the advocates of specific intervention to manage incentives and markets (say on the South Korean model) or those who see no *a priori* reason for public sector or cooperative enterprises to be more inefficient than private sector alternatives agree that much state intervention and many public sector enterprises and co-operatives have, in fact, been inefficient.[11] Given the present constraints upon both financial and managerial resources, SSA governments, with few exceptions, appear over-extended and will need both to cut back and to determine priorities.

A ninth factor—political in nature—has been the very uneven degrees of national solidarity, political system acceptability, and public policy operationality of SSA states. These phenomena are not identical, e.g. Somalia has a high degree of national solidarity (at least vis-à-vis external actors) but extremely little operationality in its domestic economic and social policy. Perhaps only Botswana can be given high rankings on all three criteria.

Flowing from this last factor is a tenth—domestic discontent, up to and including both civil wars and violent changes in government. Whatever their specific causes, both extreme discontent and sudden, disorderly changes of government have high dislocation costs (usually involving increased 'security' spending) and tend to push economic policy to the periphery of attention. Attempted economic reforms whose initial impact is to rend the fabric of society and to erode the political foundations of the government seeking to implement them are, for this reason alone, likely to prove both unsustainable and counter-productive,[12] e.g. Zambia 1985-87.

An eleventh factor is primarily historic—African states and economies are with few exceptions open and lack a well articulated network of domestic intra-sectoral linkages. Modern states (both politically and technically) are very recent; indeed most are post colonial creations of the last quarter century and are still heavily externally dependent for knowledge, technology, policy patterns and—less uniformly—specialized personnel. Medium and large scale economic units (for production and infrastructure) are a comparatively modern innovation. A majority have been begun during the past two decades. Their interaction with the small scale economic sectors which still supply the bulk of agricultural output and services and provide nine-tenths of the opportunities for employment and self-employment are imperfect, little understood, fragmentary and often fragile. A sudden fall in import capacity can have a massive multiplier effect in preventing utilization or even maintenance of much of the capital stock, in reducing real government revenue (usually highly dependent on imports, exports and domestic manufactured products) and in setting off a cumulative process of economic and political weakening, disintegration or even collapse—a process from which the small scale sector is only very partially immune.

A twelfth and (for this list) final factor is also historic. Most SSA economies are small in terms both of population and of economic magnitude. A majority have populations less than 10 million and gross domestic products of under $2 billion. Even a small United States town, such as Walla Walla, Washington, has a larger gross economic product (and tertiary educational enrollment) than several African economies (e.g. Gambia, Seychelles, and probably Togo and Benin) and a regional metropolis such as Seattle, Washington, almost certainly has a larger product than that of any SSA economy other than Nigeria. Small size combined with economic buoyancy can sometimes facilitate national consciousness, public policy operationality, and moderately well distributed economic prosperity, as in Burkina Faso, Togo, Burundi, Guinea Bissau, and the Central African Republic.

The balance among these factors—indeed which ones are significant—varies from state to state. Opinion on the relative weights to be attributed to external, historic, and domestic policy factors continues to vary widely, indeed wildly. A safe generalization would be that each African state and economy has been affected by several of the above factors and several by up to ten. There might also be agreement that in a context of historical newness, smallness and fragility, external shocks have both exposed existing institutional and policy weaknesses, and have further weakened the capacity of African governments to cope and of African economies to respond. There would surely also be agreement that—whatever the causes were and wherever that blame lies—no recovery is possible for most SSA economies without institutional and policy restructuring that is African-initiated and domestically sustained. It is also true that such changes will rarely be effective or even sustainable without enhanced levels of external co-operation.[13] External economic cooperation will need to encompass both a less hostile environment in such matters as commodity prices, market access, and interest rates and the attainment of recognized minimum levels of net resource inflows.

APPER and After?

It is sometimes stated that the worst is past and that SSA is set on a path toward rehabilitation and recovery. The case argued is that stabilization and adjustment programs exist in 25 to 30 countries, currency over-valuation is declining, the 1983-85 drought has passed, most Africans have survived and that the 1985-86 formulation of Africa's Priority Program for Economic Rehabilitation and Development (APPER)[14] plus its endorsement by the international community at the 1986 United Nations General Assembly Special Session will ensure the mix of policies and external resources flows needed for sustained recovery.

That is almost certainly too optimistic a reading. Only in 1984 and 1985 did SSA output rise by the same order of magnitude as population—1986 and 1987 have seen renewed per capita falls to levels below those of the early 1970s. The erosion of human and economic productive capacity which characterized the past decade has not been made good and will increasingly pull down attainable levels of output and human welfare until it is. 1987 was once again a drought year. A notable feature of many SSA stabilization and adjustment programs—however conscientiously designed—has been their failure to achieve stable resource balances consistent with even constant per capita output, let alone to set in train the self-sustaining structural dynamics which would unblock development. Even the Fund and the Bank (after earlier over-optimism about programs such as those which collapsed in Zaire, Uganda, Sudan, Zambia, Somalia, Malawi, and the Ivory Coast) are now very cautious about claiming sustained successes.

In such difficult times, survival itself is a form of success—but a limited one. In any event, millions of Africans who would be alive had the 1960-1979 infant mortality and life expectancy trends continued did not survive. Nor did a number of African governments. APPER itself does set out a coherent, if broad brush, economic rehabilitation strategy which in terms of policy choice and resource inputs should prove viable. A majority of SSA states are committed to action consistent with it. But the 1986 endorsement of APPER and a parallel fund-raising campaign campaign led by the World Bank have, to date, failed to improve the external economic environment. Net resource inflows did rise marginally over 1985-1986 but neither new flows nor debt deferrals and writeoffs were anywhere near either APPER or World Bank targets. Meanwhile, worsened global terms of trade (and, for South Africa's neighbors, heightened aggression and destabilization) more than offset these gains. The best general estimates of the medium term future prospects remain the World Bank's. With rather higher resource inflows and world growth rates than seem likely and with African policy reform (which the Bank sees as moving fairly rapidly across a broad front) such estimates show no recovery in output per capita in low income SSA through the mid-1990s, following the 20 to 25 percent deterioration that occurred between 1979 and 1987.

Toward an Identification of Operational Parameters

To plan for the future, the first requirement is to learn from the past. We seek to do that here by posing and by offering answers to what seem to us a number of important questions:

1. Was SSA economic performance uniformly unsatisfactory prior to 1979?

In retrospect, the year 1979—the year following the second oil shock— can be seen as something of a watershed. Over the 20 years prior to 1979, average annual growth rates amongst SSA countries varied from negative to over 10 percent, with most countries being in the 3 percent to 5 percent range. They were on balance higher in the early and mid-sixties, lower in the early seventies, negative over 1974-75 and highest over 1976-79. Progress was made regionally and in most countries in nutritional standards, in the ease of access to pure water and to basic health services, and in literacy and education. Obviously a sound growth rate facilitates the public funding of such services, but the rates of progress also quite clearly reflect the policy priorities of different governments. Thus it is difficult to establish any close correlation in such social advances with either initial GDP per capita levels or with rates of economic growth.[15]

The development strategies of different governments differed markedly. Both relatively free market and managed market strategies were common. Likewise some governments went for export-led growth while others pursued policies focussed on national economic integration, including promoting import substitution. In virtually all countries the direct role of the public sector was large—usually including participation in marketed production. The role of and attitude toward the private sector and in particular that of foreign private investment varied widely, as did the degree of control which governments attempted to exercise on private sector activities.

In general governments professing to policies of "African Socialism" (which was, however, often a synonym for interventionist capitalism, e.g. Kenya, Senegal) and "transition to socialism" tended to move more into direct production and distribution sometimes by extending the activities of the existing colonial created marketing boards, sometimes through national-izations, sometimes through entering "joint venture" agreements with foreign firms. Many of such nationalized industries and joint ventures have performed disappointingly—especially, though not only, after 1979—and African presidents, such as Kenneth Kaunda of Zambia, have been loud to complain over the last five years at the burden they have imposed upon treasuries. Nonetheless, prior to 1979, it was hard to find statistical evidence for arguing that one particular strategy was more effective in procuring growth than another. National outcomes seemed to depend more upon a combination of external factors—such as the price of the country's leading export, or the presence or absence of contiguous wars—and upon the efficiency with which the chosen strategy was being executed.

What is clear is that countries that consistently maintained grossly over-valued currencies and those which displayed exceptionally high inflation rates (e.g. Ghana, Zaire) were likely to be unsuccessful economically. Whether these situations (which applied only to a minority of African economies until the 1980s) were initially the causes or consequences of economic short-comings is debatable; but when policies to correct such shortcomings were not given priority, they then unquestionably became causes of continued economic deterioration. Further, lack of any sustained coherent policy at all—e.g. in Ghana over 1973-81—was uniformly linked to economic decline.

2. Is post 1979 performance uniformly dismal?

In comparison to 1976-79 the answer is yes, except for the special case of Zimbabwe, which began emerging from the conclusion of its independence war in 1980. The uniform manner in which economies turned downward from 1978-80 (except for those with oil or other atypical exports) whatever development strategy had previously been pursued or however good their earlier economic performance, strongly suggests that the initial shocks precipitating the decline must have been external. To posit uniform endogenous deterioration in 40-odd very different economies with very diverse state-structures and policies at precisely the same time is not very plausible.

But if the initial shocks were unquestionably external, it is equally undeniable that the capacity to withstand and to respond effectively to those shocks has varied greatly in a manner which has had much to do with both the structures of the states concerned and with the policies selected and implemented for dealing with adversity. On the whole those with the least coherent and disciplined policy and those with the most extended state structures responded least effectively or rapidly. It is not difficult to see why. Falls in export proceeds in SSA lead to more than proportionate falls in public revenues. Investment and development expenditures and imports tend to be cut first. Then supplies, especially imported supplies become short, leading to a declining efficiency within the public services and to under-utilization of public and private manufacturing capacity.[16] Employment and nominal salaries in the public sector were usually maintained, but only at the cost of budget deficits, domestic credit creation, accelerating inflation and declining public service real incomes, morale, and efficiency. The external value of the domestic currency was also maintained or reduced less rapidly than the rate of domestic inflation indicated to be appropriate for fear of adding to the inflation, resulting in a bias against export production and the proliferation of commercial opportunities dependent upon the issue of import and other licenses. Thus the distortions tended to grow, and the performance of the economy further to deteriorate. Nevertheless some of the results have been contrary to popular impression, e.g. post-1979 Ivory Coast performance has not been strong; over 1983-86 Tanzania (before formal external endorsement of its strategy) had positive GDP growth (below population but above the SSA average) and regained a 3.5 percent trend growth in food production.

Even greater divergences appear in the degree to which human investment (health, education, pure water, and nutrition) has been protected. Again these efforts have not been closely correlated to economic growth performances as such; they would appear to be more a reflection of the social and political priorities of particular governments.

3. What has been the degree of and cost (or gain) from public sector expansion? Has there been generalized over-expansion?

Over 1950-79 the public sector—government and enterprise—grew rapidly both absolutely and as a share of total public and private expenditure in most SSA states. This growth took place largely during the latter days of the colonial administrations and in the early period of independence. The purposes of such expenditure included the creation of the array of governmental administration services expected of a sovereign state, the expansion of health and education services promised in party programs, and investments and direct marketing and production where these seemed to be required in the public good but were not being supplied by the infant domestic or reluctant foreign private sector. In some countries a significant proportion of the public sector was comprised of enterprises that had been nationalized or partly nationalized, had been handed over by the ex-colonial state after it nationalized their parent companies (significant in the lusophone states), or which the government had acquired by purchase from foreign interests or from members of minority communities. Since 1979, in most of Africa—as elsewhere—the public sector has been in retreat. In part this reflects the decline in resources available to government and in enterprise operating profits. In part also it reflects a wide dissatisfaction with the performance of parastatals—many of which have required public subsidies where they had earlier been expected to contribute to government revenues. Partly, no doubt, this reflects a push towards privatization and an expansion of the use of markets urged by donors, including both OECD governments and the IFIs.

To the extent it is the last, its reality and sustainability are in some doubt. Increasing public enterprise efficiency is a widely shared goal as, to a slightly lesser extent, is selective reorganization of sectoral scope and objectives.[17] Wholesale privatization is not popular even in states with a high degree of commitment to the use of market forces. Indeed closure of hopelessly unviable public enterprises often attract wider political support than does selling viable ones at knockdown prices (to private interests). Even the World Bank doubts that in practice there is scope for more than modest privatization in more than a few SSA countries. The one major exception may be the actual operation of crop marketing. especially when it can be separated from export pricing and marketing floor prices, intra year reserve and food security issues, none of which requires state enterprise, rather than co-operative or private enterprise handling of physical purchasing, storage, and transport.

On average SSA government budgets—with the exception of social security and related transfer payments—are roughly the same percent of GDP (about 25 percent) as in other areas of the world.[18] Nor is there a marked average difference in their make-up by type of spending. Social security, subsidies and related transfer payments are the lowest of any region at about 2 percent of GDP. Against these appearances of "normalcy" however, must be set the consideration that it is more difficult—and often more expensive—to raise a given proportion of GDP in taxation in a low-income country than it is in a richer one. Further, compared to large low-income countries (India, China, Bangladesh, Indonesia) SSA countries suffer from diseconomies of small scale.

There are substantial variations from under 10 percent (e.g. Somalia) to over 30 percent (e.g. Botswana) and some surprising rankings, e.g. Kenya ahead of Tanzania. The most plausible explanatory sequence seems to indicate that rapid growth leads to increased public revenues, which in turn leads to large government budgets relative to GDP.

SSA public enterprise investments vary widely in operating efficiency and profitability. Those dealing with food procurement and distribution (in most cases, the lineal descendants of colonial boards) are relatively high cost and limited in their ability to distribute throughout the country. But these failings also characterize most private and co-operative enterprises dealing with food production and distribution. In most other sectors the results are mixed by country, by criterion used, and by enterprise. Like other large scale enterprises, many public ones have been very severely affected by import constraints, price distortions, and the impact of non-marginal devaluation on external debt servicing burdens.

In two senses the public sector clearly is overextended. First, the present eroded revenue and import capacity do not allow full operation or maintenance of existing capacity. In health, education, water, transport where the need is clearly for more, not less, services for economic as well as humane reasons, the cure lies primarily in restoring the revenue base. For states (e.g. Kenya, Nigeria) not facing significant external, threats, some cutbacks in defense spending may well be appropriate. Similarly, in some states the proportion of expenditure on administrative services appears unduly large.

Second, given the limited financial and personnel resources, greater selectivity in determining what the public sector should do is necessary. But we should not deceive ourselves by thinking that wholesale privatization is likely to provide a solution. Rather it should be recognized that in most cases the actual choice is not between whether a service is provided publicly or privately; it is between whether it is provided publicly or not at all. In present circumstances, a more limited range of functions carried out better would usually be desirable.

It can be seen clearly in retrospect that most public sector enterprises or parastatals in most SSA states have been affected by serious weaknesses in four interacting areas. These have been:

First, a deteriorating economic environment has reduced availability of supplies, stability of demand and ability to pay better prices to domestic suppliers or workers;

Second, inexperienced management—many of those in senior positions had had no previous experiences of operating enterprises for profit in competitive (or even non-competitive) conditions—and limited technical skills and experience—especially in accounting and finance and only slightly less in engineering—made the ability to respond effectively to a tougher context inadequate;

Third, unwarranted interference, impractical instructions, and inappropriate regulations and controls exerted or imposed by ministers or other senior political or military figures combined with effective non-accountability and lack of disciplining managers performing poorly or defying proper instructions were endemic.

Fourth, serious over-manning which tended to become even more serious in contracting economies.

Those responsible for weaknesses in each of those areas have been able to claim convincingly that it has not been their own performance that has been the cause of failure but rather the weaknesses that were all too apparent in other areas. Apart from tackling specific areas of weakness directly, policy considerations concerning the appropriate content and the proper role of public enterprises are often very complex.

For a number of sectors—e.g. rail transport, electricity generation, internal airlines, harbors—there is neither a realistic private sector alternative nor an option to close down. In others the choice is effectively between public sector African (or mixed African/foreign) and foreign private enterprise. In further cases the domestic alternative exists but in the form of communities of non-African ancestry. Their already privileged—and deeply resented—economic position, inherited from the colonial era, means that privatization to them would pose massive political and social problems (e.g. in Kenya). Further it could be very problematic indeed as to its impact on the national economy in some cases (e.g. in Sierra Leone) because of their commitment to high capital and consumption remittances and very non-market styles of securing commercial advantage.

These constraints do imply that where African private (or co-operative) enterprises can do the job—e.g. small scale industry, retail trade, most road transport—then public sector participation needs special justification. Experience elsewhere—notably in Brazil and South Korea—suggests that detailed, selective, efficient state intervention at product and enterprise level is important to achieving overall economic and export growth. Credit and import allocations are particularly critical. Whether such interventions work more efficiently with a substantial public sector in the financial and external trade fields is open to debate. The appropriate answer is likely to vary from state to state, and over time, and to be related as much to the number of qualified, experienced citizen personnel available as to ideological choices.

4. How much of SSA's failure to respond effectively flows from bad economic management?

This varies widely from country to country. Just as economic performances in the 1960s and the 1970s were very uneven so also was the quality of economic management. In every country some policy mistakes and a greater number of weaknesses in implementation and management can be cited. However, it is not convincing to argue that economic management everywhere suddenly became worse after 1979.

What clearly did happen was that it became less able to produce desired results. That, however, was true in all regions—not excluding OECD—over 1979-82. The failure was more pronounced in SSA because the external shocks were greater both relative to the physical and financial capacity to respond and to the ability of economic management to tackle harder problems than those it had previously had to face.

Failure to achieve results—for whatever reasons—is bad for morale. When repeated failures accumulate over several years, both the individual and the institutional capacity to manage deteriorates. That process has occurred already in several African states. There is a real danger that it will occur in many more if the problems which have overwhelmed SSA countries in the past eight years remain unresolved.

5. Why has public sector capacity to act declined so sharply?

The simple answer is lack of resources. For example in Zambia rural health services usually lack fuel and spares for vehicles, drugs and food for patients, equipment and kerosene for clinics. Extension services in several countries cannot sensibly advise use of fertilizer, insecticides, or improved seeds because none of these is available.

In some countries—notably but not exclusively the poorer Francophone ones—civil servants and municipal employees may be paid up to three months in arrears. Nearly everywhere price rises and cuts in subsidies imposed in the attempt to regain budgetary balance have reduced the purchasing power of government employees' pay draconically. For example, in Uganda a clerk or laborer's monthly pay as of early 1987 would barely buy one week's staple food for his family; in Zaire a secretary's salary will just about cover the cost of going to and from work. Needless to say, moonlighting, charging users for services nominally (but not actually) paid for by the salary, and overt corruption became endemic in such cases.

In other countries, as a result of two decades of intensive training backed by substantial external support, competent personnel, especially in health and education, are available. Unfortunately, lack of adequate government revenue or import capacity means that drugs, textbooks, kerosene for refrigerators, desks and chairs, paper and pencils, beds and medical equipment, vehicles and fuel cannot be provided in adequate quantities for the personnel to function properly. In extreme cases—e.g. Somalia—the whole public health and education systems are virtually non-functional with only community support and direct donor programs warding off total collapse.

6. Have the recent declines in export crop production and economic growth been the result of politicians' attempts to extract too much from rural producers?

In part and perhaps are the most probable answers. Part of the difficulty with any simple answer is that these processes are not post-1979 (or even post-independence in origin) and in most countries less extraction and redistribution has occurred in the 1980s than before. This is not a complete refutation of the theory as even reduced extraction can have increasingly negative effects if the pool from which the extractions are made is already shrinking for other reasons.

Another problem is one of definition. All taxes, fees and marketing costs (public or private) constitute extractions from the retail or export price before the balance reaches the farmer. But some are necessary costs of actual services, some unnecessary costs of necessary services, some unnecessary costs of unnecessary/undesired services, some exploitative profits and/or corruption, and some normal taxes. The impact of nominal taxation and excess marketing costs depends partly on what income is left after such taxes and how easy it is for the farmer to shift into effectively untaxable crops (e.g. most food crops in most SSA economies). It also depends on whether farmers see a reasonable proportion of total revenue being spent on the type of services and investment which they themselves desire. Sometimes this happens, sometimes it does not, and often it is very difficult to tell whether or not it is happening. Indeed even the direction of rural/urban (or urban/rural) net transfers on public and private account may be neither clear at a particular moment nor uniform over time. In numerous cases, e.g. Botswana, Tanzania, and Zimbabwe, the apparent flow is urban to rural on both accounts but changing relative price ratios may partially offset this, for instance in respect of food crop growers in Botswana in non-drought years.

7. What explains the poor growth record of SSA agriculture?

It is first necessary to enter three caveats. For a majority of SSA economies (but not for those ones in which a majority of SSA's people live) the available estimates do not show a steady declining trend in per capita *food* production but erratic, weather-related fluctuations leading to recurrent crises. The overall averages are dominated by very poor performances in four countries with large populations—Nigeria, the Sudan, Ethiopia, and Zaire. However, for domestic *industrial* crops and for *export* crops, the 1970-87 record *is* unambiguous. For SSA as a whole, and in a majority of its economies, the record is of very low growth, or of absolute decline with even sharper decline in per capita terms. Third, the data series are so shaky that output levels may easily be wrong by 20 to 50 percent and trend changes by as much as 2 percent a year—i.e. what we think we know may not be so.

That said, the dominant physical problems include the declining availability of basic inputs (including hand tools and improved seed), rising populations pushing farmers and herders on to more and more sub-marginal land, cultivation/rotation patterns adapted to long fallows of up to 20 years giving way to intensive, near permanent cultivation, and frequent breakdowns in transport, processing, and marketing services. On the human side, a major problem is the overload of demands on women's time. Health and other basic services have been weakened. Inadequate research frequently results in extension advice being either wrong or impossible to apply. In terms of farmers' incentives, the shortage of goods for their money to buy and the delays in payment for crops delivered may be as much of a problem as the poor prices which the state marketing boards tend to offer, particularly for export and industrial crops.

8. In what way are export and industrial crops different?

Overvaluation of domestic currencies serves to depress prices which farmers will be offered by official marketing boards for export and industrial crops. By-passing low official prices is difficult because there are few alternative buyers, and attempts to sell illicitly or on parallel markets may be risky as well as expensive. Further the global real prices of these crops have tended to fall, so that even in the absence of domestic currency overvaluation and excess marketing costs the real grower prices would have fallen by up to 50 percent since the late 1970s.

Depending upon crop and country, there are sharp differences in the proportion of export proceeds received by growers. In countries with real exchange rates now below late 1970s levels, adjusted for relative inflation, the grower price for tree crops is about 30 percent of export value in Ghana (cocoa), 50 percent in the Ivory Coast (coffee and cocoa), and nearly 70 percent in Tanzania (coffee).

For the marketing of domestic food crops the position is very different. Probably no more than 10 percent are sold through official marketing channels since about 65 to 75 percent are consumed by their producers, 15 to 20 percent are crops or animals for which there are no official channels, and 5 to 10 percent are sold on parallel markets. Official channels (whether marketing board or co-op) do not exist for the marketing of all crops—indeed they are virtually unknown for root crops and plantains, and for many livestock and livestock products, and for vegetables and fruit. With few exceptions such channels as do exist can be by-passed readily whenever official prices fall below private market prices or if—as often happens—private buyers pay cash while official ones pay with chits that take a long time to convert into cash.

Consequently most SSA economies' effective grower and consumer food prices have between 1970 and 1987 risen at least as rapidly as those of other products, and much faster than industrial and export crop prices. Exceptions are limited to those occasions (decreasing in frequency) when large volumes of imported food are made available at highly subsidized prices, e.g. in Zambia and in Somalia. Such subsidies may be provided by the exporter, through the medium of currency overvaluation, by the domestic government directly, or by food aid sold at an unrealistic exchange rate (as in Somalia).

Inefficient public marketing and high profit margin private marketing both give rise to real economic costs. Scarce resources are wasted, government deficits are raised (e.g. notably so in Kenya and Malawi), and food prices are driven up to levels which weigh heavily on the urban poor, and upon those of the rural poor who have to buy food. What is more doubtful, however, is whether inefficient and high cost public marketing does in fact create actual price disincentives for domestic food crop growers. The evidence suggests that growers choose between official or parallel channels depending on which pays more, and the absence of adequate import capacity decouples domestic market prices from the impact of currency overvaluation. This is in marked contrast to what happens with industrial and export crops for which low official prices really do lower grower incomes, encourage smuggling (massively in pre-1984 Ghana and post-1975 Uganda), and divert production away from export crops and toward food crops.

9. If price is not an adequate means to increasing agricultural production what else can be done in the short or medium term?

First basic inputs need to be restored. Second, infrastructure and operating capacity in transport, processing and storage require urgent rehabilitation and expansion. Third, basic services need to be restored as incentives to remain in rural areas, to reduce the time required to fetch water and reach health points and to lower levels of sickness. Poor health significantly reduces the amount of work which rural households can put into production. Fourth, widely sought consumer and construction goods (from cooking oil through beer, thread through cigarettes, roofing sheet and cement through radios and bicycles, soap through cloth—in most places about 20 to 30 basic items) need to be available in rural shops to create real incentives for peasant households, i.e. desired products that actually can be bought for crop proceeds.

These steps could raise output at least 20 percent in most SSA economies independently of changes to grower price or in technology. Most of such steps could also have an impact on the growth of food for household self-provisioning (the so-called "subsistence sector") on whose output price incentives alone have little direct impact. Taken with the 2 to 3 percent trend growth coming from the rising numbers of growers and some slow technological improvements already taking place, the measures cited above could be expected to buy a decade of growth in output of 4 percent a year, or perhaps a little more, which would be sufficient to ease over that period the increasingly severe food scarcity that had been such a tragic feature of the past decade.

10. What of the longer term?

A remarkable feature of SSA's agricultural problem is how little about it is securely known. This ignorance must be dispelled by the late 1990s if output growth above population increase rates is to be sustained.

The first requirement is to procure even reasonably accurate output data. The Asian model of sample crop cutting surveys—virtually unknown in SSA—would appear to be a priority.

The second is to know more about present production patterns and methods and about the gender division of labor. Many indigenous African techniques —e.g. interplanting, and soil scratching (hoeing) as opposed to deep ploughing—are now becoming recognized as more appropriate starting points than imported ones. Further, the variation in output among peasants over quite small distances is frequently high, suggesting that learning from peasants and extending "best known practice" could itself boost output substantially.

Rural women face severe work overloads in Africa.[19] They do nearly all the food processing, water and fuel collection, and caring for the sick on top of more than half of total farming time spent in the field. Improvements—e.g. in rural water and health service access and cheap time-saving innovations in food processing—could simultaneously reduce their burdens and allow them time to produce more. Analyzing accurately which tasks men perform and what tasks are done by women would allow more sensible targeting of extension advice, as would recognition that perhaps a quarter of all rural households are female headed. Those are the aspects of women's liberation of most immediate concern to millions of rural African women.

The third requirement is to create a body of locally-tested, user-friendly, producer cost-effective innovations. At present these are notable by their absence—except for a handful of export crops, certain grains, and in a very few countries (e.g. Zimbabwe). Agricultural researchers have estimated that applicable knowledge in SSA is currently about one-tenth that in South and Southeast Asia. Until that gap is redressed, high growth in output per person or per hectare employed is most unlikely to be sustained.

While action on all three fronts (crop data, production patterns, innovations) is needed at once to provide for the future, substantial gains from research on the first two issues probably cannot be anticipated in under five years. The Asian record from research results suggests a decade's lag between a coherent, targeted program's commencement and any high, generalized payoff. In SSA the time required may be longer because poorer soils, much more dependence on rainfall and greater inter-year (and intra-year) weather variations are characteristic of Africa. Comparable Asian areas—e.g. Bihar—have been the ones for which it has proven hardest to develop relevant innovations.

11. Is increased food output a sufficient condition for overcoming hunger?

Physical availability of food is a necessary condition for adequate nutrition but not a sufficient one.[20]

The majority of the very poor and malnourished (perhaps 75-80 percent) are members of food growing households whose food production levels and other income cannot meet both minimum nutritional standards and other essential needs requiring cash, e.g. cloth, school and medical fees, simple construction materials, soap, farm tools. Until these poor rural households are enabled to produce more they will remain malnourished and poor no matter how much additional output large farmers and agricultural enterprises produce.

The other 20 to 25 percent of the very poor and malnourished are food buyers—largely but not exclusively urban. They too will not benefit from an increased physical availability of food until higher productivity and a more buoyant macroeconomic context make if possible for them to raise their incomes—or until food production costs fall so much from enhanced productivity that lower real food prices and higher net real farmer incomes are attainable at the same time.

Because most African households have separated—not unified—budgets, which member of the household gets the additional income also matters. In general expenditure on child care and food dominate female, but not male, budgets. Thus if reduction of malnutrition and improved child welfare are priorities, so too are raising women's income earning opportunities and productivity levels.

12. How important is price policy?

Very important but unevenly so. The most important price substantially subject to government control is that of foreign exchange (i.e. the exchange rate). Serious (say over 20 percent) and growing overvaluation has widespread detrimental effects including smuggling, lower export production, and erosion of the state revenue base. Correcting it—especially without very serious side effects—is difficult, painful, and can be politically dangerous. Yet the longer these distortions are left uncorrected, the more difficult the process of correction becomes.

Much the best advice is "Don't let serious over-valuation of your domestic currency occur in the first place." Once it has occurred, a phased return to plausible rates (e.g. by managed auctions or by an actively sinking crawling peg) will be required, along with a strong resolution—if possible backed up by institutional safeguards—that major overvaluation should not recur.[21]

The real price of labor is also crucial but in practice is only peripherally within state control. In most SSA countries, only a minority of workers are in formal employment—or are even wage employees at all. "Informal" sector real incomes are virtually totally determined by (very imperfect) markets, with the main spillover from formal sector wages being via wage-earner purchases from the "informal" sector. Even private sector real wages (including allowances and benefits in kind) are only tenuously influenced by state wage policy.

Public sector wages and salaries are—in general—too low. At present levels they cannot sustain minimally adequate household consumption levels. This clearly reduces productivity (whether from malnutrition and related illnesses or from working fewer hours for the government or public enterprise in order to have time to earn other incomes) and inevitably leads to informal "user charges," theft from employers and overt corruption.

However, raising public sector salaries and wages at the same time as public sector deficits are reduced will almost inevitably mean trimming the size of the civil service and government casual labor force. That again will not be politically easy or even cheap—any more than rather less draconic and better compensated restructuring and retrenchment was for the World Bank itself.

Real interest rate levels for most—not by any means all—sources of credit are subject to some state control. As inflation is both hard to predict and raised by higher interest rates, the degree of control over *real* interest rates is far less than that over *nominal* rates. However, serious questions arise as to the functionality of very high nominal interest rates given that there is little evidence that they increase savings and a good deal of evidence that they make it more difficult to reduce inflation. Cost push considerations start to operate while simultaneously banks and governments start to ration credit on considerations other than willingness to pay the going rate. If these processes limit the growth of output, inflationary pressures may be further increased.

Advocates of government non-intervention, and of leaving prices to be settled by markets, often make an exception of the three prices (foreign exchange, labor, and capital) discussed above. In theory, such intervention as does occur should be used to regain market clearing levels. In practice, most critics want most SSA governments to increase the prices of foreign currency and of credit, and to depress the price of labor without empirical analysis of actual or of equilibrium real levels, of present disequilibria or of the dynamic process of moving from one to the other. But it may be hazardous or even perverse to apply general precepts to specific economies without taking the trouble to work through what the effects on actual production, distribution, and inflation in a particular, given situation are likely to be.

Price management is largely non-functional in SSA today. In the past,—when for example price control was administered on a reasonable cost plus basis—price management may have sometimes limited excessive growth in actual costs and /or profit margins in imperfect markets. But it can do so only when supplies at the official price are near demand at that price, or when there is effective rationing down to consumer levels. These conditions are now met only for a handful of goods in a handful of countries (e.g. for staple grains in good crop years). Less sophisticated price controls either prevent production, turn it into parallel channels, or simply benefit a favored minority who are able to procure at official prices and resell at uncontrolled market prices.

13. What is the single most general constraint on SSA countries' ability to produce or even to maintain their existing capital structures?

With the exception of a handful of economies (e.g. Botswana), the answer is import capacity. For half of SSA's economies import strangulation is an appropriate as well as a graphic descriptive term.

In many SSA economies, absolute real import levels are half (or even less) those of the late 1970s. The bulk of the cuts have come in intermediate inputs into production, spares for maintenance, and capital goods for replacement or new investment. The costs show in capacity utilization. Current output in manufacturing is often under one-third of rated capacity and under one-half of the actual output levels attained in the late 1970s. Proper maintenance has become impossible, resulting in a steady erosion of usable capacity, culminating in breakdown. Replacement investment is not made. This in turn leads to capital stock shrinking, and diminishes the ability to clear bottlenecks or to begin any required alteration in the structure of production possibilities.

Contrary to popular impression, these results are not necessarily most severe when initial import to GDP ratios are high. In those cases a cutback of consumption imports with only a limited impact on domestic output is likely to be possible. On the contrary, the lower the ratio of the imports to domestic value added, the greater the domestic output cost of a $1 cut in intermediate goods imports is likely to be. For example, if intermediate and spares operating inputs are 20 to 25 percent of ex-factory value of manufactures (broadly the case in, e.g. Zimbabwe and Tanzania) every $1 of imports reduced is likely to cost $3 to $4 in lost domestic production ex-factory, and there will be additional indirect tax, transport, and distribution losses.

14. How can import capacity be restored to minimally adequate levels—say the real per capita import levels of 1980 as proposed by the World Bank?

That would imply an overall import rise for SSA of the order of 33 to 40 percent—over 50 percent for a significant number of states and over 100 percent for some. To achieve that before the end of the century requires parallel (and coordinated) action on three fronts—increasing export earnings (measured in import capacity terms), reducing ratios of necessary imports to production by building up domestic economic linkages (including efficient import substitution) and raising the levels of net external resource inflows (by higher gross inflows plus more external debt rescheduling and writeoffs).

It has to be recognized that expanding exports cannot do the job single handed. In the first place restoring and increasing export levels will require high prior levels of imports. Second, market prospects for most SSA exports are poor in terms of growth in demand, price, and access to overseas markets.[22] In consequence, a 3 percent real export earnings growth will be extremely hard to sustain, except in those few, fortunate places where new natural resource exports, large relative to present levels, can be opened up— itself an import intensive and time consuming process. Third, SSA's production structures are rigid as well as fragile so that—with few exceptions, e.g. Mauritius and Zimbabwe in goods and the Gambia in tourism—rapid absolute growth of non-traditional exports is likely to need to be preceded by a decade of hard work, structural shifts, and higher imports. Indeed, many of the most promising future exports, e.g. processed forms of existing raw materials plus some simple manufactures, will face severe competition from better financed current producers. High tariffs and other access problems (the so-called "new protectionism" or subsidized self-sufficiency of the North)—if they continue at present levels or burgeon—will simply present further formidable obstacles to breakthroughs.

Encouragement of efficient production of tradeables for the domestic market needs to go hand-in-hand with efficient export promotion. It should not be regarded as its antithesis but as its integrally linked counterpart, as the experience of South Korea and Brazil with import substitution and domestic production integration convincingly demonstrates. Such policies over two to three decades have laid the base for a subsequent rapid growth in non-traditional exports in the cases cited. The need is to devise similar strategies and priorities relevant to SSA contexts and potentials. Food, energy, and manufactures with a high content of local resources and labor are evident candidates. Related infrastructural and bottleneck breaking investments should also be undertaken along with a programmed production of selected intermediate and capital goods. Import substitution of final consumer goods with low initial domestic value added is usually not sensible, because SSA labor costs per unit of output are unusually high for such products and because the initial import capacity to allow production while a slow buildup of domestic inputs took place is not there.

Insofar as this represents a necessary change in strategy, it must be recognized that such a domestic use production strategy will take time to plan and to implement. It takes time to identify suitable products (whether that is done by private or public enterprises), to create institutions, to train people, to acquire knowledge and to create capacity to shift production structures. It will also be import intensive. The direct and indirect import cost of fixed investment in SSA (excluding small scale agriculture) is probably about 67 percent. Even in Zimbabwe, which has relatively well-developed capital goods and construction sectors, it is above 50 percent.

It follows that higher net real resource inflows are even more necessary for adjusting structures of production, imports, and exports than for simple short-term survival or partial recovery within the existing structures. Unfortunately these flows—at net level—have fallen drastically since the late 1970s. For the private sector and for the IMF they have turned negative. For official bilateral flows (including export credits) the net positive balances narrowed. Only for the multilateral official—dominated by the World Bank group and more particularly the International Development Association (IDA)—have they risen significantly.[23] Increasing net flows will in most cases require both increases in net inflows—especially quick disbursing ones targeted on reviving operating input and spare parts import capacity—and debt rescheduling and writing off to reduce outflows.

15. How can human and institutional competence be increased?

This question cannot be answered operationally outside specific national, sectoral, and local contexts.[24] Many SSA countries have made very substantial achievements in basic and higher education. Middle level training—e.g. of artisans, bookkeepers, mechanics—(including functional education to follow-up basic literacy) is much weaker. This often results in inadequate support for high level persons, or a misallocation of their time to inappropriate tasks.

Institutional weaknesses flow partly from newness, partly from personnel weaknesses and partly from the overuse of short stay expatriates in managerial and coordinating roles. This last may prevent an institution from being seen as—or even seeing itself as—truly national. It may also destroy continuity and historic memory without which it is very difficult for any institution to learn from its own experience. This failing is exacerbated when parallel institutions are created and staffed by external bodies supposedly to assist weak national ones. In practice they marginalise and destroy the morale of the national institutions and externalise key policy decisions—e.g. the 1975-80 Marketing Development Bureau's incompetent hegemony over most aspects of agricultural policy in Tanzania.

Similarly, loss through transfer or emigration of trained citizen personnel has nullified many educational achievements and turned institutions into empty shells. One reason is inadequate—below survival—pay; over 80 percent of qualified Ghanaian doctors are practicing outside Ghana, and in Somalia the chief value of a nursing or primary teaching certificate has been to obtain a job "over the water" (predominantly in Saudi Arabia) not in Somalia.

However, pay is not the only explanation. Tanzania with low (but not Ghanaian or Somalian) real wage and salary levels also has a low brain drain; lower it would appear than Kenya's. Many of the African professional diaspora have good reason to doubt their welcome or even their safety should they return home. Ability to do a job seen as useful, respect from society, political stability, and professional freedom appear to be equally crucial factors.

16. Do stabilization and structural adjustment provide adequate frameworks for economic rehabilitation in SSA?

Stabilization (closing of gross imbalances) and structural adjustment (altering output and use mixes) are inevitable. That is the first and truly basic point.

The question which follows is whether such stabilization and adjustment will be planned and managed or imposed by events. The latter path is likely to be the more protracted and expensive, and to create new imbalances and distortions as fast as it extinguishes the old, e.g. Ghana 1973-1981.

Second, there are alternative stabilization and structural adjustment approaches. The idea that there is one simple, always appropriate Fund/Bank package is not accurate. Indeed it is arguable that in any specific case the Fund's concentration on short term, demand constraining, macro monetary management and the Bank's emphasis on medium term, supply expanding, real sectoral issues and policies are at least as likely to conflict as to complement each other.

Third, our ability to compare the results of Fund and/or structural adjustment programs is poor. One cannot prove empirically that a cross section of economies with programs have done better absolutely or in contrast to immediate pre-program results than a cross section without. For example, Togo, Madagascar, Zambia, Sudan, and Zaire have had program after program without attaining stability, significant structual change, or sustainable growth. On the other hand, Ghana's program and the (national not Fund/Bank) Zimbabwe program have at least partially achieved those ends.[25]

Because stabilization and structural adjustment are so necessary, more satisfactory program design and implementation must be worked for. Among the elements in improved programs are likely to be greater flexibility, more built-in mechanisms for adjusting to unforeseen exogenous events, more specific relationships to varying contextual constraints and opportunities, longer time horizons (i.e. in the case of at least the twenty-odd most severely affected economies a decade or more), greater and more articulated attention to expanding supply (including export supply) and more adequate levels of appropriate external funding.

The last issue is in some cases the most critical. Import capacity/external funding levels estimated as the minimum needed for success by the World Bank seem to be met in very much less than half the programs. Further, inappropriately high cost, short term finance, e.g. seven to eight percent, three year grace and three to five year repayment loans (including export credits and IMF drawings) form a dangerously high proportion of many finance packages. It is rational on pure economic grounds for Nigeria not to have drawn on its Fund standby and for Tanzania to have agreed to negligible net levels of Fund finance (other than from the much softer Structural Adjustment Facility). Nigeria views World Bank loans as superior because of longer maturities and Tanzania sees high interest, early repayment finance for general capacity utilization and rehabilitation as part of the problem, not part of the answer.

17. Does "Adjustment With A Human Face" make economic sense in SSA?

"Adjustment With A Human Face"[26] is an approach which stresses the need for early improvement in the access to basic services, the consuming power, and the earned incomes of poor people. It addresses the fact that these are not at present priorities in most stabilization and adjustment programs, albeit since 1985 they have won verbal endorsement from international institutions (including the fund and Bank) and most OECD governments.

The argument is not that poor people would have been better off without stabilization and adjustment. Nor is it primarily that stabilization and adjustment policies themselves make poor people poorer—albeit this can and does happen. Rather it is that national stabilization and adjustment must pay attention to Adam Smith's conclusion that no nation can be great and prosperous the majority of whose people are poor and miserable.

The approach centers on access to basic services (health, education, and pure water), on food security, and on increased production by poor people. Based on evidence from programs which did stress these, it concludes there is no necessary contradiction between these goals and those of macroeconomic growth and restructuring. Poor, illiterate, sick people and, especially, women worn out by caring for the sick and fetching inadequate quantities of impure water over long distances, cannot work very long, very hard or very productively.

The human investment/labor productivity case for universal access to basic services is a strong one. Enhanced production by poor people (whether as farmers, urban self-employed, or employees) is often the lowest cost way of raising output and also the only way in which poor people can be sure to benefit since distribution is integrally linked not only to growth of production but to the production that grows.

Both work related uses of food aid (e.g. in employing the otherwise unemployed in the creation of infrastructure that will improve food security) and community involvement in operating basic services are consistent with this approach. It is not an attempt to import a rich economy welfare system into SSA, but a deliberate attempt to increase production (as well as social and political stability) by augmenting the human conditions of poor people.

18. Is more policy dialogue needed?

Yes, but only if it really is a dialogue with a Northern willingness to listen and to learn, to advise, and to support rather than simply to preach and to require. Unwise external advice acted on by SSA economies played a substantial part in the creation of present problems and could do so again.

There are no simple, generally and instantly applicable answers to SSA's overall economic problems—except wrong ones. Simple panaceas enforced on SSA countries by technical assistance and through the leverage exerted by offering access to financial resources are a prescription for continued disaster. No strategy or policy package which is not based on detailed contextual knowledge and which is not understood and genuinely supported by the relevant African leadership (and at least passively assented to by a broad range of households and workers) has any chance of success. Nor does a strategy stand much chance of success if it is jerked up by the roots for examination every year and radically changed if it does not produce dramatic results within two years.

19. What implications for United States policy?

United States policy toward SSA is inevitably subject to three major constraints. First, United States concerns in SSA—and especially southern Africa—are not solely, perhaps not even primarily, economic. Second, the United States policies which affect SSA's chances for economic rehabilitation are not necessarily either primarily economic in themselves (e.g. spin-off of East-West issues) nor particularly SSA oriented (e.g. backwash of rising protectionism aimed primarily at newly industrialized countries, Japan, and the European Economic Community). Third, the United States is facing a period of declining real resource availability for support of all its external policies and SSA is not viewed as a top priority area by many except sub-Saharan Africans themselves and their most committed supporters.

However, there are three counteracting points. Continued economic disintegration in SSA will have major human consequences which—as evidenced by the widespread reaction to the television pictures of 1984-85 drought—do matter to many Americans. And the United States has consistently perceived the accompanying political instability as contrary to its political interest. Second, a bankrupt Africa unable to export, import, or service debts will be a drag on the world economy. In the context of a threatened recession, such a drag would be detrimental to the United States' economic interests.

Third, the United States does—through military and economic support and by its other contributions bilaterally and through multinational agencies—spend substantial sums on overseas assistance, including not insubstantial amounts in SSA. Just as SSA countries are regularly advised to review the consistency, attainability, and rationality of their goals and to reorganize them in relation to fresh priorities and to available resources, so too should the United States in relation to SSA review its policies and the basis of its assistance to SSA. Sub-optimal resource deployment is not a failing unique to African governments.

A Checklist of Priorities—Adjustment Approaches
The first priority is to take a hard look at what is actually happening and why. Both friends and critics in SSA frequently doubt the accuracy of official United States economic (or for that matter political) perceptions and interpretations. One special area of concern is evaluating the actual consequences of stabilization and adjustment packages, most (not all) of which are failing in their own terms. Clearly a more flexible contextual process of learning from experience and "adjusting adjustment" is needed.

Enhancing Efficiency: Public and Private
A second related priority is to treat economic efficiency and privatization as parallel and, perhaps, related issues, not as a single issue. There is little disagreement that the former is needed nor that government and public enterprises will continue to play major economic and social roles and, therefore, that improved efficiency on their part is crucial. The actual scope for privatization or, given the low growth and extreme foreign exchange constraints, new foreign private investment is much more contentious and non-homogenous. Even the World Bank doubts that it is very great over the short and medium term in more than a handful of SSA economies. Clearly ideological, broad brush demands for wholesale dismantling of public services and public enterprises produce negative counter-reactions even from businesslike governments whose economies are dominated by healthy private sectors, such as Botswana.

One form of economic assistance which would be generally welcome and which would support the private sectors of SSA economies is the establishment of revolving funds to pre-finance imports of spares and intermediate goods to help produce exports. Such programs do work and do assist efficient private sector enterprises. Until halted for reasons unrelated to its economic results, the U.S. AID program of this type in Zimbabwe was viewed as of major value by both the private enterprise sector and the government.

So long as public enterprises were not excluded, very few SSA governments would reject such programs on ideological grounds. On the contrary, they would be likely to be welcomed as a means to expanding exports.

Financing Adjustment Appropriately

A third priority is longer term, more appropriate and in most cases larger support for well designed stabilization/adjustment packages which do embody national priorities and which are actually believed in and backed by the SSA governments presenting them. Rolling commitments stretching three to five years ahead (which need not be binding contractual obligations) are needed. The World Bank is quite correct in viewing substantial structural adjustment as a seven to ten year exercise not adequately addressed by annual or even two year projections and programs.

Because present capacity is underutilized and undermaintained, more import support for intermediate goods and spares, more rehabilitation and deferred maintenance finance are needed and less new projects other than those which are central to breaking bottlenecks and adjusting the makeup of production. Balance of payments support in the context of a majority of SSA economies should not be viewed as subsidies for consumption, but rather as the provision of the complementary resources necessary to put people back to work.

The need for more finance for adjustment applies both to USAID spending and to the United States contributions to international agencies. IDA, African Development Bank (ADB), International Fund for Agricultural Development (IFAD), International Labor Organization (ILO), World Food Program (WFP), UNICEF, United Nations Development Porgram (UNDP), and the Structural Adjustment Facility of the IMF are important components in most of the SSA rehabilitation and recovery efforts which are functioning effectively. All have been hampered by freezes, cutbacks, or delays in United States funding. Attempts by the United States government to encourage other OECD members to play a larger proportionate role are handicapped by the United States already having the lowest ratio of net concessional resource transfers to GDP amongst any of the large OECD countries and one which has been falling.

Knowledge Transfers and Institutional Support

The gaps in SSA specialized knowledge, entrepreneurial and management competence, and institutional capacity (including the capacity of the private sector and of voluntary organizations) deserve to be addressed more specifically and effectively within United States assistance to SSA. Generalist advisory and review teams and long stay senior personnel (except in new, highly technical activities) are no longer the most common need, nor are unselective overseas educational programs.

Short stay specialist personnel (for mutually agreed purposes), funding for applied research by Africans (as pioneered by the Rockefeller Foundation), support (including specialist personnel and equipment) for African training institutions at regional and national levels, and assistance to facilitate direct institutional links (government, enterprise, university, and non-governmental organizations [NGOs])—these are the types of initiatives likely to prove most productive in most SSA countries today. They may also prove to be cheaper as training in the United States costs more than it does in SSA, and senior expatriate technical assistance personnel are very expensive.

The Peace Corps' evolution toward a more specialized and less homogenous set of roles provides an example for broader application. However, direct institutional links (e.g. southern United States agricultural faculties and SSA agricultural faculties, African power corporations and USA counterparts) and NGO-run programs linked to grass roots African bodies are not invariably effective. Detailed specification of intended goals and approaches, two-way familiarization, and mutual respect are as important (and as hard to achieve) at these levels as at the government to government level. The country programs and/or projects (e.g. in nutrition, basic health, immunization, productive employment creation) of several of the smaller international agencies—including IFAD, UNICEF and ILO—are in some respects similar to NGOs in reaching poor people and their community bodies directly and at low cost, while often being able to deploy sounder contextual knowledge and technical expertise than some NGOs.

Disaster Relief: A Continuing Disaster Area
Disaster relief—not only that provided by the United States—urgently requires refashioning. The aims are clear enough—to relieve suffering during disasters, to contribute to the rehabilitation of those affected, and to reduce future vulnerability. Separate logistical units for disaster relief may be necessary but care needs to be taken since separate analysis and program planning can lead to a form of tunnel vision and to cadres for whom (however unintentionally) disaster is their bread and butter.

Most disasters cast long shadows in advance. Early warnings and at least rough estimates of need can commonly be given. Early responses—crucial to having assistance in time to allow those affected to remain in their homes and not be driven into camps or urban slums—are much less common. Pre-existing coordinating committees chaired by governments but including donors (like that in Botswana) are rarer still. Disaster aid is not currently linked to many key aspects of future loss limitation (e.g. the supply of veterinary drugs in Somalia), to subsequent rehabilitation (including the provision of interim wage employment while agricultural output is rebuilt), or to measures to reduce future risk. U.S. AID could and should take a lead in promoting rethinking along these lines by SSA governments and by the other agencies making major contributions to disaster relief.

Exports and Adjustment

SSA needs to export more if structural adjustment is ever to narrow the large export/import gaps afflicting at least half of Africa's economies. It is in the interests of the United States that this happens. SSA cannot become a promising growth market for United States exports until it occurs. If export growth with reasonable prices cannot be achieved, there is a genuine danger that SSA could become a permanent problem area requiring continuous external support and with little sign of any return to sustainable growth, let alone development.

Simply raising the volume of most present SSA commodity exports rapidly is likely to contribute more to a lowering of world prices than to raising overall SSA export earnings measured in import capacity. The recent history of commodity price management like that of industrial economy commodity to output ratio shifts does not suggest any easy answers to these structural problems. However, the coffee and cocoa agreements are marginally useful in averting sudden catastrophic price collapses and in exerting some influence on tendencies toward overproduction. Continued United States membership in them and advocacy of major consuming or producing (e.g. Malaysia in the case of cocoa), non-members joining would be useful to SSA and further the United States interest in economic stability in SSA and Latin America.

However, such measures will do more to reduce risks of sudden price falls than to raise export earnings or the net value per unit of commodity production. Research directed toward production and transport cost reduction, facilitation of more effective marketing, additional pre-export processing, and manufacturing can open up more promising ways forward for a number of SSA economies. US Aid should be willing to finance research and pilot programs as well as resultant operational projects in these fields. However, to be fully effective, such support should be paralleled by review of United States tariffs and other trade policies which place higher barriers on manufactured and processed imports from SSA countries than on the importation of the raw primary commodities on which they are based.

Similar considerations apply to other non-traditional SSA exports. United States trade restrictions aimed at major exporters are likely to be especially serious for new SSA entrants or would-be entrants into global markets even though their exports to the United States could hardly damage United States industries or contribute significantly to the United States trade deficit. Some form of exemption scheme (e.g. for specialty textiles, furniture, and shoes) should be possible for low and lower middle (up to $1,250 per capita GDP) SSA.

Conclusion

These recommendations recognize that United States resources are limited and that SSA is a middle level, not a top, priority area for United States external and especially external economic policy. Therefore, to a large extent they embody suggestions for using resources more efficiently or taking low cost initiatives.

That said, the United States has one of the lowest ratios of concessional external economic transfers to GDP of OECD members and within it a lower than average proportional allocation to SSA. A case for rearranging priorities exists on both counts. The reasons are of necessity mixed—humanitarian, political, and economic—even if the means and ends discussed above are primarily economic.

Notes

1. For fuller accounts see World Bank, *Toward Sustained Development in Sub-Saharan Africa - A Joint Programme of Action* (Washington, 1984); Torre Rose (ed.), *Crisis and Recovery in Sub-Saharan Africa* (Paris, 1985); Philip Ndegwa, Leopold Mureithi, and Reginald Herbold Green (ed.), *Development Options for Africa in the 1980s and Beyond* (Nairobi, 1985).

2. For fuller accounts see World Bank, *Financing Adjustment with Growth in Sub-Saharan Africa, 1981-90* (Washington, 1986); United Nations Economic Commission for Africa (ECA), *The Human Dimension as the Test of and a Means to Achieving Africa's Economic Recovery and Development* (Addis Ababa, 1988).

3. For a review and case studies see Christopher Colclough and Reginald Herbold Green (eds.), "Stabilisation—For Growth or Decay? Short Run Costs and Long Run Uncertainties in Africa," *IDS Bulletin*, XIX, 3 (1985), 1-5.

4. *Ibid.*

5. See, e.g. World Bank, *Sustained Development* and *Financing*; Ndegwa, *Options*; Caroline Allison and Reginald Herbold Green (eds.), "Sub-Saharan Africa: Getting the Facts Straight," *IDS Bulletin*, XVI, 3 (1985), 1-6.

6. See also Ndegwa in Ndegwa, *Options;* Green, "Malaise to Recovery: An Overview," in Reginald Herbold Green (ed.), "Sub-Saharan Africa: Towards Oblivion or Reconstruction," *Journal of Development Planning*, 15 (1985), 9-41.

7. For fuller discussion see Carol Lancaster and John Williamson (eds.), *African Debt and Financing* (Washington, 1986); Stephany Griffith-Jones and Green in Rose, *Crisis and Recovery* .

8. See UNICEF, *Children on the Front Line* (Washington, 1987), especially annexes to Southern African chapter and, more generally, Reginald Herbold Green, "Killing the Dream: The Political and Human Economy of War in Sub-Saharan Africa," IDS *Discussion Paper* 238 (Falmer, 1987).

9. See Michael Lipton in Rose, *Crisis and Recovery*.

10. See editorial and Charles Harvey, "Non-Marginal Price Changes: Conditions for the Success of Floating Exchange Rate Systems in Sub-Saharan Africa" in Colclough, "Stabilisation," 67-74.

11. See Ndegwa, *Options;* Ndegwa, Mureithi, and Green, *Management For Development: Priority Themes in Africa Today* (Nairobi, 1987).

12. See ECA, *Human Dimension*, for fuller discussion.

13. See World Bank, *Sustained Development* and *Financing*; Lancaster, *Debt and Financing*; Organisation of African Unity, *Africa's Priority Programme For Economic Recovery, 1986-1990* (Rome, 1985) for broadly similar argumentation and supporting analytical exercises.

14. *Ibid.*

15. ECA, *Human Dimension*. See also Giovani Andrea Cornea, A. Richard Jolly, Frances Stewart (eds.), *Adjustment with a Human Face: Protecting the Vulnerable and Promoting Growth* (Cambridge, 1987).

16. For a fuller account, see Green "From Deepening Economic Malaise toward Renewed Development: an Overview," in Green "Oblivion or Reconstruction?", 9-43; Rose, *Crisis and Recovery*.

17. See Ndegwa, *Options* and *Management*.

18. See Colclough, "Competing Paradigms in the Debate about Agricultural Pricing Policy," in Allison, "Getting the Facts Straight," 39-46.

19. See ECA, *Human Dimension*; Allison in Ndegwa, *Options*; Weeks-Vagliani in Rose, *Crisis and Recovery*.

20. See Cornea, *Human Face*; ECA, *Human Dimension,* for more detailed discussion.

21. See Colclough "Stabilisation," especially editorial and article by Harvey.

22. See Martin Godfrey, "Trade and Exchange Rate Policy in Sub-Saharan Africa," in Allison, "Getting the Facts Straight," 31-38.

23. See World Bank, *Financing,* Lancaster, *Debt* for fuller accounts.

24. See Ndegwa, *Management,* for a number of contextual and sectoral studies.

25. See Colclough, "Stabilisation" for several case studies.

26. Cornea, Jolly, Stewart volume by this title represents a wider body of work including, e.g. ECA, *Human Dimension*.

27. See economic cost estimates in UNICEF, *Children on the Front Line.*

4: The Debt Problem in Sub-Saharan Africa:

Causes, Consequences, and Possible Solutions

BY JOHN UNDERWOOD

1. Introduction and Summary

Virtually everyone who writes about debt eventually cites (perhaps apocryphally) John Maynard Keynes: "If you owe the bank one thousand dollars, it's your problem. If you owe the bank one million dollars, it's their problem." If you change these numbers to one hundred million and one hundred billion, you have something of the essence of the African debt problem. Africa owes simultaneously too little and too much. Sub-Saharan African countries owe too little to commercial banks to present a danger to the world financial system and, thus, to draw attention to their plight. Yet, relative to the earning power of their own economies, many of these countries are deeper in debt than Brazil or Mexico.

Sub-Saharan African debt now stands at about $100 billion (See Table 1 on page 74). By contrast, Brazil and Mexico owe over $100 billion each. United States bank exposure (their claims not guaranteed by a third party outside the debtor country) in sub-Saharan Africa is less than $2 billion (See Table 2 on page 75). Excluding Nigeria and the Ivory Coast, which come under U.S. Treasury Secretary James Baker's well-publicized 1985 initiative for highly indebted middle income countries, United States bank exposure

Table 1

Sub-Saharan Africa's External Debt as a Share of Total Developing Country Debt at the End of 1986

(Figures given are in billions of U.S. dollars)

		(Percentage Share)
Sub-Saharan Africa[1] of which:	102	8.6%
IDA-eligible countries	57	4.8%
Other countries of which:	45	3.8%
Nigeria	22	1.8%
Ivory Coast	11	0.9%
Latin America[1] of which:	399	33.5%
Brazil	111	9.3%
Mexico	102	8.5%
Other Developing Countries[1]	691	57.9%
All Developing Countries	1,192	100.0%

[1] Estimates for countries, such as Angola, that do not report external debt data to the World Bank are included under "Other Developing Countries."

Source: World Bank, *World Debt Tables,* 1987-88 edition.

Table 2

United States Bank Claims on and Exposure to Sub-Saharan Africa: March 31, 1987

(Figures given are in millions of United States dollars)

	Claims	Less Amounts Guaranteed By External Entity	Plus Amts. Externally Guar. by Borrower	Equals U.S. Bank Exposure
Non-Oil Africa	2,734	806	46	1,974
Less:				
Egypt	546	337	31	240
Morocco	845	99	8	754
Tunisia	134	42	0	92
Plus:				
Nigeria	864	274	28	618
Gabon	41	9	0	32
Equals:				
Sub-Saharan Africa	2,114	611	35	1,538
Ivory Coast	367	7	6	366
Sub-Saharan Africa Less Nigeria and Ivory Coast	883	330	1	554

Source: Federal Financial Institutions Examinations Council Country Exposure Lending Survey: March 1987, released August 5, 1987.

is a mere $600 million. By contrast, United States bank exposure is $24 billion in Mexico, $23 billion in Brazil, $8 billion in Venezuela, $6 billion in Chile, and $78 billion in all of Latin America. While European banks are more active in Africa, with roughly $23 billion in claims ($13 billion excluding Nigeria), many of their loans carry the guarantees of European official export credit agencies (ECAs) and do not represent private bank exposure to Africa.

This relatively small amount of debt by the standards of Latin America is too large for many African countries. A World Bank study outlined below indicated that, for a dozen low income African countries, scheduled debt service in 1986-90 was about 67 percent of projected exports, far higher than levels that developing countries have been able to meet under the best of circumstances. Reschedulings (actual and anticipated) reduce the debt service to 40 percent of expected exports, but leave the volume of imports 13 percent below the already depressed levels of 1980-82, given likely levels of new borrowings, and grant aid. In per capita terms, imports are projected to fall by 30 percent. The sharp decline in projected imports puts in doubt the export projections because, without new capital goods and spare parts, which many African countries cannot currently produce in sufficient quantity, production for export is endangered. These countries are projected to enter 1991 with scheduled debt service averaging almost 60 percent of exports and with depressed import and growth prospects. This is far from a creditworthy situation, despite years of adjustment and debt rescheduling designed to restore creditworthiness.

These dozen debt distressed countries have per capita incomes in the $100 to $400 per year range, far below the $2,000 average for Latin American countries. Further compression of consumption to generate the resources to increase investment is not possible in most cases. In order to resume growth, external financing of investment is crucial. New resources, in the form of new concessional aid or extraordinary debt relief or a combination of both are needed to allow these countries to achieve rates of growth and eventual creditworthiness.

This chapter is split into three parts. The first briefly reviews the history of the debt build-up in sub-Saharan Africa. The second examines the current situation and outlook with regard to the external debt of these countries. The third weighs the merits and demerits of various proposals for dealing with the very serious debt problems of a group of low-income African debtor countries.

Two important points must be highlighted at the outset. First, Africa's problem is not exclusively, or even predominantly, an external debt problem. The debt problem in Africa is a symptom of low rates of investment and low rates of return on the investment that was undertaken. Africa's growth and debt problems predate the interest rate and terms of trade shocks of the 1980s that have precipitated the debt crisis in other regions. Much of Africa's debt is fixed-rate and concessional and was only marginally and gradually affected by rising real interest rates. Any permanent solution to Africa's debt problems must involve major policy changes—changes that result in an increase in the productivity of investment. Second, a majority of African countries face a manageable debt service situation over the next decade. Low-income African countries with extremely serious external debt service problems of a prolonged nature probably number 20 or fewer.

This chapter uses a country classification system that is helpful in discussing sub-Saharan Africa. The region is divided into those countries eligible to receive credits from the International Development Agency (IDA), the soft loan facility of World Bank, and those that are too rich and too creditworthy to borrow from IDA. There are 33 IDA-eligible countries and 12 non-IDA countries. One of these latter countries, Angola, would be eligible for IDA if it were a member of the World Bank. Countries in both groups have serious debt servicing problems, but because the composition of debt in the two groups of countries differs markedly, the likely solutions will be different. The non-IDA countries with debt problems fall under the category of Baker initiative countries, where private banks play a major role.[1]

II. A Short History of the Debt Build-up

Any attempt to delineate general causes for the debt service problems of Africa must, of course, abstract them from the very complex economic, political and social factors at work in each country. But most analysts list several overlapping and related factors as important in the evolution of the current debt service problems in Africa.[2]

The factors at work in the debt build-up include:

1. Commodity price booms that were thought, or at least wished, to be permanent and that proved to be transitory.

2.   Expanded access to nonconcessional credit from banks, most often with guarantees from official export credit agencies such as the United States Export-Import Bank.
3.   Public expenditure expansion financed by the boom in exports and by nonconcessional loans.
4.   External factors that turned negative during and after the second oil shock.
5.   Failure to recognize and adjust to the new, more hostile external economic environment, leading to external payments interruptions and, consequently, to a disruption in inflows from external loans.

A majority of the IDA countries experienced a cycle of commodity price boom and bust in the 1970s: Niger (uranium); the Central African Republic, Tanzania, Kenya, and several others (coffee); Togo (phosphate); and the Gambia and Senegal (peanuts). Because of government-run marketing boards or because of export or other taxes, these higher prices led to higher government revenues and great pressures to increase government expenditures. Expectations of even higher future revenues led to pressures for external borrowing that allowed increases in both current consumption and current investment. In some countries, the 1970s were mainly a bust, but they did not escape debt problems either. Low copper prices hurt Zambia and low iron ore prices hurt Mauritania and Liberia. But all three countries borrowed to maintain government expenditures on the expectation that prices would rise to historical levels in the near future.

The expanded access to credit came about for two reasons. First, the banking system spent much of the 1970s recycling the current account surpluses of the OPEC countries. The Eurocurrency market became an important source of financing for some of the richer IDA countries, including Senegal, Togo, Zambia, and Liberia. Even some poorer countries—Malawi is an example—borrowed from banks. Second, export credit agencies, pushed by developed-country governments facing rising unemployment and sluggish demand, increased their lending and guarantee activities at a 35 percent per year rate between 1972 and 1980. A third feature of credit availability, important in a few countries, was direct lending by public and private entities in OPEC countries to favored countries in Africa. The major recipients included Mauritania, Sudan, and Somalia.

Public sector borrowing was directed mainly into large public investment projects. Some of these were in categories for which the economic return is either negligible or very long-term: new capitals, conference centers (Liberia), or elaborate new universities (Madagascar). So-called white elephant projects included luxury hotels, steel mills, oil refineries, and sugar mills. Often, borrowed funds were used for recurrent expenditures, meaning that no productive assets were put in place to service the debt. Another factor that must be mentioned is capital flight. Often, the borrowed funds ended up in the overseas accounts of local residents. The assets are gone but the debts remain.

The contribution of external factors, other than low commodity prices, to debt problems was less important in Africa than elsewhere. Higher real interest rates had less of an impact on the IDA countries in Africa than on Latin America. Africa has much less floating rate debt. The share of Africa's debt, including short-term, at floating rates is about 33 percent, mostly in non-IDA countries, compared with 76 percent in Latin America. Until recently, virtually all guaranteed export credits carried fixed rates. Development aid (known as official development aid, or ODA, in the trade) in the form of loans carries low and fixed rates—and ODA is increasingly in the form of grants. However, the fall in interest rates since 1985 has also helped Africa less. As Africa's predominantly fixed-rate debt rolls over, often through rescheduling, the nonconcessional component picks up higher interest rates. This built-in lag means that many IDA countries face higher, not lower, average interest rates on their debt over the next few years.

III. The Current Debt Situation

The 40 or so countries of sub-Saharan Africa owe approximately $100 billion to their creditors. That is about $200 per person. African debt is small when compared to the debt of, say, Latin America, which stands at about $400 billion or about $1,000 per capita. Unfortunately, sub-Saharan Africa's ability to produce income is also small. GNP per capita averages about $400 per year in Africa, as opposed to close to $2,000 per year in Latin America, making the debt to GNP ratios about the same in both regions. Africa's scheduled debt service, as a fraction of GNP, is slightly smaller than Latin America's because Africa's debt is more concessional.

Yet, one can make a case that the burden of debt is potentially larger in Africa because incomes are lower. Each one percentage point of its very

low income that must be devoted to debt service imposes a greater pain in
Africa than in Latin America.

The Creditor Composition of Sub-Saharan Africa's Debt

The composition and concentration of Africa's debt is also different from
that of Latin America. About 70 percent of Africa's debt represents claims
against official creditors, comprising the IMF, other multilateral organza-
tions, and official bilateral creditors. (See Table 3 on pages 82-87.) Only about
20 percent of Latin America's debt represents claims on official creditors.

These numbers lack precision because of the way data are recorded in the
World Bank's Debtor Reporting System (DRS), the major source of developing country external debt data. Suppose a United States bank finances an
export to an African country but seeks a guarantee from the United States
Export-Import Bank (Exim Bank). The debtor country would report the debt
as owed to a private bank. The country is unconcerned with, and may be
unaware of, the external guarantee. The guarantee becomes apparent to the
debtor only if payments on the loan are missed. The guaranteed portion of
those payments then become the claim of the guarantor.

Given the lack of access of most African countries to the market for commercial bank syndicated credits, it is likely that a relatively high percentage
of the claims of private banks are guaranteed by an official agency in an
industrial country. United States banking statistics show that 29 percent of
United States bank claims on sub-Saharan Africa carry external guarantees,
as opposed to about 5 percent in Latin America. The externally guaranteed
portion jumps to 37 percent if Nigeria and the Ivory Coast, the two sub-
Saharan African Baker initiative countries, are excluded.

United States Claims on Sub-Saharan Africa

United States claims data reflect the predominance of official claims in
sub-Saharan Africa's debt. United States government claims are $4.3 billion,
or about five percent of total sub-Saharan African debt, enough to make
the United States government one of Africa's largest official bilateral
creditors, but indicative of the wide dispersion of African debt by source.
(See Table 4 on page 88.) United States claims are about evenly split between export credits, official aid (including military), and credits in support
of United States agricultural exports. Over $1 billion of these claims are on
IDA-eligible countries with serious debt problems. United States commercial

bank exposure in sub-Saharan Africa is only $1.5 billion. Excluding Nigeria and the Ivory Coast, both middle income Baker initiative countries, United States bank exposure in the region is tiny, less than $600 million.

Debt Service

Data on debt service (payments of principal and interest on external debt) also illustrate the importance of official creditors in Africa. Seventy-five percent of the debt service due on the long-term public debt of the IDA-eligible countries of sub-Saharan Africa in 1986-87 was owed to official creditors. (See Table 5 on pages 90-95.) The IMF accounted for 20 percent of total debt service due and other multilateral creditors for another 17 percent. The remaining 38 percent was scheduled to be paid to individual bilateral creditor governments.

Total scheduled debt service of the IDA-eligible countries in 1986-87 averaged about $5.7 billion dollars per year, about 40 percent of estimated exports of goods and services. As in the past, actual debt service was much lower, because of rescheduling and rising arrears. In 1984, these countries were scheduled to make debt service payments equal to 35 percent of exports of goods and services. Their actual ex post debt service payments were 22 percent of exports.

Since 1975, 23 sub-Saharan African countries have negotiated a total of 71 rescheduling agreements with official creditors, about half of all Paris Club rescheduling agreements during this period. (See Chart 1 on pages 108-109; the Paris Club is the name for the forum in which official bilateral creditors meet with debtor countries to discuss debt rescheduling.) Fifteen sub-Saharan African countries have negotiated 29 rescheduling agreements with commercial banks. To again demonstrate the relatively small magnitude of sub-Saharan African debt, $31 billion was rescheduled in these 100 agreements, about nine percent of the total dollar volume of $350 billion of developing country debt rescheduled over the last decade. Excluding Nigeria and the Ivory Coast, the rest of sub-Saharan Africa accounted for only five percent of the volume of debt rescheduled since 1975.[3]

The Official Creditor Problem

There are two aspects to the predominance of official creditors in external claims on Africa that add to the difficulty of solving their debt service problems. First, multilateral claims are traditionally exempt from rescheduling, the standard remedy to a debt service problem. Fifteen IDA-eligible countries

Table 3a: External Debt by

(Figures are in millions of United States dollars)

| | Public and publicly guaranteed long-term debt | | | | |
| | Total Liabilities (Including IMF purchases) | Official sources | | Private sources | |
		Total	IBRD	Suppliers' Credits	Financial Institutions[a]
IDA-eligible countries with prolonged debt problems					
Benin	685	100	0	20	261
Gambia	280	48	0	10	23
Liberia	1,027	343	100	3	157
Madagascar	1,952	814	28	63	334
Mali	1,095	579	0	19	11
Mauritania	1,327	720	57	62	61
Niger	947	282	0	12	144
Somalia	1,429	742	0	0	59
Sudan	7,201	3,765	40	40	905
Tanzania	3,329	1,135	281	171	290
Togo	776	342	3	4	94
Zambia	4,775	1,552	338	225	405
Sub Total	24,822	10,421	846	630	2,744

Note: Rows may not add to totals because of rounding.

a. Includes a small amount of private financing from nonfinancial institutions.

b. Arrears on long-term principal payments are included in long-term debt,

Source at the End of 1984

Total public and publicly guaranteed long-term debt	Private nonguaranteed long-term debt	Estimated short-term debt & arrears	IMF	Debt as percentage of GNP	Debt as percentage of exports of goods and services
582	0	..	0	72.5	292.5
161	0	..	27	169.8	325.9
757	0	..	208	92.6	209.2
1,636	0	..	148	80.2	517.9
960	0	..	64	109.7	502.3
1,171	0	..	30	183.6	383.6
678	0	..	44	83.3	259.4
1,233	0	..	102	104.8	1,538.6
5,659	0	..	598	79.5	913.2
2,594	61	..	24	86.9	733.2
659	0	..	49	115.1	306.0
2,779	23	..	698	181.0	476.89
18,867	246	3,718	1991	99.0	527.3

and some short-term arrears may be included in short-term debt; as a result, there may be some double-counting.
Source: Financing Adjustment with Growth in Sub-Saharan Africa, 1986-90 (Washington, D.C., 1986).

Table 3b: External Debt by

(Figures are in millions of United States dollars)

| | Public and publicly guaranteed long-term debt | | | Private sources | |
	Total Liabilities (including IMF purchases)	Official Total	sources Total	Suppliers' Credits	Financial Institutions[a]
Other IDA-eligible countries					
Burkina	437	110	260	7	30
Burundi	346	102	209	0	24
Central African Rep.	262	99	98	24	2
Chad	115	13	72	14	10
Ethiopia	1,526	681	522	57	124
Ghana	1,014	523	473	123	3
Guinea	1,287	763	227	136	43
Guinea-Bissau	180	58	58	9	14
Kenya	3,811	909	1,240	63	4,221
Lesotho	138	10	112	2	11
Malawi	885	146	457	19	109
Rwanda	281	54	190	0	0
Senegal	2,026	860	498	10	187
Sierra Leone	463	128	124	65	24
Uganda	1,031	261	344	27	42
Zaire	5,001	2,764	608	139	573
Sub-Total	19,803	7,480	5,503	696	1,618
Total: IDA-eligible countries	44,625	17,901	10,576	1,326	4,362

Note: Rows may not add to totals because of rounding
a. Includes a small amount of private financing from nonfinancial institutions.
b. Arrears on long-term principal payments are included in long-term debt

Source at the End of 1984

Total public and publicly guaranteed long-term debt	Private nonguaranteed long-term debt	Short-term debt	IMF	Debt as percentage of GNP	Debt on percentage of exports of goods and services
407	0	..	0	48.3	255.3
334	0	..	0	36.1	270.6
224	0	..	24	44.0	166.7
109	0	..	4	38.3	78.1
1,384	0	..	75	32.5	249.7
1,123	0	..	468	41.6	329.3
1,168	0	..	11	65.3	330.9
149	0	..	4	111.0	1,284.7
2,633	428	..	380	64.5	234.6
134	0	..	0	45.3	32.6
731	0	..	113	66.1	231.2
244	0	..	0	17.6	153.7
1,555	10	..	201	84.9	270.8
342	0	..	74	46.2	298.7
675	0	..	315	20.5	229.7
4,084	8	..	579	159.9	264.9
15,297	446	1,812	2,248	56.4	245.0
34,165	692	5,529	4,239	74.1	348.9

and some short-term arrears may be included in short-term debt; as a result, there may be some double-counting.

Sources: Financing Adjustment with Growth in Sub-Saharan Africa, 1986-90 (Washington, D.C., 1986).

Table 3c: External Debt by

(Figures are in millions of United States dollars)

| | Total Liabilities (including IMF purchases) | Public and publicly guarnateed long-term debt | | Private sources | |
		Official sources Total	Total	Suppliers' Credits	Financial Institutions[a]
Other countries					
Cameron	2,729	727	638	82	290
Ivory Coast	7,431	835	1,152	272	2,576
Nigeria	19,744	1.072	1,111	350	9,283
Zimbabwe	2,124	295	188	19	944
Sub-Total	32,028	2,929	3,088	723	13,094
Botswana	281	81	158	7	30
Congo	1.603	562	263	64	507
Gabon	975	191	66	46	422
Mauritius	560	89	158	1	106
Swaziland	195	60	110	8	178
Sub-Total	3,614	984	754	118	1,072
Total: Other countries	35,642	3,912	3,843	842	14,166
TOTAL	80,268	21,814	14,418	2,168	18,527

Note: Rows may not add to totals because of rounding.

a. Includes a small amount of private financing from nonfinancial institutions.

b. Arrears on long-term principal payments are included in long-term debt,

Source at the End of 1984

Total public and publicly guaranteed long-term debt	Private nonguaranteed long-term debt	Short-term debt	IMF	Debt as percentage of GNP	Debt as percentage of exports of goods and services
1,738	609	..	0	37.3	109.3
4,835	1,350	..	591	112.9	246.7
11,815	895	..	0	26.1	159.5
1,446	78	..	256	41.8	153.9
19,834	2,932	8,415	847	33.8	166.2
276	0	..	0	28.5	32.6
1,396	0	..	0	81.0	123.7
724	0	..	0	28.8	43.5
354	13	..	154	54.4	110.3
178	0	..	10	40.2	52.1
2,928	13	509	164	45.9	68.4
22,762	2,945	8,924	1,011	34.7	145.2
56.927	3,636	14,455	5,250	49.3	214.9

and some short-term arrears may be included in short-term debt; as a result, there may be some double-counting.
Source: Financing Adjustment with Growth in Sub-Saharan Africa, 1986-90 (Washington, D.C., 1986).

Table 4: Outstanding Long-Term Debt of Sub-Saharan African Countries to the United States Government as of September 30, 1986
(U.S. dollars, millions)

	Exim Bank	Foreign Assist.	USDA	CCC	Other	Total
All of Africa	2,080	2,465	1,7711	270	13	6,538
Less:						
Algeria	459	-	-	-	-	459
Morocco	100	522	335	184	-	1,131
Tunisia	70	450	128	9	-	657
Sub-Saharan Africa	1,450	1,493	77	13	4,291	
Ivory Coast	89	11	1	-	-	101
Nigeria	294	63	-	-	-	357
Other SSA	1,067	1,419	1,258	77	13	3,833

Source: U.S. Treasury:
Office of the Assistant Secretary for International Affairs, *Status of Active Foreign Credits of the United States Government, September 30, 1986.*

in sub-Saharan Africa owed 40 percent or more of scheduled 1986-87 service on public debt to the IMF and multilateral creditors. Debt service to multilateral creditors sometimes exceeds 25 percent of export earnings. Second, there is a great diversity across African countries in the makeup of debt owed to bilateral creditors. In some countries, the important bilateral creditors are the OECD countries that traditionally reschedule at the Paris Club. In others, notably Guinea, Mali, Mauritania, Somalia, Sudan, and Guinea-Bissau, the principal bilateral creditors are OPEC countries. In a few, debt to centrally planned countries predominates. This diversity among bilateral creditors adds to the difficulty in achieving negotiated solutions to the debt service problems of low-income African.

A Projection Exercise

Over the next several years, many countries in Africa face debt service payments that are much higher than the actual payments they have been able to make in the past. In order to assess the longer-term implications of the debt problems of these countries, the World Bank undertook a projection exercise that looked at export prospects, relative to future debt service payments. These include payments on: existing debt; assumed new credits; and on rescheduled debts. The base year for the projection exercise was 1984.[4]

The projections of exports of goods and nonfactor services were based on export volume projections made by the World Bank's country economists. These projections take as a starting point a common set of external assumptions, including developed-country growth rates, primary commodity prices and world demand, prices of manufactured imports, and changes in the exchange rates of industrial country currencies. The projections were made assuming the "most likely" domestic policies to be followed by each developing country. In case of sub-Saharan Africa, these policies are, in most instances, assumed to be much improved as compared with the past decade.

Gross disbursements were held at 1980-82 levels in real terms through 1990. The distribution of new disbursements among grants and concessional and nonconcessional credits was assumed to be the same as in 1984. As a result, the terms of projected new commitments are, in general, somewhat softer than the terms of the 1980-82 commitments. New IMF purchases were set at half the level of repurchases due in each year. End-1984 arrears were

Table 5a: Debt Service Payments Due on

(including IMF Repurchases and Charges)

	1984 debt service		Scheduled debt service, 1986-87		
	Scheduled	Actual			
	As percentage of exports goods and Service	As percentage of GNP	As percentage of exports of goods and services	Millions of dollars	As percentage of projected exports of goods and services
IDA-eligible countries with prolonged debt problems					
Benin	38.3	9.5	16.4	86	34.9
Gambia	20.8	10.9	13.6	25	30.8
Liberia	20.8	9.2	16.7	184	35.1
Madagascar	80.9	12.5	40.5	285	59.3
Mali	33.3	7.3	11.4	109	53.1
Mauritania	30.7	14.7	16.1	176	45.7
Niger	17.8	5.7	18.3	110	30.4
Somalia	145.9	9.9	25.7	185	97.2
Sudan	96.4	8.4	25.0	948	150.9
Tanzania	47.1	5.7	18.3	110	30.4
Togo	55.8	21.0	29.9	114	33.1
Zambia	55.2	20.9	24.6	620	59.0
Sub-Total	54.4	10.2	22.8	3,122	61.8

Note: Debt service excludes interest on short-term debt and arrears and payments on private nonguaranteed debt. Rows may not add to totals because of rounding.

a. Interest and exchange rate fluctuations, as well as reschedulings, debt

Public Debt Outstanding at the End of 1984

| Percentage share of total debt service due in 1986-87 | | | | |
| Official | | Private | | |
Bilateral	Multilateral	Suppliers' Credits	Financial Institutions	IMF
10.8	16.4	2.2	70.6	0.0
16.3	25.5	7.5	18.8	31.9
17.1	20.0	0.6	28.8	33.5
43.7	9.0	5.1	27.9	14.2
59.0	17.8	3.1	2.7	17.4
63.4	20.3	4.6	7.1	4.6
31.1	16.1	2.8	39.5	10.4
35.4	44.1	0.0	4.2	16.3
44.9	7.1	0.6	30.5	16.9
31.1	16.1	2.8	39.5	10.4
35.4	44.1	0.0	4.2	16.3
27.5	15.1	9.7	15.1	32.6
39.6	15.6	4.1	22.9	17.8

forgiveness, and the accumulation of arrears, affect the difference between scheduled debt service and actual payments.

Source: Financing Adjustment with Growth in sub-Saharan Africa, 1986-90 (Washington, D.C., 1986).

Table 5b: Debt Service Payments Due on

(including IMF Repurchases and Charges)

| | 1984 debt service | | Scheduled debt | |
| | Scheduled | Actual | service, 1986-87 | |
	As percentage of exports goods and Service	As percentage of GNP	As percentage of exports of goods and services	Millions of dollars	As percentage of projected exports of goods and services
Other IDA-eligible countries					
Burkina	20.9	2.5	12.7	38	19.4
Burundi	18.9	2.5	17.5	32	16.3
Central African Rep.	17.7	4.7	13.1	26	12.9
Chad	8.8	4.3	3.8	5	5.4
Ethiopia	20.1	2.6	19.3	149	19.9
Ghana	19.0	2.4	18.6	217	25.9
Guinea	31.0	6.1	27.2	151	20.2
Guinea-Bissau	4.3	0.4	27.9	16	84.6
Kenya	26.9	7.4	26.8	470	25.5
Lesotho	4.7	6.6	5.0	10	2.0
Malawi	29.1	8.3	29.4	104	25.3
Rwanda	3.7	0.4	3.3	13	6.4
Senegal	29.0	9.1	16.9	294	31.9
Sierra Leone	33.1	5.1	20.2	57	29.2
Uganda	36.1	3.2	35.1	192	30.2
Zaire	24.1	14.6	24.0	766	36.0
Sug-Total	23.8	5.5	21.7	2,539	25.7
Total: IDA-eligible countries	35.0	7.4	22.1	5,661	37.9

Note: Debt service excludes interest on short-term debt and arrears and payments on private nonguaranteed debt. rows may not add to totals because of rounding.

a. Interest and exhange rate fluctuations, as well as reschedulings, debt

Public Debt Outstanding at the End of 1984

| Percentage share of total debt service due in 1986-87 | | | | |
| Official | | | Private | |
Bilateral	Multilateral	Suppliers' Credits	Financial Institution	IMF
29.6	49.3	5.1	16.0	0.0
36.7	42.5	0.0	20.9	0.0
45.6	23.3	13.5	0.2	17.4
34.5	62.0	3.5	0.0	0.0
42.9	15.7	9.5	18.5	13.4
23.1	20.7	5.0	0.3	50.9
66.4	15.1	$0.9	3.6	4.0
41.3	34.1	14.4	6.4	3.8
18.8	30.9	3.9	23.1	23.3
11.7	72.8	4.0	11.5	0.0
15.5	24.1	4.1	28.3	28.0
38.2	61.8	0.0	0.0	0.0
39.8	16.8	0.7	23.2	19.6
22.0	20.3	14.0	5.0	38.7
27.9	14.8	8.0	4.5	44.7
50.9	7.5	5.1	18.2	18.2
37.1	18.5	5.4	16.0	23.0
38.5	16.9	4.7	19.8	20.1

forgiveness, and the accumulation of arrears, affect the difference between scheduled debt service and actual payments.
Source: Financing Adjustment with Growth in sub-Saharan Africa, 1986-90 (Washington, D.C., 1986).

Table 5c: Debt Service Payments Due on

(including IMF Repurchases and Charges)

| | 1984 debt service | | Scheduled debt service, 1986-87 | | |
| | Scheduled | Actual | | | |
	As percentage of exports goods and Service	As percentage of GNP	As percentage of exports of goods and services	Millions of dollars	As percentage of projected exports of goods and services
Other countries					
Cameroon	11.3	3.9	8.9	275	9.9
Ivory Coast	40.1	18.3	35.9	1,173	32.9
Nigeria	28.3	4.6	25.5	3,670	36.2
Zimbabwe	26.3	7.2	22.4	408	25.6
Sub-Total	27.8	5.6	24.8	5,526	30.6
Botswana	4.4	3.8	3.8	48	4.3
Congo	24.0	15.7	19.4	324	30.3
Gabon	11.7	7.7	11.4	189	9.7
Mauritius	23.2	11.4	24.6	102	16.4
Swaziland	5.8	4.5	5.6	27	7.1
Sub-Total	14.2	9.5	13.0	698	13.5
Total: Other countries	24.8	5.9	22.2	6,215	26.8
TOTAL	23.3	6.5	22.2	11,875	31.1

Note: Debt service excludes interest on short-term debt and arrears and payments on private nonguaranteed debt. Rows may not add to totals because of rounding.

a. Interest and exchange rate fluctuations, as well as reschedulings, debt

Public Debt Outstanding at the End of 1984

| Percentage share of total debt service due in 1986-87 | | | | |
| Official | | | Private | |
Bilateral	Multilateral	suppliers' Credits	Financial Institutions	IMF
32.6	31.5	8.0	27.9	0.0
11.2	16.5	6.0	54.2	12.1
5.0	6.3	3.3	85.4	0.0
9.0	8.8	1.1	61.2	19.8
8.0	9.9	3.9	74.1	4.0
22.5	68.1	2.0	7.3	0.0
20.6	10.0	5.9	63.3	0.0
17.3	5.9	8.9	67.8	0.0
13.4	27.2	0.0	20.5	38.8
18.5	56.9	0.7	8.2	15.6
18.7	17.3	5.4	52.2	6.4
9.2	10.7	4.1	71.7	4.3
23.2	13.7	4.4	46.9	11.8

forgiveness, and the accumulation of arrears, affect the difference between scheduled debt service and actual payments.
Source: Financing Adjustment with Growth in sub-Saharan Africa, 1986-90 (Washington, D.C., 1986).

Table 6a: Total Debt Service and Projected Import Capacity
(including IMF Repurchases and Charges)

(figures are annual average in millions of United States dollars)

	Actual debt service, 1980-82			As percentage of exports of goods and services
	Interest	Principal	Total	
Other IDA-eligible countries with prolonged debt problems				
Benin	10	9	19	5.2
Gambia	5	4	9	13.4
Liberia	32	16	48	8.7
Madagascar	52	44	97	22.4
Mali	10	7	17	7.8
Mauritania	30	26	56	17.7
Niger	83	100	183	33.3
Somalia	10	22	32	13.5
Sudan	171	104	276	25.7
Tanzania	83	77	160	22.0
Togo	33	14	47	10.3
Zambia	225	252	477	37.1
Sub-Total	745	677	1,422	22.6

Note: Debt service includes interest on short-term debt and payments of private nonguaranteed debt and arrears. Rows may not add to totals because of rounding. Chad, Guinea, Guinea-Bissau, and Swaziland are excluded

of IDA-eligible Sub-Saharan African Countries

Projected debt service, 1986-90			As per-centage of exports of of goods services	Annual imports of goods and noninterest services in 1980 dollars	
Interest	Principal	Total		1880-82	1986-90
47	11	58	21.9	488	455
17	9	26	28.2	170	162
69	59	128	24.2	700	614
130	55	185	33.0	1,159	773
40	27	67	25.5	495	481
57	42	99	23,5	600	661
70	52	121	29.5	1,103	989
58	66	123	50.8	569	606
475	157	632	71.3	1,639	1,562
165	69	234	36.1	1,293	1,107
50	18	67	17.0	569	532
395	232	627	51.9	1,813	1,229
1,572	796	2,268	39.9	10,599	9,171

because data were not available.
Source: Financing Adjustment with Growth in Sub-Saharan Africa, 1986-90
(Washington, D.C., 1986).

Table 6b: Total Debt Service and Projected Import Capacity
(including IMF Repurchases and Charges)

(figures are annual average in millions of United States dollars)

	Actual debt service, 1980-82			As percentage of exports of goods and services
	Interest	Principal	Total	
Other IDA-eligible countries				
Burkina	10	1	20	9.7
Burundi	4	4	8	6.3
Central African Rep.	4	5	8	5.4
Ethiopia	28	26	54	9.7
Ghana	59	54	112	12.2
Kenya	241	247	488	27.2
Lesotho	5	4	8	2.1
Malawi	54	40	94	30.2
Rwanda	4	2	6	3.2
Senegal	81	73	154	19.1
Sierra Leone	18	40	58	27.6
Uganda	18	53	71	21.9
Zaire	217	179	396	22.2
Sub-Total	741	737	1,478	19.0
Total: IDA-eligible countries	1,486	1,413	2,900	20.6

Note: Debt service includes interest on short-term debt and payments of private nonguaranteed debt and arrears. Rows may not add to totals because of rounding. Chad, Guinea, Guinea-Bissau, and Swaziland are excluded

of IDA-eligible Sub-Saharan African Countries

Projected debt service, 1986-90			As per- centage of exports of goods and services	Annual imports of goods and noninterest services in 1980 dollars	
Interest	Principal	Total		1980-82	1986-90
17	29	46	20.7	532	553
14	10	24	11.7	283	274
11	9	20	8.4	303	366
44	110	154	18.5	883	1,074
87	178	265	25.2	1,142	995
266	365	631	29.9	1,413	2,242
4	7	11	1.8	516	714
47	67	115	20.4	448	633
8	11	19	8.9	366	391
139	80	219	19.6	1,279	1,578
26	26	52	21.9	430	347
44	126	170	26.0	432	772
334	169	503	20.4	2,072	2,498
1,042	1,187	2,229	21.2	11,089	12,437
2,614	1,983	4,597	28.0	21,688	21,609

because data were not available.
Source: Financing Adjustment with Growth in Sub-Saharan Africa, 1986-90
(Washington, D.C., 1986).

Table 6c: Total Debt Service and Projected Import Capacity
(including IMF Repurchases and Charges)

(figures are annual average in millions of United States dollars)

	Actual debt service, 1980-82			As percentage of exports of goods and services
	Interest	Principal	Total	
Other countries				
Cameroon	168	155	323	15.0
Ivory Coast	635	556	1,191	37.8
Nigeria	1,155	585	1,741	8.7
Sub-Total	2,045	1,344	3,389	12.5
Botswana	10	4	14	2.0
Congo	84	80	164	14.4
Gabon	131	235	366	15.0
Mauritius	45	28	73	13.7
Sub-Total	269	348	617	12.9
Total: Other countries	2,314	1,692	4,006	12.6
TOTAL	3,801	3,105	6,906	15.0

Note: Debt service includes interest on short-term debt and payments of private nonguaranteed debt and arrears. Rows may not add to totals because of rounding. Chad, Guinea, Guinea-Bissau, and Swaziland are excluded

of IDA-eligible Sub-Saharan African Countries

Projected debt service, 1986-90			As per-percentage of exports of goods and services	Annual imports of goods and noninterest services in 1980 dollars	
Interest	Principal	Total		1980-82	1986-90
195	239	434	14.1	2,340	3,592
1,025	588	1,613	40.2	4,270	5,244
2,373	875	3,248	28.9	22,211	12,256
3,778	1,981	5,759	28.3	30,923	23,273
32	32	64	4.9	1,093	1,431
204	73	277	23.3	1,441	1,487
98	138	236	11.1	2,020	2,192
51	90	141	14.6	638	957
385	333	718	12.9	5,192	6,067
4,163	2,314	6,477	25.0	36,115	29,340
6,776	4,298	11,074	26.1	57,803	50,948

because data were not available.

Source: Financing Adjustment with Growth in Sub-Saharan Africa, 1986-90 (Washington, D.C., 1986).

assumed to be rescheduled at the same terms as the other debt or, for the nonrescheduling countries, paid off in equal installments over the 1986-90 period.

Reschedulings were judged to be necessary in most cases where projected debt service ratios significantly exceeded ex post debt service ratios of the recent past. These past ratios were assumed to be a rough indicator of a country's ability to service debt over the next five years. No reschedulings were deemed necessary in countries where likely capital inflows would result in a substantial increase in import capacity without rescheduling. Of the 33 countries studied, 20 were deemed very likely to reschedule debt in the 1986-90 period. Most of these countries have already rescheduled debt at least once.

The terms assumed for the reschedulings are fairly standard:

1. A ten-year repayment period with five years of grace.
2. Interest rates at or near market rates for rescheduled private debt and for export credit agency claims.
3. Interest rates at the original rates for rescheduled loans from official development agencies—note that this is the main concessional element in the current Paris Club rescheduling process: stretching out the maturity of a below-market-rate loan increases its concessional element.
4. A contract cut-off date of December 31, 1984; that is, only loans contracted before the end of 1984 were rescheduled. (Most creditors would be reluctant to make new loans that they knew were likely to be rescheduled almost immediately.)
5. Rescheduling of 100 percent of principal payments due on all private and official bilateral credits.
6. Rescheduling of 50 percent of interest payments due to official bilateral creditors, but as is standard practice, no rescheduling of interest payments due to private banks. Banks were not assumed to make new money loans in lieu of rescheduling interest, as they are expected to do in the Baker countries.
7. Rescheduling of payments due under previous reschedulings, for reschedulings undertaken before December 31, 1984, the contract cut-off date.

These terms are not far out of line with those agreed to in recent Paris Club and commercial bank negotiations with African countries. In fact, terms have often been more generous. The Paris Club has rescheduled 100 percent of principal and interest payments due in a number of cases in Africa.

Results of the projection exercise are shown in Table 6 on pages 96-101. We find that, for the majority of the countries of sub-Saharan Africa, the debt situation, while it may be difficult, appears to be manageable. Projected reschedulings reduce debt service rations to levels in line with the past in these countries. For the IDA countries in this category, imports of goods and non-interest services are projected to rise by 13 percent over their 1980-82 levels. This implies an 11 percent drop in per capita import capacity and emphasizes the need for increased resource flows to Africa if investment and growth are to rise.

However, for 12 countries in sub-Saharan Africa the debt situation is more desperate. After rescheduling, their debt service ratios are likely to remain significantly higher than ex post ratios in recent years. Their import capacity is likely to be lower in 1988-90 than in 1980-82 and far lower, 25 percent or more, in per capita terms. Moreover, their situation does not improve over the period. Projections of scheduled debt service payments in 1991 are far above the levels that these countries could meet without further rescheduling. Without additional concessional capital inflows or additional debt relief, the prospects for these countries are dismal.

These projections were done on the basis of a more favorable external environment for African countries than exists today. Lower prices for a number of commodities have cut export prospects. The fall in the dollar has added to the debt service burden, since only about half of sub-Saharan African debt is denominated in dollars, compared with about 90 percent in Latin America. As the dollar fell, debt and debt service payments, measured in dollars, rose. Export earnings, also measured in dollars, have not risen as rapidly, thus increasing the burden of debt service. These reversals in the economic situation and outlook for sub-Saharan Africa would probably add six to eight countries to the list of IDA-eligible debt distressed countries given in Table 3 on pages 82 to 87.

IV. The Dimensions of a Solution

Any solution to the debt service problems of sub-Saharan African countries must have two aspects. First, it must relieve the immediate constraint on resource availability that is evident in the very high ex ante debt service ratios. Ex ante annual debt service in the IDA countries with serious debt service problems currently averages over 50 percent of exports. None of these countries can afford to devote a major share of their export earnings to debt service. They also cannot meet debt service payments out of normal market borrowing; the same combination of low per capita GNP and poor growth outlook that led to the debt problem means that they are not creditworthy in world financial markets. That is the key to the second aspect of a solution: it must leave these countries in a reasonably creditworthy situation at the end of the process. Creditworthiness, in this context, means that, at the end of the program period, the country can meet debt service payments out of expected export earnings, expected new voluntary capital inflows, and a modest level of grant aid, with import levels compatible with growth.

These two aspects are not independent. As Dooley argues, the debt overhang, until resolved, discourages investment and contributes to the lack of long-run creditworthiness. All potential new investors must share the expected loss on old credits. The rate of return on new projects must be very high to cover this extra cost, limiting investment to the few most lucrative projects.[5]

Annual reschedulings may meet the first requirement, cash-inflow improvement, without meeting the second, long-term creditworthiness. Many of these debt distressed countries have had repeated reschedulings covering up to twelve consecutive years of debt service. (See Chart 1 on pages 108-109.) The failure of the reschedulings to return these countries to creditworthiness has been blamed on policy failures in the rescheduling countries. While policy failures have definitely played a role, the inability of more than one or two countries that have rescheduled to escape from the cycle of arrears build-ups and further rescheduling indicates that other factors are also at work. Rescheduling of previously rescheduled debt, something the Paris Club did not allow in the 1970s, has become the norm for low-income Africa in the 1980s.

These annual reschedulings cause a bow wave effect in the debt service of countries that grow slowly. The immediate burden of debt service is reduced through the rescheduling of 100 percent of principal and interest due and accumulated arrears, including payments due and arrears on previous reschedulings. The accumulated capitalized and recapitalized interest payments on the debt at commercial terms begins to predominate. The average rate on commercial debt rescheduled at the Paris Club is currently above eight percent, or about four percent in real terms, and has been higher in earlier years. The real dollar value of GNP or exports in these countries has rarely grown at that pace over the last decade. Therefore, external debt has grown faster than GNP or exports; and ex ante debt service ratios have risen. Hence, while annual reschedulings may go a long way toward relaxing the short-term external resource constraint, they may lead to an exponential growth in the debt overhang, further discouraging investment and growth.

In some cases, reschedulings may not even meet the first requirement of a solution. Countries in economic decline sometimes find their debt service, after rescheduling, beyond their capacity to pay. Moratorium interest payments on rescheduled debt (interest due on rescheduled principal and interest payments) plus payments to preferred creditors exceed 50 percent of exports in some low income African countries with serious debt problems.

In countries such as Sudan and Zambia, debt service payments and arrears to preferred creditors, mainly multilateral agencies, are more than the country can service, given current levels of exports, capital inflows, and grant aid. Resource availability in these countries is a problem even if all debt service payments, including moratorium interest, on private-source and bilateral official debt are rescheduled.

Assuming that the first requirement, adequate external resources to allow investment and economic growth without further cuts in already low levels of consumption, can be met through rescheduling and an increase in concessional aid, the second requirement may remain out of reach. Merely postponing the day of reckoning is not a solution since, as argued above, the debt overhang frustrates attempts to increase investment and exports. Some method of reducing the debt overhang or subordinating old claims, relative to new claims, must be found. Many solutions are possible. Increased grant aid flows to cover all or part of debt service payments (as opposed to reschedulings), concessional reschedulings, total or partial debt writeoffs, and debt buy-backs financed by donors (as undertaken in Bolivia) have all been proposed.

The Policy Response to Date

The African debt crisis has elicited a series of policy responses. Secretary of the Treasury Baker's famous 1985 debt initiative was twofold. The first component dealing with the major debtor countries—the Baker 15—received the most attention. The second component dealt with low-income debtors, mainly the IDA-eligible African countries. The IMF Structural Adjustment Facility (SAF) was a direct outgrowth of this proposal. It uses reflows from the earlier Trust Fund loans to provide ten-year low interest (one half of one percent) loans with five years of grace to IDA-eligible countries with severe balance of payments problems. The SAF programs require close cooperation between the IMF and World Bank. The two organizations prepare a joint policy framework document that lays out the adjustment program and the expected sources of finance. Secretary Baker hoped that this joint framework would be the catalyst for additional financing from bilateral sources. An Enhanced Structural Adjustment Facility (ESAF) has recently been established by the IMF. The additional funds, more than $8 billion, come from contributions made by major donor countries. The United States did not contribute to the ESAF.

The recent IDA replenishment agreement took into account the special problems of low-income African countries. Up to half of the $12 billion dollars to be committed over the next three years will go to sub-Saharan Africa. For countries with serious debt problems, a large percentage of new IDA credits are likely to be in the form of quick-disbursing loans in support of adjustment programs.

The official bilateral creditors and donors have also responded positively to the African debt crisis. The June 1987 Venice summit meeting of the leaders of seven major industrial countries recognized the problem. Their communique stated that, "For those of the poorest [African] countries that are undertaking adjustment efforts, consideration should be given to the possibility of applying lower interest rates to their existing debt and agreement should be reached, especially in the Paris Club, on longer repayment and grace periods to ease the debt burden." The Paris Club has already responded to this directive in its agreements with Mozambique, Mauritiana, Senegal, Somalia, and Uganda. Mozambique and Somalia both received 20-year maturities with 10 years of grace. The other three countries received 15-year maturities with 6 years of grace.

The interest rate issue has proved to be more problematic. Normally, interest rates on rescheduled debt are determined in bilateral meetings between debtor and creditor governments following the Paris Club meeting. ODA claims are usually rescheduled at the original, concessional, rate of interest. Nonconcessional export credits or military loans are normally rescheduled at rates related to current market rates, often the creditor government's cost of borrowing plus a spread. Some creditors argue that rescheduling export credits at less than market rates would require budgetary transfers from the central government to the ECAs at a time of budget stringency in most creditor countries. Others, notably several European countries, are willing to reschedule the debts of the poorest African countries at below-market rates, but only if other bilateral official creditors do the same.

The African countries themselves have asked that creditor countries implement the 1978 UNCTAD resolution calling for the conversion of outstanding concessional bilateral loans to grants, but the net effect of this "retroactive terms adjustment" will be relatively small. A number of creditor countries converted all ODA loans to grants in 1970s. Other ODA loans have been rescheduled at their original interest rates, increasing their concessionality (the longer the maturity the greater the concessionality of a below market rate loan). Canada is one country which has announced a new program of retroactive term adjustment. The Canadian government announced early in 1987 a five-year moratorium on ODA debt service payments from sub-Saharan African countries. Recently, Canada went beyond the moratorium and announced the forgiveness of $70 million of claims on African countries.

The IMF has announced an enlargement of the resources available to the SAF to SDR 9 billion (about $12 billion at present exchange rates) from the current level of SDA 2.7 billion. These new resources would need to be additional to the resources in current aid budgets, if the SAF is to benefit the debt distressed countries without drawing resources away from other developing countries. A possible source of additional funds would be IMF gold sales.

Implications for U.S. Policy.

The United States government has a series of policy decisions ahead that are important for the debt distressed sub-Saharan African countries. One of the most important is the United States contribution to the eighth replenishment of IDA. The recent budget compromise has resulted in the appropriation of $915 million of the $958 million the United States had agreed to contribute. While this amount is commendable, given the squeeze in other parts of the development aid budget, the remainder must be appropriated if IDA-8 is to meet Africa's needs, as other donors may withhold funds pending a full United States contribution. Negotiations are to begin soon

Chart 1: Debt Relief Agreements of Sub-Saharan

	1975	1976	1977	1978	1979	1980
Central African Republic						Ar
Congo						
Ivory Coast						
Equatorial Guinea						
Gabon			Ar	1		
Gambia, the						
Guinea						
Guinea-Bissau						
Liberia						<--
Madagascar						Ar
Malawi						
Mauritania						
Mozambique						
Niger						
Nigeria						
Senegal						
Sierra Leone		Ar<--	--1--	-->	Ar<--	2.---
Somalia						
Sudan					Ar<.1----	
Tanzania						
Togo				Ar	<-1--	----
Uganda						
Zaire	<----	-1.---	2--3->		Ar<-4----	
Zambia						

Source: World Bank, International Finance Division.

Notes: Dashed lines indicate the length of consolidation periods. "+" line indicates portion of agreement cancelled. "Ar" indicates arrears on

African Countries with Official Creditors, 1976-1987

1981	1982	1983	1984	1985	1986	1987	1988

long-term debt consolidated. Number indicates number of
agreement. Vertical bars indicate separate tranches.

on the ninth replenishment of IDA. The special needs of Africa's debt distressed countries must be considered in the determination of the size of IDA-9.

The United States also needs to make a decision on interest rates applied to rescheduled United States claims on low-income debt distressed countries in Africa. Without a reduction in the present value of external claims, through forgiveness or below market rate reschedulings, or an increase in highly concessional aid, many poor African debt distressed countries are unlikely to resume growth and eventually restore creditworthiness. Interest rate relief has been used in the past in similar situations. In 1970, bilateral official creditors, including the United States, rescheduled Indonesian debts over 30 years at a zero rate of interest. Ghanaian debt was rescheduled in 1974 at a rate of interest of 2.5 percent. The United States Eximbank might conceivably improve its eventual rate of return on its approximately $600 million of loans and contingent claims (in the form of guarantees) to debt distressed countries by reducing the interest rates on these loans in concert with other lenders. The reduced debt burden could accelerate the rate of investment and growth of these countries. With United States support, a proposal to decrease interest rates on the bilateral official debt of IDA-eligible African countries with severe debt problems would probably be accepted by all bilateral official creditors.

The question of precedent should not become an issue. Concessional debt relief, mainly from official bilateral creditors, for countries with per capita incomes below $400 per year does not imply similar treatment for middle income debtors, whose debt problems and growth prospects differ markedly from those of the debt-distressed low-income African countries. The middle-income countries' debts are owed mainly to commercial banks. Settlements involving rescheduling at less than market rates may not be necessary; if they are, the direct use of public funds is not likely to be an option.

Another issue is the increase in the resources available to the IMF ESAF. The United States government should reconsider its decision not to contribute or should explore other alternatives, including authorizing the IMF to sell additional gold to finance a larger ESAF.

United States aid flows are also a crucial element in any solution to the debt crisis in low-income sub-Saharan African countries. Ideally, aid flows should be expanded, with most of the increase in the form of quick disbursing grants to countries with adjustment programs, endorsed by the IMF, World Bank, and the major donor countries.

The United States government has pressed African countries to undertake adjustment programs encompassing a smaller role for the public sector, freer markets for goods, and reforms of the financial sector, reducing the amount of allocated credit and setting interest rates at realistic levels. Many African countries have responded positively to these pressures and have adopted market-oriented policies. If the size of the debt burden and inadequate external financing causes reform programs to fail, these policies could be severely discredited. The United States will find it in its own interest to ensure that reform programs in Africa have the external finacial support they need.

Notes

1. IDA loans to countries with per capita incomes below $400 per year carry a maturity of 40 years and a grace period of 10 years. The interest rate on IDA loans is 0.75 percent per year, plus a small (0.5 percent) commitment fee.
2. See Kathie Krumm, *The External Debt of Sub-Saharan Africa* (Washington, D.C., 1985), for a careful review of the debt build-up in Africa. Much of the analysis in this section is drawn from that source.
3. The Paris Club is the name given to the forum in which creditor governments meet with a debtor government in order to arrange the general framework of a rescheduling of debt owed to or guaranteed by an official government agency in creditor countries. The actual reschedulings are formalized in a series of bilateral agreements. See Alexis Rieffel, "The Paris Club, 1978-1983," *Columbia Journal of Transnational Law,* XXIII (1984), 83-110, for a good summary of the operations of the Paris Club. See Thomas Klein, "Debt Relief for African Creditors," *Finance and Development,* XXIV (1987), 10-13, for a discussion of the evolution of the relationship between the Paris Club and debtor countries in Africa.
4. The World Bank, *Financing Adjustment with Growth in Sub-Saharan Africa, 1986-90* (Washington, D.C., 1986), 49-56.
5. Michael P. Dooley, "Market Valuation of External Debt," *Finance and Development,* XXIV (1987), 6-9.

5: Population, Resources, and Famine in Sub-Saharan Africa

BY MOHAMED T. EL-ASHRY
AND DORSEY BURGER

Introduction

Three years after the last tragic famine, Ethiopia seems to be sliding into another food emergency. The rains have failed in the north and central highlands, and about five million people are estimated to be at risk. As many as one million people in Ethiopia alone may have perished during the 1984-85 famine, only ten years after the widespread Sahelian famine of 1970-74. Recurring famine and death notwithstanding, five million African children die and another five million are crippled for life every year because of malnutrition and hunger, according to United Nations reports.[1]

For centuries, Africa was able to feed itself and survive occasional droughts through subsistence farming and herding. While most of the soils tend to be shallow, low in nutrients, and deficient in moisture, many indigenous

African cultures developed production systems that are well-adapted to these constraints. Known as "shifting cultivation" or "bush fallow," these agricultural methods allow fields to rest and recover nutrients and moisture for lengthy periods after two or three seasons of crop production. Many traditional systems of farming also integrate livestock production into agriculture; livestock are fed on crop residues and tree fodder, and animal wastes are used as organic fertilizer for fields and gardens. Similarly, pastoralists in drier Sahelian regions where farming is not productive lived in balance with nature by moving their herds around in search of water and vegetation. However, these traditional production systems have been increasingly disrupted by rapid population growth; changing social, political, and economic policies; and inappropriate Western-style development schemes.

In the past decade, Africa has experienced a 20 percent decline in per capita food production. Food production increased at 1.5 percent per year in the 1970s and at only 1 percent in the 1980s. Such small increases in production have been outstripped by a population growth rate of 3 percent, the highest in the world today. At such a growth rate, the United Nations estimates that the current population of sub-Saharan Africa's 42 countries, some 450 million, will more than triple to 1.4 billion in the next 40 years.[2]

Climatic extremes have been conveniently blamed for Africa's failing food production and the recent famine. Yet, poor weather and droughts have hit sub-Saharan Africa repeatedly over the last 2,500 years without the massive and disastrous effects of recent times. In Ethiopia, for example, it is estimated that a local drought occurs every year, a regional drought every three or four years, and a widespread drought every eight to ten years. Severe droughts are definitely a trigger for occasional food shortages; however, recent events have been exacerbated by overexploitation and mismanagement of a fragile resource base. Growing human and animal populations, development policies which do not address local needs, insecure land tenure, and a burdensome foreign debt have all contributed to the degradation of forest, soil, and water resources and reduced agricultural productivity. Yet, the response of Western nations and international organizations was largely directed to what was perceived as a short-term emergency, not to the long-term underlying problems of a rapidly deteriorating natural resource base and the associated population and development policy issues.[3]

Fortunately, much more is presently known about the functioning of Africa's natural and cultural environment. This knowledge provides a sufficient basis for the formulation of policies and programs to restore or maintain resource productivity and simultaneously enhance economic prospects for the improverished rural majority. Human actions, from the peasant's conservation of soil and water to the policymaker's commitment to sustainable development, are the key to long-term food security. In recent years, discussions of natural resource issues in Africa have broadened to consider linkages between population and environmental degradation on the one hand, and agricultural productivity, economic development, trade, and security issues on the other hand. These are two-way linkages; environmental factors are both cause and effect. While the connections are often complex, an understanding of their interactions is vital to the development of coherent national and international policy alternatives.

Population

Discussions of population issues in Africa often present the situation as a crisis in which increasing numbers of humans (and occasionally livestock) outstrip the productive capacity of the resource base. Indeed there is much cause for concern; with the average annual growth rates hovering around 3 percent, sub-Saharan Africa's present population of almost 450 million will double in less than 30 years. Population increase appears to be fastest in Kenya, Botswana, Tanzania, and Zimbabwe, where growth rates for the period between 1985 and 1990 are estimated at 4.2 percent, 3.7 percent, 3.65 percent, and 3.6 percent respectively. (See Table 1 on pages 116-17). Nevertheless, simply interpreting the data as a Malthusian crisis glosses over many of the interactions between population, resources, and economic development.[4]

Some analysts stress the positive effects of population growth on agricultural development and resource conservation. By raising demand and creating broader markets, population growth first prompts an extension of production, and ultimately makes land resources more valuable. This promotes adoption of yield-enhancing techniques and justifies investments to increase and preserve the productivity of renewable resources. By increasing the scarcity and economic value of resources, population growth also induces institutional innovations. One of the most important is clear definition of property rights governing resource usage, and the tenurial conditions essential for long-term sustainable management.[5]

In fact, some argue that Africa is an underpopulated continent and that, in many areas, underpopulation may be a major constraint to economic development. Among developing areas, Africa's population density remains below those of Central America and Asia. Africa's average population density is only 16 per square kilometer, compared to China's 100 per square kilometer and India's 225. One reason for this relative low density lies in environmental constraints in some regions. Endemic health problems limit population density in the humid lowlands of central Africa. In arid and semi-arid regions, pastoralists traditionally adapted their cultural and productive systems to scarce resources and maintained low densities.[6]

The Western assessment of the population situation as a crisis is not generally shared by African people. Less than 15 years ago, the same could be said about African politicians and planners, judging from the fact that only 3 countries had instituted population policies and 24 others have developed family planning programs. However, these government policies and programs have not been translated into a slowdown in population growth rates or fertility. For the entire continent, it is estimated that population growth has risen from 2.6 percent in 1970 to more than 3 percent presently.[7]

Kenya was one of the first countries to set up a national family planning program in 1967. Despite its efforts to curb population growth, Kenya's fertility rate has since climbed to its present level of eight births per woman, and its natural increase of four percent per year is the highest in the world. Cultural and socio-economic factors support the desire for large families. On the economic side, children provide labor for agricultural production and guarantee access to land for the mother. On the cultural side, children prove a woman's fertility, thus confirming her status in marriage and also serve to raise the father's social prestige. Minority groups often have a similar interest in seeing their absolute and relative numbers grow, since this may enhance their economic and political opportunities. High fertility also helps to overcome the high infant and child mortality rates that are common in Africa. It is estimated that more than one out of ten newborn infants dies,

Table 1. Estimated Size and Growth of Population, 1955-2000

	Estimated Population (thousands)			Estimated Average Annual Population Change (percent)				
	1960	1987	2000	1955-60	1965-70	1975-80	1985-90	1995-2000
AFRICA (Sub-Sahara)	207,852	448,545	682,491	2.31	2.62	2.97	3.02	2.99
Angola	4,816	9,220	13,234	1.64	1.52	3.39	2.67	2.82
Benin	2,251	4,307	6,532	1.20	2.06	2.77	3.12	3.24
Botswana	481	1,193	1,917	2.10	2.54	3.84	3.70	3.63
Burkina Faso	4,279	7,310	10,538	1.75	1.76	2.02	2.65	2.90
Burundi	2,927	4,999	7,226	1.76	1.45	1.80	2.84	2.80
Cameroon	5,483	10,438	15,168	1.94	2.13	2.57	2.80	2.91
Cape Verde	200	341	470	2.98	3.04	0.87	2.36	2.44
Central African Rep	1,605	2,701	3,750	1.33	1.63	2.22	2.42	2.57
Chad	3,064	5,255	7,308	1.53	1.82	2.10	2.44	2.56
Comoros	215	472	695	2.04	2.43	3.40	3.08	2.84
Congo	972	1,836	2,643	1.90	2.18	2.46	2.73	2.83
Djibouti	126	388	604	2.19	2.42	7.41	3.32	3.39
Equatorial Guinea	252	410	559	1.18	1.56	1.99	2.31	2.41
Ethiopia	24.191	45.997	66.509	2.19	2.41	2.32	2.79	2.82
Gabon	867	1,195	1,603	0.75	0.97	1.19	2.01	2.25
Gambia	374	670	898	1.36	2.24	2.15	2.13	2.30
Ghana	6,772	14.523	22,607	4.51	2.02	3.30	3.36	3.43
Guinea	3,660	6,380	8,879	1.38	1.95	2.17	2.48	2.57

Guinea-Bissau	540	925	1,229	0.73	0.06	5.04	2.08	2.21
Ivory Coast	3,731	10,529	16,006	1.58	1.415	3.77	3.34	3.17
Kenya	7,903	22,397	38,534	3.21	3.66	4.03	4.20	4.11
Lesotho	870	1,600	2,255	1.84	2.01	2.41	2.61	2.65
Liberia	1,047	2,336	3,615	2.11	2.73	3.36	3.25	3.43
Madagascar	5,362	10,605	15,550	2.02	2.32	2.70	2.90	2.95
Malawi	3,529	7,415	11,387	2.15	2.56	2.82	3.32	3.25
Mali	4,636	8,569	12,658	1.99	2.16	2.19	2.94	3.03
Mauritania	981	2,007	2,998	2.17	2.45	2.75	3.08	3.07
Mauritius	660	1,087	1,298	3.17	1.82	1.91	1.65	1.19
Mozambique	6,545	14,724	21,104	1.54	2.28	4.42	1.69	2.79
Niger	3,234	6,489	9,750	1.36	2.08	2.59	3.01	3.19
Nigeria	42,305	101,992	161,930	2.63	3.23	3.49	3.49	3.57
Rwanda	2,753	6,488	10,123	2.84	3.05	3.31	3.36	3.43
Senegal	3,041	6,793	9,765	2.03	2.89	3.46	2.71	2.82
Sierra Leone	2,475	3,741	4,867	1.25	1.38	1.59	1.93	2.07
Somalia	2,143	4,862	6,671	1.83	2.14	4.23	2.11	2.80
Sudan	11,165	22,828	32,926	1.91	2.29	3.08	2.89	2.75
Swaziland	333	691	1,048	2.35	2.39	2.90	3.14	3.23
Tanzania	10,026	24,186	39,129	2.60	3.08	3.42	3.65	3.71
Togo	1,514	3,146	4,709	1.37	4.33	2.52	3.06	3.11
Uganda	6,562	16,584	26,262	3.33	3.95	3.19	3.49	3.55
Zaire	15,908	31,796	47,581	2.44	2.11	2.86	3.04	3.12
Zambia	3,141	7,135	11,237	2.63	2.96	3.08	3.43	3.52
Zimbabwe	3,605	9,430	15,130	3.97	3.61	3.39	3.61	3.64

Source: International Institute for Environment and Development and World Resources Institute, 1987

the highest rate of any continent.[8]

One lesson from the Kenya case is that centralized family planning programs that improve the supply of family planning methods without encouraging demand for these methods will have only limited impact. Serious attempts at curtailment of rapid growth must change the perception among parents that more children are a great asset. Addressing the demand side of birth control programs entails a recognition of the socio-economic and cultural bases of high fertility and the design of institutional and educational interventions tailored to the country's realities. While many African governments and academics have criticized population programs as neo-colonial or imperialist, many implicitly recognize that the cultural values, emotions, and spiritual beliefs of African societies lie at the heart of the African population situation. Nevertheless, donor programs influence the policy environment and must be carefully designed. In particular, there is some evidence that Western countries' preoccupation with Africa's overpopulation problem may have had the unintended effect of engendering suspicion and increased resistance to family planning programs among the African populace.[9]

While Africa may appear underpopulated because of its relatively low density, this fact must be seen in the light of the productivity of the resource base and the fact that population density is a misleading measure of population pressure. One attempt to link population and resources involves the use of the "carrying capacity" concept. Carrying capacity essentially measures the ability of the resource base indefinitely to support populations of a given species. A population is ultimately limited by the availability of its scarcest vital resource. In many African countries, this may be food, but it can also be fuelwood, living space, or health conditions.

The United Nations Food and Agriculture Organization (FAO) studied food carrying capacity in Africa and estimated the maximum viable populations that could be maintained at minimum nutrition standards, assuming low, intermediate, and high levels of inputs. According to this study, at low levels of inputs (the present reality in most of sub-Saharan Africa), 14 countries with a combined population of more than half that of sub-Saharan Africa had already surpassed their carrying capacity in 1982. By 2000, 7 more countries are expected to surpass their food carrying capacities. (See Table 2 on facing page.) The relatively low carrying capacities of many African

Table 2. Human Carrying Capacity At Low Levels Of Inputs

Carrying Capacity was exceeded in 1982	Carrying Capacity will be exceeded between 1982 and 2000
Mauritania	Mali
Senegal	Ghana
Burkina Faso	Togo
Niger	Benin
Nigeria	Malawi
Ethiopia	Zimbabwe
Somalia	Swaziland
Kenya	
Uganda	
Rwanda	
Burundi	
Botswana	
Angola	
Lesotho	Source: FAO, 1982.

countries derive from their poor soils, arid climate, and the fact that an estimated 80 percent of the continent's land is uncultivable.[10]

While carrying capacity provides a rough indication of the maximum population that a particular region can support, its applicability for planning and policy has some real limitations. In particular, it does not account for improvements in food producing technologies or the flow of people, food, or energy across borders. For example, trade allows one region to make effective use of the excess carrying capacity of another. In addition, the carrying capacity of a region represents the maximum, not the optimal population; determination of the latter depends upon an array of socio-economic and political factors.

The carrying capacity of a country or region can also be adversely affected if it is temporarily surpassed. In some African countries, it appears that population levels beyond the carrying capacity have been maintained by "mining" capital in the form of natural resources (e.g. mineral deposits, standing trees, the productivity of the soil). While the economic costs of deforestation and soil erosion are rarely included in national income accounts, they often entail irreversible degradation of the resource base, permanently reducing its productivity.[11]

If exploiting the resource base is one unavoidable response to carrying capacity constraints, a second option brings population and carrying capacity into equilibrium by limiting the former and expanding the latter. This option represents the path of sustainable development. For Africa, sustainability rests upon the development of a low-input agricultural system that mimics the species structure, function, and interactions in the natural ecosystems instead of the commercial and subsistence exploitation of the resource base which has provided convenient short-term fixes for governments and individuals.[12]

Sustainable agriculture does not necessarily repudiate all systems of production based on chemical inputs in favor of organic farming. Instead sustainable agriculture is distinct from industrial-type agriculture which places exclusive emphisis on the maximization of yield per unit area. In contrast, sustainable agriculture rests on the multiple objectives of yield, stability, environmental quality, and net income to the farmer. As these latter objectives become perceived as more important over time, one can expect sustainable agriculture to become more prevalent.[13]

Despite its limitations, the carrying capacity of a nation or region provides important information relevant to strategies for sustainable development. A study of desertification in West Africa, for example, identifies strategies for development based on the ratio of actual population to carrying capacity. It concludes that no significant increases in carrying capacities within the Sahelian and Sudanian zones (350-600 millimeters of rainfall per year) can be expected without major policy changes such as: the encouragement of resettlement to the more productive Sudanese-Guinean zone; the strengthing of land laws to include conservation; and the imposition or increase of wood cutting fees. These options are not available to the rest of

Africa, however. Pressure on natural resources in Tanzania, Kenya, and elsewhere derives partly from the increasing rates of migration from high potential areas to adjacent low potential semi-arid lands. This presents more intractable problems since farmers have already cultivated the most productive arable lands.[14]

In summary, population growth in Africa has contributed to a race on which the fate of many millions will depend. Some farming practices, tenurial systems, and government policies are responding to conditions of increasing scarcity of renewable resources in ways that provide greater incentives for investment in the sustained productivity of the resource base. However, those renewable resources are deteriorating—in some cases at an accelerating rate— as the demands on them increase and the traditional institutions that govern them weaken. The net impact of population growth on Africa's renewable resources, and the future productivity of those resources, depends on the outcome of this race.[15]

Resource Degradation

Sub-Saharan Africa's inability to feed itself and improve its economic conditions can best be described in terms of the region's carrying capacity, the interactions between people and the natural resource base, the use and overuse of resources, and the competition among different sectors of society for the use of a limited and fragile resource base. Food shortages and famine are encompassed by the bigger problems of population pressure and environmental degradation. Overgrazing, overcultivation, and overcutting of trees— pushed by rapidly growing populations and inapropriate development policies—have disrupted traditional systems, reduced land productivity and contributed to food shortage and starvation (See Figure 1 on page 122).

Traditional African farming systems and cultivation techniques tend to be adapted to local ecological conditions and to be sensitive to the preservation of fragile natural resources. For example, shifting cultivators clear and often burn the natural vegetation to plant fields which are maintained for a period of around three years. By this time the harvest of a standing crop as well as the increased leaching and erosion from planted fields have usually deprived the soil of nutrients vital for crop production. Letting the fields revert to unmanaged bush allows the normal nutrient cycling process to resume, thus replenishing the soil with nutrients from decaying vegetation and increased microbial activity. As Africa's population has grown rapidly,

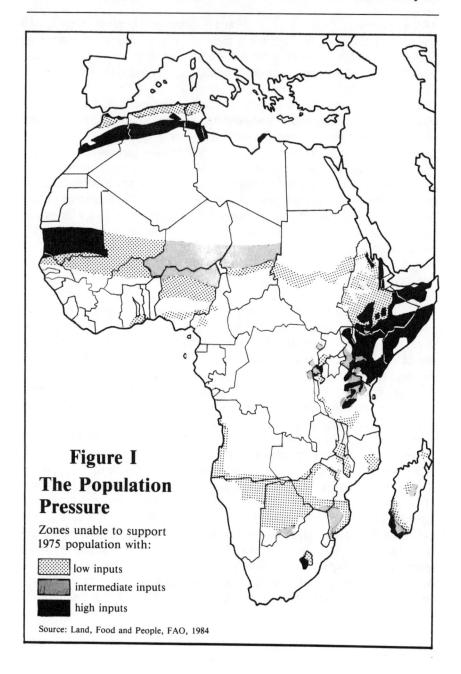

Figure I
The Population
Pressure

Zones unable to support
1975 population with:

low inputs

intermediate inputs

high inputs

Source: Land, Food and People, FAO, 1984

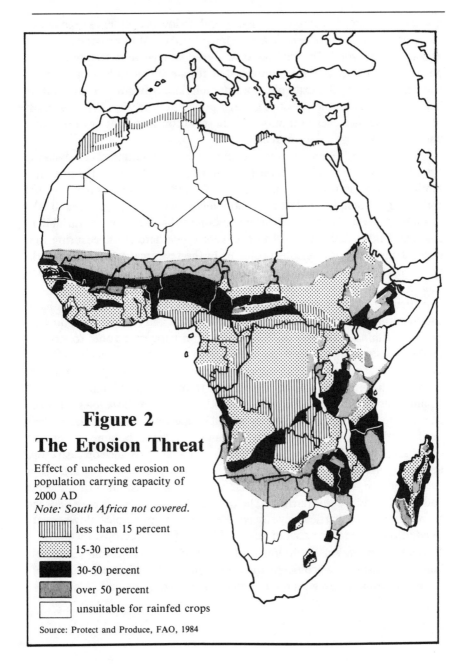

**Figure 2
The Erosion Threat**

Effect of unchecked erosion on population carrying capacity of 2000 AD
Note: South Africa not covered.

	less than 15 percent
	15-30 percent
	30-50 percent
	over 50 percent
	unsuitable for rainfed crops

Source: Protect and Produce, FAO, 1984

making increasing demands on available land, fallow periods have been reduced in many areas whereby they are no longer sufficient to provide adequate grazing or fuelwood. In other regions, a gradual change in technology and an increase in inputs have compensated for declining fallow periods. In southeast Nigeria, for example, considerable intensification of agriculture has occurred under the pressure of high population density. But over most of Africa the increases in inputs and conservation measures have not kept pace with rising population densities.[16]

Similarly, traditional forms of pastoralism maintained a dynamic equilibrium with a highly variable environment and often operated in a symbiotic relationship with shifting cultivation. In the semi-arid zones unsuited for farming, nomadic herders conventionally ranged over large areas to take advantage of rainfall and vegetation resources that were highly variable in space and time. Cultural mechanisms kept down herd sizes, ensuring that overgrazing was not a serious problem. In the few areas where these traditional mechanisms remain intact, the pastoralists had much more resiliency than more "modern" herders in dealing with recent droughts.[17]

Agricultural practices that are not adapted to the fragile tropical soils of sub-Saharan Africa significantly degrade the land and reduce its productivity. Indiscriminate transfer of technology from temperate zones to tropical regions has seriously accelerated soil erosion as well as the conversion of forest into grass-savanna and sterile steppes. In short, many development projects in Africa have done little to restore the traditional production systems' equilibrium with the environment. Livestock projects and boreholes for water transformed pastoralists' life—they settled in one place, built the size of their herds, and put great pressure on the land. Firewood became scarce and overgrazing caused extensive desertification. Similarly, reliance on cash crops actually increased soil erosion and decreased soil productivity. Cash crops such as cotton, tobacco, and peanuts, consume large amounts of nutrients and thereby reduce soil fertility. The thin topsoil which is left bare between growing seasons is particularly susceptible to erosion by tropical downpours. In addition, with large areas of good soils used for cash crops, farmers are forced to cultivate smaller holdings of increasingly marginal and vulnerable lands for subsistence crops. At the same time, pastoralists are pushed off their traditional grazing land and end up overgrazing the limited and more

Table 3. Export Dependence of Selected African Countries

Country	Export product	Percent of all export earnings from that product
Burundi	coffee	93
Rwanda	coffee	71
Somalia	live animals	71
Ethiopia	coffee	69
Mauritius	sugar	68
Sudan	cotton	65
Mali	cotton	47

Source: Africa Faith and Justice Network, 1984.

fragile rangelands available to them. The result is severe declines in productivity and food carrying capacity due to erosion. (See Figure 2 on page 123.)

Heavy reliance on cash crops for export has not helped African countries' trade and debt situation either. Most African countries are dependent on exporting a small number of raw materials and agricultural products. Table 3 (see above) lists some countries which are highly dependent on the export of just one commodity. Thirty-seven African countries, with more than 60 percent of Africa's population, obtain over 50 percent of their total export earnings from primary commodity exports.[18]

Prices for raw materials tend to stagnate or decline over time relative to those of manufactured imports, thus contributing to fiscal crises for the com-

Table 4. Real Growth of Commodity Prices, 1950-84

Commodity	Average annual percentage change
Total Agriculture	-1.03
Beverages	-1.13
Cereals	-1.30
Fats and oils	-1.29
Raw materials	-0.08
Metals and Minerals	-0.09

Source: World Bank, 1986.

modity exporting countries. (Table 4) shows that all major commodities exported by less developed countries suffered real price declines
since World War II. At the same time, prices of manufactured goods from
industrialized countries averaged annual real increases of 5.4 percent between
1965 and 1973 and 11 percent between 1973 and 1980.[19]

Similarly, a burdensome foreign debt induces government policies that
promote exploitation of the natural resource base for foreign exchange. The
need to increase short-term economic gains is forcing many countries to ignore
their own assessments of the extent of resource degradation and delay implementation of rehabilitation programs. At the same time, national policies continue
to encourage the commercialization of natural resources, which contributes to
further land degradation. This is perhaps clearest in the case of forest management in the humid zone. In several West African countries, for example, under-
taxation of timber and generous concession terms encourage timber companies
to clear the forest without placing restriction on the method of logging. The
duration of the terms of agreement (between 5 and 15 years) is much shorter
than the regeneration period of the forest. As a result, logging companies
retain no interest in the land after the agreement expires; there is
virtually no incentive to maintain the productive capacity of the forest.
The results are predictable. In West Africa, the rate of clearing of the

productive closed forest since 1975 has been the highest in the world, 3.7 times the average rate for all tropical countries. The rates are highest in Ivory Coast and Nigeria; these countries cleared an average of 290,000 and 300,000 hectares respectively each year between 1981 and 1985.[20]

Land competition between small holders and commercial farmers has also placed more burdens on the shrinking resource base in sub-Saharan Africa. In the central Sudan, millions of acres of grasslands have been cleared for mechanical cultivation of nonfood crops. This practice leads to severe soil erosion, weed infestation and fertility declines, and the progressive degradation forces farmers to abandon their fields. Lack of an effective land use policy in the Sudan has brought 'suitcase' farmers to those areas with clay soils—some with short-term leases and others unauthorized. These farmers have no incentive to implement conservation practices or sustain these agricultural lands.[21]

Land tenure systems may also exacerbate degradation by making the connection between land users and their holdings more tenuous. Such systems include short-term cultivation rights, sharecropping tenancies, and absentee landlords. In addition, government ownership of farmland, rangeland, forests, and wildlife resources undermines community and private control. As population and livestock densities increase, so does the pressure on these common resources. Each individual takes what he can from these "commons" before others do, thus accelerating the degradation and eventual destruction of the resource base.

Closely tied to Africa's agricultural problems is the continent's acute energy shortage. Many countries depend overwhelmingly on fuelwood and other forms of biomass for more than 90 percent of their energy and construction needs. The savanna woodlands and forests are being cut down at an alarming rate with devastating effects on the soil and the entire ecosystem. In the Sudan, the total biomass deficit is 33 million cubic meters and the problem is particularly acute in the northern provinces. Some 31,000 square kilometers of wooded land are lost each year. Studies by the National Energy Authority in the Sudan suggest that by the year 2000, and at current rate of consumption, 77 percent of all tree cover in the northern regions (Northern, Central, Eastern Khartoum, Kordofan, and Darfur) will have been destroyed. In Khartoum, Central, and Eastern provinces, all tree cover could be lost in 1987.[22]

At one time, over 40 percent of Ethiopia was covered with forests. Two decades ago, 16 percent of the land was still forested; the area presently occupied by forests is only 3.1 percent. Devegetation of the land for fuelwood and charcoal production is degrading millions of acres more of sub-Saharan Africa's watersheds, causing severe soil erosion, and disrupting the delicate water balance. Urban charcoal producers tend to strip the landscape of all vegetation. This practice degrades biomass resources more severely than the rural practice of collecting deadwood and lopping branches. Fuelwood sources for Mogadishu, Somalia, are fully 500 kilometers to the south. In the Sudan, the charcoal sources for Khartoum have moved 450 kilometers to the south and the city is at the center of a denuded zone 70 kilometers in diameter.[23]

The increasing scarcity of fuelwood leads to the use of alternative sources of fuel, including grass, dung, and crop residues. This use upsets the ecological equilibrium by depriving the indigenous production system of materials normally used as fertilizers for nutrient replacement and mulches for soil conservation and water retention. In Ethiopia, many farmers have substituted dung for wood as a household fuel in the face of severe forest depletion. This dung no longer provides the nitrogen, phosphorus, and other nutrients which formerly sustained soil fertility. Extensive afforestation programs are vitally needed to avoid a breakdown of the agricultural production system. However, the Ethiopian government policies provide little incentive for the individual farmer—who lacks ownership of the land as well as the trees—to practice this afforestation or other resource conservation.[24]

A fragile ecosystem exploited beyond its carrying capacity eventually breaks down. Whether in the United States dust bowl or in some parts of Africa, the results can be tragic. Major symptoms of desertification in the Sahelian countries include sand dune encroachment, deterioration in rangelands, forest depletion, and deterioration of irrigated systems. Deforestation, overgrazing, expanding rainfed agriculture, and other practices have combined to severely degrade many watersheds and to accelerate soil erosion. The Sudan and Ethiopia have some of the highest clearing rates of agricultural lands per family. Figures for soil erosion in Ethiopia as high as 450 tons per hectare per year are not unusual. In all, about 6.9 million square kilometers are threatened by desertification in sub-Saharan Africa and 16.5 percent of Africa's existing rainfed cropland will be lost by the end of the century if conservation efforts are not taken.[25]

With all the problems facing rainfed agriculture, large-scale irrigation is often promoted as the answer to Africa's food problems. A study by FAO shows the vast potential for irrigation in many sub-Saharan countries. The Sudan and Somalia, which depend heavily on large irrigation schemes for much of their agricultural production, exploit 53 percent and 92 percent respectively, of their irrigation potential. By contrast, Tanzania has developed only 6 percent and Ethiopia 13 percent of the land suitable for irrigation. There are a number of reasons for slow progress in expanding irrigated acreage in sub-Saharan Africa. These include: the high cost of developing surface irrigation (which can be as high as US $25,000 per hectare), the uncertainties of the groundwater resources, the lack of deep-rooted tradition and expertise in irrigation, the vast distances between rural villages, and poor communications.[26]

The challenges confronting existing irrigation systems in countries like the Sudan and Somalia, on the other hand, center on the age and inefficiency of the structures, and on the improper management of irrigation water. Large-scale irrigation began in the 1920s in the Sudan, much of it for cotton production, and progressed throughout this century. Many of these systems are deteriorating and in need of expensive rehabilitation. The World Bank is currently funding a number of rehabilitation projects, but many more are needed. Additional problems which confront existing irrigation systems in the Sudan and Somalia include salinization and waterlogging, increasing population pressure on the land, and health hazards from water-borne diseases. In the Sudan, immigrants doubled the human and livestock population of irrigated areas, increasing the risk of severe degradation. Health risks present a heavy cost of irrigation projects that are rarely included in economic assessments. In one area of the Sudan, irrigation brought a 267 percent increase in malaria cases and 77 percent increase in bilharzia—both water related diseases.[27]

In addition, increasing sedimentation, linked to indiscriminate agricultural clearing and degradation of watersheds, is threatening the viability of irrigation systems. According to a recent World Bank report, the capacity of the Khasm El Girba dam in Sudan was reduced due to silting from 1300 million m^3 to 718 million m^3 in 1976 and is expected to reach 500 million m^3 in 1997. For the Roseires Dam, the rate of siltation recorded was over two times greater than design estimates. In addition, this reduced storage capacity in the Roseires has resulted in a decreased hydroelectric potential necessitating a costly heightening of the dam and dredging of accumulated silt. Siltation problems in the Roseires reservoir stem in part from upstream activities in the Blue Nile watershed in Ethiopia. Policy formulation and effective strategies become more difficult in these cases where transnational river systems are involved.[28]

Policy Considerations

Despite these massive problems, Africa's situation is not hopeless. Land degradation and fertility declines have been successfully curtailed in some regions. In the Sudan, high yielding varieties of sorghum have doubled the yields of this staple grain. Encroachment of sand dunes in Somalia has been halted with the participation of entire communities. "No till" methods in Ghana have reduced runoff by up to 90 percent of that from conventional ploughing methods. Water harvesting techniques in the Katheka-Kai cooperative settlement in Machakos, Kenya, have increased grain yield two to seven times. Ethiopia has mobilized a large labor force for the purpose of soil conservation; hills with steep slopes are terraced and planted with trees. Cameroon is now fully food self-sufficient with food output increasing by 50 percent in five years. However, these projects and accomplishments only begin to address the widespread environmental degradation and reduced agricultural productivity in Africa; all of the successful methods and practices await large-scale replication.[29]

Helping Africa increase its food production and prevent future crises will be a long and difficult process. Future strategies must include the development of new agricultural systems and technologies designed for the region's soils and climate, and appropriate to its cultural, educational, and financial conditions. This requires more adaptive agricultural research to be conducted in Africa itself. These research activities must involve smallholders as an integral element in the design of new technologies. In that way, feedback from local farmers would be immediate and field tests could be conducted on the farm and with farmer participation. A few research centers already exist in Africa. With adequate funds, staff, and technical assistance, they could contribute significantly to improving agricultural productivity and resource management. They include the International Crops Research Institute for the Semi-Arid Tropics (ICRISAT), the International Institute of Tropical Agriculture (IITA), and the International Livestock Center for Africa (ILCA). They are part of the network of the Consultative Group on International Agricultural Research (CGs).

The CGs have received considerable attention lately as the institutions with the greatest potential for bringing the so-called "green revolution" to Africa.

The green revolution is based on the increased output that is obtainable from increased inputs and improved crop varieties. Until now, similar efforts in Africa have largely floundered, as declining per capita agricultural output indicates. However, the starting conditions for the green revolution in much of Asia and Mexico included substantial irrigated areas, fertile soils, large amounts of fertilizers and pesticides, and strong national research programs. These conditions are absent in Africa. The CGs planned emphasis on food crops and livestock therefore seems appropriate, as does their concentration on biological and technical aspects. The CGs mandate is to come up with the technological interventions to improve productivity; these can then be made available to national and regional extension services for dissemination.

Several objections to the CGs system, however, highlight some of the problems of transferring Asia's agricultural advances to Africa. The reliance on high-yielding varieties (HYVs) can exacerbate the division between rich and poor farmers, since in many cases only those who are better off can make the initial investment. Neither are the physical attributes of HYVs appropriate for all situations. When extensively monocropped, the lack of diversity may increase susceptibility to crop epidemics. The replacement of traditional staples by higher yielding corn, for example, has led to weed infestation in the West African savanna, cutting harvests by up to 90 percent. HYVs may also prove unacceptable to small holders because of their fuel and labor requirements or because of their lower quality taste. Finally, many CGs operate in isolation from the farmers whose problems they purport to address. For example, only about 20 percent of research funding goes to intercropping, despite its prevalence among smallholders. In addition, by concentrating the best personnel and equipment on one place, the CGs become susceptible to a real or perceived elitism that threatens their relevancy to African agriculture.[30]

A green revolution based on the elements that made it successful in Asia will have very little chance of success in Africa. On the other hand, "an indigenous agricultural revolution," one that is built upon local farming and natural resource management knowledge as demonstrated in the gains made in Cameroon, Zimbabwe, and Rwanda, among others, would have a better chance of success. It is feared that prevailing pessimistic assumptions about indigenous agriculture "could lead to the rejection of several centuries of solid progress towards an improved agriculture adjusted to African ecological

**Table 5. Yields With and Without Intercropping
(Plateau State, Nigeria)**

	Value-cost ratios	
	Fertilizer ± farmers' cultivation practices	Fertilizer ± 'improved' cultivation practices
Monocrop		
Sorghum	5.6	10.2
Maize	4.1	12.2
Intercrop		
Maize/Sorghum	20.2	17.7
Yam/Maize	77.3	24.6
Sorghum/Cowpea	13.5	8.4

Source: Richards, 1985, 71.

conditions in favor of the importation of an inappropriate agricultural revolution.''

Evolutionary changes in indigenous agricultural systems and practices respond to population increases by cutting fallow time, eventually adopting permanent agriculture, penning livestock as agricultural land spreads to former pastureland, adopting soil conservation practices, and experimenting with new crops and mixes of crops, including agroforestry. These innovations do not necessarily rely on external inputs. In Rwanda, for example, agricultural productivity increases have taken place amid very high population growth rates (3.8 percent) and despite the remoteness of the country. Many imports and exports are prohibitively expensive in this landlocked country due to transportation costs. Rwanda is the most densely populated country in Africa, and average land holdings for a farm family are only around one hectare. Also all arable land is farmed. Yet despite these constraints, changes in government agricultural policies have resulted in crop yield increases beyond population growth rates, and in reductions in land degradation, a serious hazard in the mountainous terrain.

One of the characteristics of indigenous farming systems is the prevalence of intercropping. Although largely regarded as inefficient during colonial times, recent research suggests that intercropping is an especially viable alternative in regions of land shortage or low soil fertility. In these areas, yields from intercrops commonly surpass those from monocrops. (See Table 5 on facing page.) The reasons for higher productivity include: complementarity among crops grown, effectively minimizing competition and enhancing nutrient cycling; and increased resistance to insect populations, plant diseases, and weeds stemming largely from plant diversity. Agroforestry can be considered an extension of intercropping, with the identical objectives of maximizing total productivity and income while preserving the capacity of the resource base. The system is not limited to humid areas as windbreak projects in the Sahel demonstrate.[31]

The range of technical solutions for increasing agricultural productivity in Africa is impressive. Besides agroforestry and intercropping, they include alley cropping, reduced or no-till farming, integrated livestock and crop production, nitrogen fixation by legumes, improved crop rotation, and physical means of soil erosion control. However, the main bottlenecks to sustainable agriculture in Africa are institutional rather than technical. National governments and international assistance organizations need to recognize that inappropriate policies and weak institutions are responsible for many of Africa's resource productivity problems. Food subsidies, for example, often exacerbate rural poverty and urban migration. By reducing the prices paid to farmers for their crops, governments remove much of the incentive to increase, or even maintain, agricultural production. As a result, land users have little rationale for conserving a resource base dedicated to the production of underpriced commodities. Rural livelihoods become increasingly difficult and rural to urban migration grows, compounding the problem of urban poverty and unrest.[32]

The small private farmers are by far the most important component of Africa's economy. Yet government policies divert most resources and attention to large state-owned farms. In Ethiopia, for example, while private farmers account for 40 percent of the gross national product, 85 percent of exports, and 80 percent of employment, according to World Bank figures, state-owned farms absorbed about 40 percent of all government expenditure on agriculture between 1980-1985 while contributing about five percent of total food production.[33]

In order to address the complexities of resource degradation and food deficits in sub-Saharan Africa, policy reforms must simultaneously strive toward:

(1) increased productivity of traditional farming systems;
(2) greater participation by communities and non-governmental organizations in development projects and policy formulation;
(3) slowed population growth;
(4) the easing of land tenure constraints; and
(5) the resolution of domestic and international conflicts.

The creation and expansion of local-level organizations of smallholders is one of the most efficient means of institutionalizing conservation-based strategies in African agriculture. Incorporating substantial participation, for example, ensures strong local interest in projects that are oriented to the needs and concerns of the community. Much of the success of sand dune stabilization projects in Somalia, for example, is due to community involvement. By contrast, Ethiopian land conservation projects proceed within a technocratic and top-down framework, an approach that limits success by alienating many farmers from projects that are intended to benefit them in the first place.

Bilateral and multilateral assistance and lending agencies can help African governments achieve these goals through improved coordination among one another and through reform of their own policies. The proliferation of donors and projects that began in the 1970s is crippling the major governmental institutions of many African countries. Instead of working on comprehensive national development policies and plans, government officials spend enormous amounts of time meeting donors' approval and reporting requirements. In 1980, Zambia had 614 projects supported by 69 donors; in 1981, tiny Lesotho had 321 projects backed by 61 donors; and Mali had 188 projects supported by 50 donors. As a result of this donor multiplicity, as well as of rapidly changing policies, more money is spent on administrative expenses than on-the-ground projects. Eighty percent of the global program to combat desertification, for example, was spent on administration and support activities. Similarly, African governments spend an average of 37.8 percent of their agricultural budgets on administration; in comparison, Asia and Latin

America spend 2.6 percent and 11.5 percent respectively.[34]

Foreign assistance, designed to foster economic growth, is becoming increasingly strategic. It is also declining in real terms. The United States is a case in point. Development assistance has declined, in real terms, by more than one-half since 1961, when the Agency for International Development was created. Today, non-military assistance equals only 2.4 percent of the gross national product (GNP) which puts the United States at the bottom of aid giving among the industrialized countries. At the same time, of all United States aid to Africa, 63 percent goes to Egypt; and of the aid to African countries other than Egypt, 48 percent goes to just five countries containing 12 percent of Africa's population: the Sudan, Somalia, Liberia, Kenya, and Zaire. These are not examples of democratic regimes, but they do have naval bases or other strategic assets.[35]

Instead of focusing foreign assistance solely on economic growth and building massive projects, it could focus on building up local capacities and institutions. Instead of dictating what direction development should take in the Third World, foreign assistance could pay more attention to what the recipient countries and their people want. Donor agencies could play a catalytic role in bringing about the preparation of comprehensive, yet flexible, participatory development plans for these poor countries. The Marshall Plan did just that for Europe after World War II. However, Europe was well educated and had the necessary institutions to implement needed programs. But there does not seem to be much confidence at this time in Africa's ability to carry out such plans.

The industrialized countries can play a major role in providing technical assistance to overcome these difficulties. Working with national governments, they can assist in the formulation of economic policy reforms and in establishing certain criteria for development programs and projects to which they and the receiving governments adhere. The Development Group for Alternative Policies has drawn up a list of 15 suggested criteria. High among them: (1) Participation: Is the beneficiary group involved in the planning, design, implementation and evaluation of the project? (2) Decentralization: Do outside participants disengage themselves from the project over time? Do indigenous institutions assume increasing responsibility? (3) Scale: Is the size of the project appropriate to the stage of development of the beneficiary group? Is the size of the project appropriate to the implementing institution? (4) Participant Education: Does wide participation in the project enhance the beneficiaries' understanding of their environment, of their relationship to it, of the causes of their poverty, and of their capacity to induce change?[36]

National governments and international assistance agencies have a primary responsibility in reversing Africa's environmental decline and in increasing agricultural productivity through appropriate policy reform and efficient resource conservation strategies. Policies initiated now to achieve these goals will go a long way toward narrowing the growing gap between supply and demand for food and other agricultural products, and will have lasting benefits for the future health and welfare of the people of sub-Saharan Africa.

Notes

1. The authors wish to thank Andrew Maguire, Robert Repetto, Robert Rotberg, and Michael Wells for reviewing an early draft of the manuscript and for their valuable comments. However, the views, conclusions and any errors therein, are the sole responsibility of the authors.

2. UNEP, Report of the Executive Director. African Environmentsl Conference (Cairo, 1985); World Bank, *Toward Sustained Development in Sub-Saharan Africa.*

3. M.T. El-Ashry, "Famine: Some Additional Aspects," *Science,* (Letters), 236 (1987) 1503-4; D. Mackenzie, "Ethiopia's Grains of Hope," *New Scientist,* 115 (1987) 20-21.

4. International Institute for Environment and Development (IIED) and World Resources Institute (WRI), *World Resources* (New York, 1987).

5. National Academy of Sciences, *Population Growth and Economic Development: Policy Questions* (Washington, D.C., 1986); Robert Repetto, "Population, Resources, Environment: An Uncertain Future. *Population Bulletin,* 42(2) (1987).

6. D. Diallo, "Overpopulation and Other Myths about Africa,"*Christian Science Monitor,* April 22, 1986.

7. Blaine Harden, "Ethiopia Faces Famine Again, Requests Massive Food Relief," *Washington Post,* Sept. 14, 1987.

8. Geoffrey McNicoll, "An Interpretation of Fertility and Population Policy in Kenya" (New York, 1987)

9. D. Diallo, "Overpopulation and Other Myths about Africa," *Christian Science Monitor,* April 22, 1986.

10. FAO, *Potential Population Supporting Capacities of Lands in the Developing World* (Rome, 1982).

11. Repetto, "Population, Resources, Environment."

12. D.J. Mahar (ed.), "Rapid Population Growth and Human Carrying Capacity," World Bank Staff Working Paper (Washington, D.C., 1985).

13. M. Dover and L. Talbot, *To Feed the Earth: Agro-Ecology for Sustainable Development* (Washington, D.C., 1987).

14. World Bank, *Desertification in the Sahelian and Sudanian Zones of West Africa* (Washington, D.C., 1985; M.B.K. Darkoh, "Population Expansion and Desertification in Tanzania," *Desertification Control,* 6 (1982), 26-33.

15. D. Anderson and R. Fishwick, "Fuelwood Consumption and Deforestation in African Countries." World Bank Staff Working Paper 704 (Washington, D.C. 1984).

16. IIED and WRI, *World Resources.*

17. J.T. McCabe and J.E. Ellis, "Beating the Odds in Arid Africa," *Natural History,* 96 (1987), 42-51.

18. K. Danaher, "Can the Free Market Solve Africa's Food Crisis?" *TransAfrica Forum,* 4 (1987), 1-16.

19. World Bank, *Sudan Forestry Sector Review* (Washington, D.C., 1985), Annex III and VIII. World Bank, *World Development Report 1986* (Washington, D.C., 1986), 25.

20. M. Gillis, "West Africa: Resource Management Policies and the Tropical Forest," in *Public Policy and the Misuse of Forest Resources* (New York, forthcoming).

21. L. Berry, "Land, People, and Resources in Sudan" (Washington, D.C., 1987).

22. Ibid.
23. D. Finn, "Land Use and Abuse in the East African Region," *Ambio,* 12 (1983), 296-301.
24. K. Newcombe, "An Economic Justification for Rural Afforestation: the Case of Ethiopia." World Bank Energy Department Paper, 16 (Washington, D.C., 1986).
25. P. Freeman, *Natural Resources in Sub-Saharan Africa: Review of Problems and Management Needs,* (Washington, D.C., 1986); J. Mabbutt, "A New Global Assessment of the Status and Trends of Desertification," *Environmental Conservation,* 11 (1984), 103-113.
26. P. Richards, "Ecological Change and the Politics of African Land Use," *African Studies Review,* 26 (1983), 1-72.
27. L. Berry, "Land, People, and Resources in Sudan" (Washington, D.C., 1987).
28. World Bank, *Sudan Forestry Sector Review* (Washington, D.C., 1985), Annex III and VIII. World Bank, *World Development Report* (Washington, D.C., 1986), 25.
29. Paul Harrison, *The Greening of Africa,* (Washington, D.C., 1987).
30. M.A. Altieri, "The Significance of Diversity in the Maintenance of the Sustainability of Traditional Agroecosystems," *ILEIA Newsletter,* 3 (1987) 3-7; International Institute of Tropical Agriculture (IITA), "Combating Striga Infestation in Maize" *IITA Research Highlights,* (1983), 48-50.
31. R. Winterbottom and Peter Hazelwood, "Agroforestry and Sustainable Development: Making the Connection," *Ambio* 16 (1987), 100-110.
32. Food and Agricultural Organization, "African Agriculture: The Next 25 years." Executive Summary, (Rome, 1986).
33. Harden, "Famine."
34. A. Abubakar, "Managing Rural Development: the Role for Local Governments" *Ceres,* 20 (1987), 25-28; M.T. El-Ashry, "Resource Management and Development in Africa," *Journal '86,* (1986), 5-12.
35. J. Hamilton and J. Sullivan, "Penny-wise, Pork Foolish—Poor Nations Need Real Development Help, Not Pet Projects." *Washington Post.* Sept. 13, 1987.
36. Mark Satin (ed.), "Alternative to Terrorism: Siding with the World's Poor," *New Options,* May 30, 1986, 1-4.

6: The Potential Impact of AIDS in Africa

By Charles N. Myers
and Albert E. Henn

Introduction: Progress at Risk

In the decades since the period of independence, health conditions in much of sub-Saharan Africa have improved despite slow to negative growth of per capita product and government health expenditures ranging from $1 to $10 per person per year. Infant and child mortality have decreased and life expectancy at birth has lengthened. Now this progress, and economic growth itself, may be threatened by the impact of AIDS.[1]

The twenty-one sub-Saharan countries classified by the World Bank as "low-income economies" had an average per capita product of $210 in 1984, with an average annual decrease of 0.1 percent since 1965. Yet, life expectancy at birth in the same period increased from 42 to 48 years, infant mortality dropped from 155 per 1,000 live births to 129, and child mortality from 36 to 26. The eight sub-Saharan countries classified as "lower middle income economies" had an average growth of 2.4 percent since 1965. Life expectancy increased from 42 to 50; infant mortality dropped from 168 to 107, and child mortality from 33 to 10.[2]

This reduction of infant and child deaths is the result of social and economic changes and of a combination of biomedical advances, such as: oral rehydration therapy for diarrheal disease and multi-vaccine immunizations; innovations in delivery and surveillance such as cold chains for vaccines and growth monitoring of nutrition status; training of health professionals; and the building of primary health care and other service delivery structures. Problems persist. Mortality and morbidity rates are still high. Half of all deaths in Africa each year are of infants and children under five. Health budgets are declining in per capita terms in some countries. Leading causes of death and illness—malaria, malnutrition, diarrhea, respiratory infections and tetanus—are preventable, controllable, or treatable. But the progress already made under adverse conditions—and the special contributions of United States scientists and foreign assistance to this progress—should not be understated or undervalued.

This progress may now be jeopardized by AIDS. In Central and East Africa, it is estimated that AIDS could increase infant and child mortality by at least 20 percent; and mortality rates among young adults by 60 percent—thus reducing or erasing the progress in child survival and in overall life expectancy of the past quarter century and altering the age distribution of mortality.[3] The potential demographic and economic consequences of such outcomes and the policy issues and options for the United States are the focus of this chapter.

AIDS in Africa: Available Information

There is much that is not known about AIDS. What is known is worrisome and has prompted a global research effort of such growing intensity and diversity that nothing published about AIDS can be up-to-date. New findings may make the policy conclusions of this chapter seem too optimistic, others hopefully will make them seem the reverse.

AIDS is not a single distinct disease, but rather a complex of illnesses which results from immune deficiency. The causal agent is the Human Immuno-deficiency Virus—now abbreviated as "HIV 1" to distinguish it from a related but so far apparently less dangerous virus recently identified in West Africa: HIV 2. The HIV 1 virus is transmitted by sexual intercourse (vaginal, anal, and oral), by blood or blood products, by contaminated needles and syringes, and by infected mothers to children during pregnancy or at birth. Heterosexual transmission and mother-child transmission are apparently the major modes in Africa. But blood transfusions may account for 10 to 15 percent of cases; and since it is common in sub-Saharan Africa to administer most medication by injection, needles and syringes used by clinics and hospitals and also by unlicensed practitioners may account for an important proportion of infection among children and adults, including sexually active adults.[4] Other transmission modes hypothesized in Africa and elsewhere but not yet demonstrated are via breast milk of infected mothers and through the traditional practices of scarification and circumcision.

Available information about AIDS in Africa is sketchy and anecdotal, and, where more scientific, is based on small samples of populations and institutions with probable bias. Further, the characteristics of AIDS—the long latency period and infectiousness of apparently healthy adults—mean that fully accurate information on the extent of infection today will be available only retrospectively, years later. With due caution then, the only choice is to analyze and act on the available information while simultaneously seeking quickly to improve it.

Problems of Definition and Diagnosis

Total AIDS cases reported to the World Health Organization (WHO) by all African governments in mid 1987 were 4,924, compared to 39,263 in the United States. The United States Centers for Disease Control (CDC) estimates that there are 1 to 2 million infected individuals in the United States. The same ratios of cases to infected but asymptomatic individuals yield estimates of 123,000 to 246,000 infected individuals in Africa—an infection rate of less than 0.1 percent of the total population. But differences in intensity and difficulty of diagnosis in the capacity of reporting systems, even in governments' willingness to report, make these African numbers too low. In 1986, WHO estimated that there were "at least" 2.5 million infected individuals in Africa and that in five years the number of AIDS cases would be between 200,000 and 600,000.[5]

AIDS is diagnosed by testing an ill patient's blood for the presence of antibodies to HIV 1 and/or by an illness or a complex of illnesses associated with previously confirmed cases. Diagnosis in Africa is made difficult by limited capacity to perform the currently used blood tests for HIV 1 antibodies and by the greater diversity of illnesses which may affect African patients.

Immunologically, AIDS in Africa is identical to AIDS in North America and Europe, with marked depression of T-helper cells and cell-mediated immunity. But there are some differences in the typical illnesses HIV 1 infected individuals subsequently contract. The most common opportunistic infections in AIDS patients in Africa are oro-esophageal candidiasis, crytococcal meningitis or sepsis, cytomegalovirus chorio-retinitis, mucocutaneous Herpes simplex, and tuberculosis. Pnenmocystis carinii pneumonia is not common (in contrast to the United States and Europe where approximately 50 percent of AIDS patients develop this infection). Kaposi's sarcoma in Africa in its classical endemic form is not related to HIV 1 infection, although there are recent reports from African countries showing an increase in an aggressive form—disseminated Kaposi's sarcoma—which is related to HIV 1 infection and which is similar to that seen in AIDS patients in the United States.[6] Neurological disease including dementia may also affect a similar proportion of AIDS patients in Africa as in the United States, but diagnosis is difficult and data are not yet available.[7]

It is also possible that Africans who are immunosuppressed as a result of HIV 1 infection and who live in areas with other endemic diseases might manifest these diseases, e.g.: leishmaniasis, filariasis, trypanosomiasis, schistosomiasis, and leprosy. A small random sample of patients in West Africa found an association between leprosy and HIV 1 infection.[8] No association has yet been found between HIV 1 infection and malaria.[9] A syndrome of wasting, recurrent fever, and diarrhea known as "Slim disease" in Uganda, is commonly seen in HIV 1-infected individuals. Clinical diagnosis of AIDS in children is particularly difficult because poor health, malnutrition, diarrheal disease, and respiratory infections are common in infants and children in Africa with or without concurrent HIV 1 infection.

An attempt has been made by WHO to draw up a clinical case definition of AIDS suitable for use in African countries.[10] In this definition, AIDS in adults can be diagnosed by the single presence of generalized lymphadenopathy, disseminated Kaposi's sarcoma, or cryptococcal meningitis. In the remainder of cases, AIDS is diagnosed by the presence of at least two major signs in association with at least two minor signs, when there is no other known cause of immunosuppression in the patient concerned. The major signs are: weight loss greater than 10 percent by body weight; chronic diarrhea longer than one month; and fever longer than one month (intermittent or constant). The minor signs are: persistent cough longer than one month, generalized pruritic dermatitis, history of Herpes zoster during the past five years, oropharyngeal candidiasis, or chronic progressive and disseminated Herpes simplex.

The WHO case definition will no doubt improve diagnosis and reporting of AIDS cases in Africa—at least of those cases which reach levels in the health care system able to use the guidelines with the care and diagnostic sophistication required. For example, the WHO definition was tested with inpatients at the Mama Yemo Hospital in Kinshasa and correctly identified 74 percent of the patients infected with HIV 1.[11] But for now, the only basis for estimating the current and prospective size of the AIDS problem in Africa is from the results of blood tests of sample populations undertaken—by mid 1987—in at least 20 sub-Saharan countries.

Evidence from Surveys: Prevalence of HIV 1 Infection

Many of the sero-prevalence surveys undertaken in Africa to date have concentrated on high risk populations such as prostitutes, patients at sexually transmitted disease (STD) clinics, individuals with multiple sex partners, and/or other sub-populations unlikely to be representative of the population as a whole, such as patients in tertiary care hospitals, urban mothers attending well-baby clinics, urban blood donors, and so on. Control groups are tested in some of these studies, but they are most often a control group representative of the sub-population surveyed rather than the population as a whole. For all of these reasons—and small sample sizes as well—the data must be used with care. A summary of selected results by country is as follows:

RWANDA: In 1985, van de Perre, et al., reported that 18 percent of healthy adults in Kigali, and 4.5 percent of healthy adults in rural areas were infected.[12] More recent estimates are that 10-20 percent of the adult population in Kigali is infected.[13]

BURUNDI: Galli, et al., reported that 13.2 percent of 158 hospital out-patients, including 65 with STD, in a remote rural area without roads, were infected.[14]

UGANDA: Lloyd, in 1985 and 1986, found 27 percent of 100 randomly selected hospital inpatients in Kampala, 11 percent of 370 blood donors in Kampala, 14 percent of 1,011 antenatal women in Kampala, and 30 percent of 100 outpatient attenders in Masaka were positive.[15] In 1986, Carswell reported 15.4 percent (110/716) of healthy adults in Kampala were infected, but only 1 out of 71 adults in West Nile province.[16] In a rural community in southwest Uganda, Naamara in 1987 found HIV 1 infection in 67.7 percent of 184 high-risk persons, 17.7 percent of 124 normal risk persons, and 1.1 percent of 92 children.[17] De Lalla, working in a rural district in northern Uganda, found an increase in sero-positivity from 0.9 percent (1/111) in 1984, to 13.2 percent (58/441) in 1986.[18]

ZAMBIA: Hira, et al., found 17 percent of healthy persons in Lusaka were sero-positive in 1985.[19] Melbge, et al., reported 17.5 percent of 1,078 hospital patients, 18.4 percent of blood donors, and 19 percent of hospital workers were infected.[20] Ryder reports that the current prevalence in Lusaka is approvimately 20 percent.[21] In the "copper belt" on the Zambian border north of Lusaka, Buchanan, et al., found infection in 11 percent (3/28) of technical students, 13 percent (7/54) of office staff, and 22 percent (14/62) of a random sample of hospital patients.[22]

ZAIRE: At a well-child clinic in Kinshasa, Mann, et al., found that 8 percent of 191 mothers and 4 percent of children were infected. They stated that among healthy adults in Kinshasa the sero-prevalence is 6.7 percent.[23] Ryder estimated prevalences in Kinshasa of 4-8 percent in adults and 2 percent in children under 3 years old.[24] Outside Kinshasa, Surmont, et al., in Dungu in a rural area in northeast Zaire, found sero-positive rates of 24 percent (8/33) of adults with links with the local capital, 5 percent (9/170) of sedentary adults, and 0.4 percent (1/222) in a nearby village.[25] In Aru, a town on a busy road near the Ugandan border, Aktar, et al., tested 319 asymptomatic subjects over the age of 15, and found a rate of 5.3 percent.[26]

TANZANIA: In Tanzania, the epidemic seems to be mainly in the northwest. In Kagera district in northwest Tanzania, Forthal, et al., in 1985 found 31 percent of 78 barmaids and 32 percent of 34 controls positive.[27] Mhalu, et al., in Bukoba, the capital of Kagera district, in 1987 reported rates of 16 percent of 100 pregnant women and 14 percent of 32 blood donors.[28] By comparison the rates that they reported in Dar es Salaam were 3.6 percent and 4.4 percent respectively.

KENYA: Comprehensive data from Kenya, apart from high risk groups, are lacking. 31 percent to 80 percent of female prostitutes in three surveys were found to be positive.[29] Kriess, et al. reported an infection rate of 2 percent in 42 healthy medical personnel in 1985.[30]

CONGO: In 1985, in a survey of randomly selected households, Merlin, et al. found that 5 percent of 368 persons in Brazzaville and none of 360 persons in Pointe-Noire were sero-positive.[31] In 1987, Georges-Courbot, et al. reported a rate of 4.6 percent in 368 randomly selected sera from Brazzaville.[32]

CENTRAL AFRICAN REPUBLIC: Merlin, et al. in a random survey of households in Bangui in 1985 found 4 percent of 1263 subjects tested positive.[33] In a three year survey in randomized populations in the same city, Georges-Courbot, et al. reported increasing rates of 2.1 percent in 1985, 4.04 percent in 1986 and 7.8 percent in 1987.[34]

MALAWI: Gutler, et al. in 1987, found sero-positivity rates of 4 percent in 96 pregnant women, 30 percent of 32 male prisoners, and 56 percent of 265 female prostitutes.[35]

ANGOLA: In Luanda, Bottiger, et al. reported that 4 percent of 94 medical inpatients were sero-positive. Rates were 1 percent for other inpatients and less than 1 percent for other groups. In Cabinda, 11 percent of 38 maternity inpatients were positive compared to 2 percent for other patients and 0 percent for blood donors and villagers.[36]

MOZAMBIQUE: A rate of 2.5 percent was found in 131 prostitutes in Maputo by Georges-Courbot, et al.[37]

CAMEROON: In 1986, Durand, et al. tested 1,273 persons in a random household survey and found a sero-positivity rate of 1 percent.[38]

GABON: In 1987, Delaporte, et al. tested 383 subjects including children in Libreville, and found rates of 1.8 percent in adults and 0 percent in children.[39]

SENEGAL: M'Boup, et al. reported rates of less than 1 percent for HIV 1 but rates of up to 45 percent for HIV 2, depending on the region and population tested.[40]

BURKINA FASO: Sangare, et al. tested sera from 776 subjects including patients, prostitutes, prisoners, and pregnant women, and found rates of 4 percent for HIV 1 and 8.6 percent for HIV 2.[41]

IVORY COAST: Leonard, et al. in 1987 reported rates of 8.95 percent of 1,200 persons with multiple sexual partners, 6.1 percent of persons receiving multiple injections, and 2.7 percent of a control population without risk factors, including 300 children and 850 adults.[42]

Although comprehensive data from all areas and for all groups are lacking, some patterns and trends emerge from these studies. The most affected area appears to be a region of Central Africa which includes Rwanda, Burundi, Uganda, and Zambia. In these countries there are a number of cities and rural areas where 20 percent or more of surveyed adults are infected.[43] In Zaire, Congo, Central African Republic, and Tanzania, around 5-10 percent of surveyed adults and 2 percent of surveyed children under 3 years old are infected in cities and a few rural areas. The initial studies indicated that infection was confined primarily to larger cities and a few rural areas in southwestern Uganda and northwest Tanzania. There is now evidence of spread of infection to other rural areas in the most affected countries. In 1986, Quinn, et al., estimated that the annual incidence of AIDS in Central Africa was 550 to 1,000 cases per million adults, with age and sex specific rates highest in women under 30 and men over 40 years of age.[44] There is also evidence of spread southward to Malawi, Angola, and Mozambique. In West Africa, the studies suggest that in most countries 1 percent or less of surveyed adults are infected with HIV 1, although numbers are increasing in the Ivory Coast, Burkina Faso, and Nigeria.[45]

Prevalence of HIV 2
The studies also show a high prevalence in West Africa of infection of the surveyed adults with HIV 2—a recently identified "new" virus similar to HIV 1, apparently spread by the same modes as HIV 1. Kanki, et al. found HIV 2 infection in surveyed adults in Senegal, Guinea, Guinea Bissau, Burkina Faso, and the Ivory Coast, ranging from averages of 1 to 16

percent in the general population and from 15 to 64 percent in high risk individuals—female prostitutes and STD patients. In cross sectional surveys and longitudinal studies of registered prostitutes, however, no association has so far been found between infection with HIV 2 and any of the complex of immunodeficiency-related illnesses associated with AIDS and HIV 1. All West African AIDS patients tested were infected with HIV 1; most were Central Africans or had traveled there. A few West African AIDS patients were found to be infected by both HIV 1 and HIV 2, but there was no way to establish which came first or the full nature of any interactions. Kanki, et al. did find that while HIV 2 infected individuals can later become infected with HIV 1, some of the characteristic responses to HIV 1 infection may be attenuated in individuals previously infected with HIV 2. Further laboratory work on these interactions and longitudinal analysis of HIV 2 infected populations at high risk for subsequent HIV 1 infection are anticipated.[46]

Evidence from Surveys: Rates and Risk for AIDS

There is very limited evidence on rates of progression in Africa from infection with HIV 1 to AIDS-related Complex (ARC) and full blown AIDS. Such rates are important for estimating the demographic and economic consequences of the disease. After following 67 sero-positive individuals for 16 months, Mann, et al. reported a rate of development of generalized lymphadenopathy in Kinshasa of 10.4 per 100 person-years, and a rate of development of AIDS of 1.3 per 100 person-years.[47] Ngaly, et al., also in Kinshasa, found a rate of development of ARC of 20.4 per 100 person-years in sero-positive hospital workers.[48] These rates are similar to those found in homosexual populations in the United States but may also reflect some selection bias in the African samples. If, as seems likely, the hospital workers followed in both studies were of higher social class, better educated, and otherwise more healthy than the average AIDS patient in these cities, then the rates of progression to ARC, AIDS, and death, now and in the future, may be higher. Rates of progression from infection to ARC, AIDS, and death among infants are much higher than among adults; Bulatao estimates annual rates of progression to AIDS of 25 to 35 percent of infected infants.[49] Older adults infected by any mode and children infected via blood transfusions may also progress to ARC and AIDS at faster rates than younger adults.

There is better evidence concerning the populations at special risk from AIDS. The distribution of HIV 1 infection is bimodal with a peak in infancy and another peak in sexually active adults with cases equally or nearly equally distributed between males and females. Peak risk of infection among adults is between ages 15 and 29 for females and between ages 25 and 35 in males.[50] Thus deaths from AIDS can be expected to increase among women in their twenties and thirties; men in their thirties, forties, and fifties; and among infants and young children.

This distribution is the primary evidence that the mode of transmission in Africa is predominantly through heterosexual intercourse and vertical perinatal transmission from mother to child. The evidence for heterosexual transmission includes the equal numbers of males and females infected, the incidence among sexually active adults, high rates of infection among individuals with multiple sexual partners and with contact with prostitutes, and the very high rates in female prostitutes. An association between HIV 1 infection and other sexually transmitted diseases (STD) has been noted in many studies. Rates of HIV 1 infection are higher among repeat STD patients than first time patients, and higher among those with other current STD infections than those without.[51] Thus it seems likely that concurrent sexually transmitted diseases represent an independent risk factor, and that genital lesions may make transmission of HIV 1 during intercourse more likely. It is also probable that there are high correlations between prostitution and STD infections, and between STD infections and the number of injections received from licensed and unlicensed practioners and clinics. Thus, in some proportion of cases, needles and syringes may be the modes of transmission rather than the "high risk" behavior itself.[52] The distinction is critical for policy, but the proportion of cases transmitted by needles in Africa among sexually active adults is unknown.

Infants and children are at risk because sero-positive pregnant women have about a 50 percent chance of transmitting the virus to their child, either transplacentally or at birth.[53] HIV 1 has also been isolated in breast milk. But so far there is only anecdotal evidence that this is an additional mode of transmission and risk for sero-negative children of sero-positive mothers.

There is some suggestion in the surveys in Central Africa of disproportionate infection among individuals who are the more highly educated, of higher social standing, and spatially mobile.[54] The acknowledged death of Zambian President Kenneth Kaunda's son from AIDS has been widely reported, increasing the concern that a generation of highly educated Africans in central African cities may be at risk. Melbge, et al. found high education attainment to be independently associated with HIV 1 infection in a sample of 1,078 hospital patients in Lusaka.[55] Yet these individuals are also more likely to seek treatment in hospitals for health problems and thus to be sampled in studies of institutional patients. Whether high educational attainment or higher social standing are independently associated with HIV 1 infection among all infected individuals in Lusaka or elsewhere has not yet been established. On-going work in Zaire suggests that there may be an inverse correlation between educational attainment and probability of infection in Kinshasa.[56] Kreiss, et al, found HIV 1 infection rates of 66 percent in female prostitutes of low social status in Nairobi and 31 percent in female prostitutes of higher social status.[57] But this finding is confounded by the likelihood that prostitutes of low economic status have more sexual partners—itself a risk factor. Clearly, the questions of whether AIDS mortality will occur disproportionately among urban élites and whether dementia will be a significant proportion of AIDS morbidity are critical for estimating the potential impact of AIDS on African societies.

The general population is at risk from blood transfusions and the use of unsterilized needles and syringes, all of which play a lesser but significant role in transmission of HIV 1 in Africa. Risk is greater among those more likely to need care in hospitals and clinics, including young children, adults with other sexually transmitted diseases, and among those with access to services involving transfusions and injections—primarily but not exclusively urban and higher income individuals. Mann, et al.,[21] in a study of mothers and children in hospitals and attending a well-child clinic in Kinshasa, found that 61 percent of sero-positive children had sero-positive mothers. In the remaining 39 percent there was a significant association with number of medical injections, previous blood transfusions, and hospitalizations.

Routine immunizations could explain some of this risk where these injections are not given by well-trained staff with sterile procedures. But many medications are given by injection in Africa. Unsterile injections could be received by children and adults in clinics or hospitals which treat both, by adults in STD clinics and by children and adults from licensed practitioners and from numerous unlicensed practitioners. In a sample in the Ivory Coast in 1987, Leonard, et al. found infection rates of 8.95 percent of persons with multiple sexual partners, 6.2 percent of persons receiving multiple injections, and 2.7 percent of a control population without risk factors, including 300 children and 850 adults.[58] If the subsamples with multiple sex partners and multiple injections were mutually exclusive, then multiple injections may be a major mode of infection in Africa, particularly in cities.

Blood transfusions in hospitals and clinics are also widely used in Africa, the most common indication in childhood being anemia due to severe malaria. A number of studies have shown high rates of infection in healthy blood donors.[59] As many as ten percent of available blood units are infected and will transmit the HIV 1 virus.[60]

Children and youth may also be at risk from traditional practices of scarification and circumcision performed in some regions of Africa. Although these represent possible modes of transmission, they have not yet been documented.

Demographic and Economic Effects

Assessment of the demographic and economic consequences of AIDS in Africa with high levels of confidence will require complex modeling and much better data than are currently available. This section summarizes the results of preliminary but indicative work by other authors and groups and some preliminary results of our own. The purpose is to give some sense of the impact of AIDS if infection rates at the lower ranges of those found in the sample surveys approximate the actual current rates in Central Africa. The questions of concern include effects on population growth and age distribution, and on economic growth and viability.

Demographic Consequences

The effect of AIDS will be to increase and redistribute mortality. Increased mortality will reduce the rate of population growth directly. Redistribution of mortality could also directly affect the age distribution of the population— for example, if adult AIDS deaths exceed child AIDS deaths by a large amount. AIDS mortality of young adults and a change in the age distribution could reduce total fertility. AIDS mortality of infants and children may also directly affect fertility rates—although the direction of the effect is debatable. All of these changes would, in turn, affect rates of population growth and—together with future AIDS mortality—the future age distribution of the population.

Research Triangle Institute and Bongaarts, Bulatao, and Way, et al. have all modeled the prospective changes in mortality and population growth rates.[61] The models and the assumptions vary but the aggregate conclusions do not: none predicts that population growth will cease in any of the countries analyzed over the 20 to 25 years that the projections cover. Bulatao estimates that the population growth rate in Zaire would drop under worst case assumptions about AIDS, but would still be 2.23 percent per year in the period 2000 to 2005. Bongaarts predicts that with spread of HIV 1 infection to 25 percent of the population of sub-Saharan countries in the next 25 years annual population growth would drop from 3 to 2 percent; a sero-prevalence of 50 percent would be required to produce a zero rate of population growth.[62] Thus, predictions popularized in the United States media that AIDS will depopulate Central Africa are supported by none of the work done so far.

The key to these findings is that fertility rates are high and declining only slowly, and that many of the HIV 1 infected adults are likely to live long enough to have offspring—even if half or less of these children survive because of vertical transmission of HIV 1. The total population would continue to grow but it would grow more slowly because of increasing AIDS mortality and, in the longer term, because none of infected infants and children would live long enough to have offspring. Bulatao's worst case estimates for Zaire show life expectancy remaining constant rather than increasing and infant mortality rising rather than dropping—as would have happened without AIDS. In the medium term AIDS projection, life expectancy improves slowly, infant mortality decreases and life expectancy increases—though both less than would have been the case without AIDS. In all projections, child and adult deaths are of approximately equal numbers; dependency ratios are little affected.[63]

None of the models currently used estimates increased mortality among sero-negative individuals from contagious diseases other than AIDS which may be spread by AIDS patients because AIDS carriers of these diseases may be more infectious—as is thought to be the case in AIDS-related tuberculosis. To the extend that these interactions are important, the projected mortality may be understated.

None of the analyses done so far assumes any changes in fertility due to AIDS mortality of infants and young children. Among the currently unanswered questions are: Will most mothers and fathers of children who die of AIDS seek to replace these children or will they despair of attempting, particularly as one or both the parents suffer onset of AIDS-related illnesses? Will an extended family structure, particularly the availability of others to care for children, make a difference in these responses? Will sero-negative parents have more children as "insurance" if they see their neighbors' children dying in unprecedented numbers, or will they have fewer and concentrate their energy on protecting those that they have? Bongaarts speculates that AIDS will increase fertility rates as mothers respond to increased infant mortality by having more children, thus delaying the demographic transition which was foreseen in Africa and which would have occurred without AIDS.[64] If this speculation is correct, then the aggregate effect of AIDS on population growth and size will be less than the models predict, but the impact on the dependence ratio would be greater.

Aggregate results are not the whole story, of course. Even a small change in total size of the population of a country compared to what it would have been without AIDS means a large increase in deaths—in Bulatao's words about Zaire—deaths in five years "in the tens of thousands," and after twenty years, "in the hundreds of thousands and still rising." [65] There will be havoc and suffering for countless households. And if these deaths are concentrated in urban areas and among the better educated and most productive adults and their children, there could be impacts on the society as a whole which are larger than the aggregate demographic effects suggest.

Potential Economic Costs

What are the prospective economic costs of the AIDS epidemic in those countries where the available data suggest that rates of infection and illness are high? We report preliminary results for Zaire based on research in progress.[66] Among the costs of illness and death are direct costs of treatment, and indirect costs of labor time lost to society. We estimate only the indirect costs and only those indirect costs which are attributable to AIDS mortality in the working age population. Costs of treatment are not estimated. Indirect costs of illness—such as AIDS-related dementia—and of infant and child deaths, are also not estimated. Finally, we have not attempted to estimate the costs and consequences of wide-spread breakdowns in the social and economic order, were these to occur. Thus, the economic consequences projected below are conservative.

Methodology and Preliminary Estimates

The analysis is done in three steps. First, we begin with a range of estimates of increased deaths by age group due to AIDS in Zaire in the period

1985-2005.[67] Estimates of cumulative labor-years lost due to AIDS deaths among the working age population are made by assuming an average retirement age of 60. These estimates are then multiplied by estimated ranges of future marginal product expressed in constant 1984 United States dollars. We have used rates of growth of marginal product of 0, 1, and 2 percent per year.

Next, it is possible to estimate the cost to society if the workers who die are disproportionately the higher skilled, better educated, and in critical sectors or jobs. We do so by assuming that their marginal product is a conservative multiple of the marginal product estimates used in the first set of estimates. Three multiples are used: 1.5, 2.0 and 3.0—far lower than those suggested by salary multiples in Zaire and other African economies.

Finally, we estimate the additional losses which could occur if the epidemic and premature deaths lower the productivity of other workers and of the economy as a whole—that is, if there are negative spill-overs or "externalities." These could include disruption of key sectors, of factor markets, particularly labor markets, and/or reduced savings and investment. We cannot forecast consequences by sectors; mortality forecasts by sectors would be needed to do so and they are not available. Some literature speculates that there will be high rates of infection, morbidity and mortality in mining, transport, armed forces, and police, and among the urban élites.[68]

Leaving aside sectoral disruptions, the impact on savings and investment could be particularly important. There may be some diversion of household savings into curative care. For example, the average direct cost to families for treatment of chronic disease (not including AIDS) in a sample of households in the Congo was equal to 12 percent of average household agricultural income; average opportunity cost for lost days of work was equal to another 12 percent.[69] In ministries of public health, there may be a diversion of health resources into curative services and away from prevention and promotional activities—even AIDS prevention. At the economy-wide level, there may be diversion of public and private resources from other capital formation to health services provision and other AIDS costs. Companies and other institutions and third party insurers which cover workers at risk may face growing costs for care and death benefits unless they renege—as some may do to avoid serious losses or insolvency. Less investment means less growth of future product. This is particularly critical in agriculture, where foreign savings cannot so easily substitute for domestic savings as in the modern sector. At a macro and simplistic level, if the average capital output ratio is 3 and the economy is growing at 4 percent—about a 1 percent per year increase in per capita GNP because of population growth—a 1 percent reduction in savings will reduce the growth rate to 3.6 percent; a two percent reduction would reduce the growth rate to 3.3 percent. Note that the decreases in savings which produce these effects are relatively modest; from a savings rate of 12 percent to rates of 11 percent or 10 percent.

To estimate the consequences of reduced savings rates on growth, we test a range from no growth in real per capita product to growth at an annual rate of 0.5 percent. (Zaire's per capita product in fact declined at an annual rate of 2.1 percent between 1965 and 1985.) For Zaire, the most logical combinations of assumptions associated with best case and worst case assumptions yield the following estimates of cumulative losses between 1985 and 2005 expressed in constant 1984 dollars:

* low AIDS, high growth,
  high multiple,
  low externalities: $ 8.6 billion

* high AIDS, no growth,
  low multiple;
  greater externalities $17.4 billion

Putting these losses in annual terms, the results for Zaire suggest that annual costs or losses in 1995 compared to what the economic situation would have been without AIDS may be $350 to $670 million—equal to 8 percent to 16 percent of 1984 GNP. By 2005 the annual loss could be $1.0 to $2.2 billion—25 percent to 52 percent of 1984 GNP. Official development assistance to Zaire in 1984 from all sources and for all purposes was $314 million.[70]

Implications of the Results
This very preliminary set of estimates suggests that the aggregate costs of AIDS in the next decade—in terms of lost product and spill-overs—although

large, are not likely to be debilitating. By 1995, the estimates mean that on average each individual in Zaire will have between $19 and $17 less income per year (in constant 1984 dollars) than they would have had without AIDS. Per capita income in 1985 was $170. These estimated losses are not nearly as high as the cost of the negative growth rates in per capita product in the past two decades which had nothing to do with AIDS. And AIDS losses at these estimated levels could be much more than offset by improved economic policies in the next decade, notwithstanding the fact that there would still be lost product due to AIDS compared to a hypothetical non-AIDS situation. If the economy were to perform better in the next decade, the lost product would have a higher value.

As time passes, losses will mount and the amount foregone each year will be larger, compared not only to a non-AIDS situation but also to the earlier years with AIDS. Larger foregone product means a greater chance that the losses will spill-over into the functioning of critical sectors or of the economy as whole and cause serious disruptions. But such disruptions are not—we think—in view for the next decade at least.

Policy Issues and Implications for the United States

The higher ranges of the estimates beyond the next decade, and the high infection rates reported in some surveys can lead to a paralyzing pessimism. Indeed, some in the Unites States have expressed the view that portions of Africa may have to be "written-off," even "quarantined"—that rates of infection have or will soon reach such levels that a full blown pandemic with high and increasing death rates and societal and economic collapse is inevitable.

This view can be rejected—not only on humanitarian grounds—but on factual grounds and on grounds of United States national interest. The available evidence is that, so far, the epidemic is most serious in countries containing about a quarter of the sub-Saharan population (exclusive of the Republic of South Africa). In those countries, it is the urban population, about a quarter of their populations or approximately 6 percent of the sub-Saharan total, that is most at risk. Rural populations—except perhaps for discrete areas in Uganda and Tanzania, and areas contiguous to major transport routes, mines, and military bases—are at much lower risk. Thus, no generalization about AIDS in Africa as a whole is valid—at least in the medium term.

Even among urban populations in the countries most affected by the epidemic, the age groups at risk are young women, middle aged men, and the fetuses of infected mothers. Older adults, including individuals now in leadership positions, are at much less risk. Non-infected children are not at risk except from blood transfusions, other blood exchanges, and contaminated needles and syringes until they become sexually active. And because of past and current high fertility rates, these children of "safe age"—under age 15—account for 40 to 50 percent of urban (and rural) populations. These percentages were not projected to decrease very much over the next 20 years, even without AIDS, because of the demographic structure and high and only gradually declining fertility rates. If adult deaths from AIDS were to exceed pediatric deaths from AIDS, the proportion of the population under age 15 would decrease less rapidly than expected. It may not decrease at all if the response to increased infant mortality due to AIDS is an increase in fertility rates. Thus, about half the population—the future labor force and future parents—is not, or need not, be at risk, even in the cities of countries where AIDS is most wide-spread.

Finally, although AIDS is believed to be fatal in all cases, the median time from infection to disease among adults is long—five to perhaps as long as 15 years depending, in part, on general health status. Asymptomatic adults can function unimpaired for many months, many years. Even adults with AIDS-related illnesses or aware that they have tested positive for HIV 1 antibodies have some incentive to work, alter behavior, make arrangements and persevere if there is high and increasing probability that their children will survive.

There is strong reason, then, for rejecting total pessimism. But the problem of AIDS in Africa is serious and growing. There are clear policy priorities and a clear and compelling case for United States involvement and leadership in helping African societies deal with AIDS problem.

The United States' Role
Arguments in favor of strong United States support for programs of research and assistance in Africa are grounded in common cause, self-interest,

and the United States's well established leadership among donors in public health in Africa.

The United States is the country most affected by AIDS outside of Central and East Africa. The current dominant transmission modes and high risk groups in the United States are different, although heterosexual transmission and pediatric AIDS due to vertical transmission are increasingly seen in the United States. The United States shares a common problem with high prevalence African countries; it thus shares common goals of improving information, scientific understanding, prevention, control, and eventually development of vaccines and a cure.

It will benefit the United States—perhaps the future health of many Americans—to understand the epidemiology and virology of AIDS in Africa, including the predominant heterosexual transmission modes, the factors which may predict or predispose infants to infection during pregnancy and at birth, the possibility of pockets of special susceptibility to or resistance to HIV 1 in African populations, and the progression of HIV 2 infection in West Africa and its interactions with HIV 1 and AIDS.

To understand these and many other aspects of AIDS in Africa will require more than research; the case for extensive biomedical and applied research is strong. It will require long-term involvement and longitudinal work which combines research with programs to interrupt transmission modes where that is possible, and to slow transmission when it is not, and which make diagnosis and screening less costly and more accurate. Intermittent research which is not related—or not seen as related—to prevention and control is unlikely to yield information of maximum benefit to Africans or Americans and is also unlikely to be welcome in Africa. The United States can learn most by helping and can help most by being and staying committed for the long term.

The United States is already a leading donor to public health activities in Africa; many of these activities, particularly child survival and family planning programs, relate directly to AIDS and may need to be modified because of AIDS. As a major donor and innovator, the United States is also able to influence the programs of other donors as they become active in AIDS control efforts and AIDS research. In addition, United States corporations, private voluntary organizations, and religious organizations are active in Africa. The corporations—in order to protect worker health and the financial viability of health insurance programs—are potential innovators of prevention programs which could be widely applicable in other African institutions and elsewhere in the world. Private voluntary organizations and religious organizations are already working in medical care, nutrition, famine relief, and refugee assistance. They have been innovators in health care delivery in Africa and will certainly become involved with AIDS prevention control and treatment, either by design or by events.

The main argument against a strong United States role—apart from the pessimism discussed earlier—is that AIDS is still highly sensitive politically in some African countries. It may be easier and more effective for the United States to cooperate through multilateral agencies such as WHO. Indeed, this was the initial strategy of the United States Agency for International Development (AID), which provided $1 million to WHO's AIDS efforts in Africa in fiscal 1987. In addition, in 1987 two Washington-based programs were funded by AID to respond to requests from developing countries worldwide for technical assistance on applied research on AIDS, on establishment and improvement of AIDS programs and AIDS public health education. These projects are initially expected to run five to eight years, with resources in excess of $50 million for that period. Finally, AID is providing more than $1 million for direct support of AIDS control programs in Uganda, Zimbabwe, Burundi, Sierra Leone, Zaire, Ghana, and Nigeria. It gives an additional 13 million for condom supplies worldwide. Clearly these approaches are not mutually exclusive and are potentially reinforcing.

A final consideration affecting future United States work on AIDS in Africa is its cost. Although there is a constituency in Congress to support AIDS prevention and control in Africa, just as there has been for the child survival programs, budget constraints are and will be a fact of life. Even support for child survival programs has been cut over the past three years. Resources devoted to prevention and control of AIDS in Africa will have to be targeted on the most critical and cost effective interventions—particularly interventions in which the United States has special skills—and to related research.

Macro Policy Priorities

The apparent concentration of high infection rates in the urban areas of Central and East Africa dictates a general strategy of assisting countries not yet affected to prevent infection, and of assisting affected countries to control infection and slow its spread. No foreign donor can substitute for national commitment and programs. Where they are lacking, WHO and private international and voluntary organizations may be the most effective external forces to help bring about needed awareness and change. Where commitment and programs exist—as in Uganda—the financial requirements are likely to be large. Public health education, supply and distribution of spermicidal lubricated condoms, establishing and monitoring of blood supply systems, and testing and counseling of high risk groups imply capital and recurrent costs that will have to be met externally. This is particularly true in those countries where the analysis suggests that AIDS may reduce economic growth. Even the low range of estimates of the economic costs of AIDS presented in this chapter suggest that the purely economic case for preventive and control measures is high—even if the effectiveness of such measures is limited. The estimated economic losses also reinforce arguments for greater concessional lending and a resolution of the debt problem in the most affected economies.

Public Health Priorities

In the near term, the highest priority and most cost effective interventions center on technologies and the transfer of hospital and medical practices that can interrupt the transmission of HIV 1 infection quickly. Such interventions ought not depend on the necessary but slower changes in public awareness and in reproductive behavior.

The Kinshasa study cited earlier found that 40 percent of HIV 1 infected children were born of mothers without HIV 1 infection.[71] There were strong associations in these 40 percent with the number of injections, prior hospitalizations, and blood transfusions. They were also disproportionately male, suggesting the hypothesis that circumcision may also have played a role. Adults, similarly, are at risk from unhygienic injections—particularly in STD clinics and from untrained practitioners—and from hospitalization, particularly blood transfusions. There are no studies of the proportions of sero-positive, sexually active adults in African populations which have, in fact, been infected by injections and transfusions rather than by sexual intercourse. Precisely because these individuals are sexually active, their cases are impossible to distinguish. But adult cases of infection by injections and transfusion share with the 40 percent of pediatric cases identified in Kinshasa the characteristic that they need not have happened and can and should be reduced quickly in the future.

These preventive measures are by far the most cost effective interventions over the near term. The United States has special competence and experience in the establishment of blood screening and blood bank programs, and can also supply materials and technical assistance to help establish sterile procedures for injections and more strict practices with respect to transfusions.

The United States is currently active in supporting child survival programs and family planning in many sub-Saharan countries. There is no basis for arguing that these activities need to be cut back and resources reallocated to AIDS. On the contrary, because of AIDS, these activities need to be sustained and increased, though modified somewhat.

Child survival programs promoted and supported by the United States and also by UNICEF consist of preventive and promotive innovations, including expanded programs of immunizations, oral rehydration therapy, growth monitoring, promotion of breast feeding, family planning to increase child spacing, malaria control and treatment, and training of health workers and the building of delivery structures to reach members of rural and urban households—primarily mothers. In fiscal year 1987, AID child survival programs totaled almost $50 million. Over the next four years these efforts are to be emphasized in eight African countries: Kenya, Malawi, Mali, Niger, Nigeria, Senegal, the Sudan, and Zaire.

It is critical to maintain and improve the health of children, particularly in the countries most affected by AIDS. Note that only two or three of the emphasis countries fall into this category. Children not infected with the AIDS virus are or should be at minimal risk until puberty. (Infected children will likely die in infancy or early childhood and can only infect other children by blood or needle contact.) These uninfected children are the future labor force and future parents. Child survival programs provide an existing structure for reaching them, not only to sustain and improve their health, but to educate them and their parents to reduce risk of AIDS infection after puberty.

Some modifications in child survival programs may be needed. Immunization of children with unsterile needles or syringes can be a mode of transmission of the AIDS virus from infected children to uninfected children. Adequate sterilization must be assured in child survival programs. Mothers need to understand not only the importance of getting these injections for their children but equally the importance of avoiding all or most other injections—particularly from untrained practitioners. More aggressive efforts in malaria control and treatment are necessary since severe malaria is a principal reason why children receive blood transfusions. Establishment of new blood supply systems will take time and are costly. The AIDS virus has been isolated in breast milk, though mother-child transmission via breast milk has not been documented. If it is, the use of breast milk banks in child survival programs will need to be reviewed.

Child survival programs reach mainly mothers and children. Family planning information and methods focus on options for women—pills, injectables, implants, and ligation. None of these methods protects against AIDS. The near unanimous conclusion among health experts is that condoms, particularly spermicidal lubricated condoms, do. Thus, if child survival programs are to be used as one mechanism for reaching people about AIDS and for slowing or preventing its spread, fathers will need to be included more than now. Alternatively, Henderson has suggested that the United States should take the lead in helping to develop an effective and inexpensive spermicide-virucide—for example, a vaginal sponge which would protect from AIDS and perhaps also serve as substitute or supplemental family planning method. The advantage would be that a method controlled by a woman is more likely to be used.[72]

The same issues pertain to family planning programs directed at young adults and which are also supported by the United States and other donors such as the UN Family Planning Agency (UNFPA). The emphasis now is overwhelmingly on women's methods of contraception. The emphasis is also overwhelmingly on child spacing, limiting, and choice about new life—not prevention of disease, particularly fatal disease. The addition of AIDS prevention to existing family planning programs is appealing, if daunting; in Kenya, for example, only 17 percent of married couples use contraceptives; less than 0.2 percent use condoms.[73] But the job is much more than simply reaching men. Other issues include whether condom use is to be promoted instead of women's methods. Or will they be used in addition to women's methods? Will there be stigma associated with condom use if it becomes a presumptive sign of infection, and will a stigma also affect methods that do not protect from AIDS? Some of these problems would be reduced if an effective and inexpensive women's method which protects from AIDS can be developed. In the field of family planning and in addressing such questions with operations research, the United States has special competence and experience.

Continued basic and applied research on AIDS epidemiology, serology, and virology is critical. Henderson has suggested that the United States should take the lead in helping to establish research centers to undertake longitudinal studies of the epidemiology and pathobiology of AIDS in Africa, to establish the relative importance of injections and other modes of infection, and to evaluate interventions to slow the spread of AIDS based on such research.[74] Other priority programs focused directly on AIDS which may be appropriate for international and bilateral support and are likely to be cost effective include the development of simplified, less expensive and more reliable blood tests, perhaps based on antigens in addition to antibodies.

The testing of vaccines in Africa under the auspices of bilateral programs would appear politically a bad choice; national or international auspices would clearly be preferable. When and if there are breakthroughs in vaccines or treatments—if, for example, genetically-engineered T-4 decoy receptors prove to be effective, safe, and economic—then major efforts would be appropriate and economically justified. Until then, there is no scientific or economic justification for bilateral support of programs to treat those already infected and ill, even though AZT or other drugs may, at high cost, slow progression rates somewhat. For the greatest human and economic impact, available United States resources must now be devoted as much as possible to assisting research, prevention, and control.

There are strong arguments to support United States assistance to African states confronted by AIDS, based on the projected impact of the disease upon their economies. There is little evidence for the argument that some countries are already so much affected that they are beyond help and that aid would be a waste of scarce resources. The most efficient and politically acceptable approach to AIDS assistance is an emphasis on the transfer of technology in which the United States has special expertise and to strengthen the child survival, maternal and child health, and family planning programs already in place. The United States is already perceived by Africa to be a valued partner in public health interventions. The United States was the major contributor to the eradication of smallpox from West and Central Africa, and United States assistance to service development, training, and research in the health sector in Africa has been an important element in the life expectancy and infant and child mortality rate gains seen in the past two decades. Our continued support of these programs and our added support of AIDS research and prevention programs will contribute significantly to a national and international effort to reduce the prevalence and impact of AIDS, not only in Africa but worldwide.

Notes

1. The authors wish to thank David Scrimgeour and Jody Heymann for research assistance in the preparation of this chapter. Any remaining errors are the responsibility of the authors.

2. World Bank, *Financing Health Services in Developing Countries: An Agenda for Reform* (Washington, D.C., 1987), App. Tables. These and other averages are weighted averages, adjusted for country population sizes.

3. Lincoln C. Chen, "The AIDS Pandemic: An International Approach to Disease Control," *Daedalus,* CXVI (1987). 184.

4. Jonathan Mann, *AIDS: The Global Impact* (Washington, D.C., 1986), 8; D.A. Henderson, personal communication (Dec. 1987).

5. Mann *AIDS: Global Impact,* 4.

6. "AIDS in Africa," editorial, *Lancet,* II (1987) 192-194; Mann, et al., "Association between HTLV-III/LAV Infection and Tuberculosis in Zaire," *Journal of American Medical Association,* CCLVI (1986), 346.

7. Mann, *AIDS: Global Impact,* 1.

8. D. Daumerie, et al., "HIV Infection and Leprosy: A Hypothetical Mutual Interference," paper presented at the Second International Symposium on AIDS in Africa (Naples, 1987).

9. O. Simooya, R. M. Mwendepole, and S. Siziya, "Relationship between P. Falciparum Malaria and HIV-Positivity," *ibid.*

10. R. Colebunders, et al., "Evaluation of a Clinical Case-Definition of Acquired Immunodeficiency Syndrome in Africa," *Lancet,* I (1987) 492-494.

11 *Ibid.*

12. P. van de Perre, et al., "HTLV-III/LAV Infection in Central Africa," paper presented at the International Symposium on African AIDS (Brussels, 1985).

13. Robert Ryder, personal communication (Oct. 1987).

14. M. Galli, et al., "Prevalence of Antibodies to HIV in a Rural Area of Burundi," paper presented at the Second International Symposium on AIDS in Africa (Naples, 1987).

15. G. Lloyd, quoted in "AIDS: A Public Health Crisis," Pl-219 *Population Reports*, XIV (1986), 219.

16. J.W. Carswell, et al., "How Long Has the AIDS Virus Been in Uganda?" *Lancet*, I (1986), 1217.

17. W. Naamara and F. Plummer, "Cross-sectional Study of HIV Infection in South-Western Uganda," paper presented at Second International Symposium on AIDS in Africa (Naples, 1987).

18. F. DeLalla, et al., "Rapid spread of HIV infection in a Rural District in North Uganda," paper presented at the Third International Conference on AIDS (Washington, D.C., 1987).

19. K.S. Hira, et al., "The Epidemiology and Clinical Manifestations of the Acquired Immunodeficiency Syndrome (AIDS) and its Related Complex (ARC) in Zambia," paper presented at the Second International Conference on AIDS (Paris, 1986).

20. M. Melbge, et al., "Evidence for Heterosexual Transmission and Clinical Manifestations of HIV Infection and Related Conditions in Lusaka, Zambia," *Lancet*, II (1986), 1113-1115.

21. Robert Ryder, personal communication (Oct. 1987).

22. D.J. Buchanan, R.G. Downing, and R.S. Tedder, "HTLV-III Antibody Positivity in the Zambian Copper Belt," letter, *Lancet*, II (1986), 155.

23. Mann, et al., "Risk Factors for Human Immunodeficiency Seropositivity among Children 1-24 Months Old in Kinshasa, Zaire," *Lancet*, II (1986), 654-657.

24. Robert Ryder, personal communication (Oct. 1987).

25. I. Surmont and J. Desmyter, "Urban to Rural Spread of HIV Infection in Dungu, Zaire," paper presented at the Second International Conference on AIDS in Africa (Naples, 1987).

26. L. Aktar, et al., "Distribution of Antibodies to HIV 1 in an Urban Community (Aru, Upper Zaire)," paper presented at the Second International Conference on AIDS in Africa (Naples, 1987).

27. D.N. Forthal, et al., "AIDS in Tanzania," quoted in *Population Reports*, XIV, L-219 (1986).

28. F. Mhalu, E. Mbena, and U. Bredberg-Raden, "Prevalence of HIV Antibodies in Healthy Subjects and Groups of Patients in Some Parts of Tanzania," paper presented at the Third International Conference on AIDS (Washington, D.C., 1987).

29. J.K. Kriess, et al., "AIDS Virus Infection in Nairobi Prostitutes: Spread of the Epidemic to East Africa," *New England Journal of Medicine*, CCCXIV, (1986), 414-418. P. Piot, "Retrospective Seroepidemiology of AIDS Virus Infection in Nairobi Populations," *Journal of Infectious Disease*, CLV (1987), 1108-1112.

30. Kriess, et al., "AIDS in Nairobi Prostitutes."

31. M. Merlin, et al., "Evaluation of the Prevalence of Anti-LAV/HTLV-III in the Central African Population: About 12 Sample Surveys," poster presented at the Second International Conference on AIDS (Paris, 1986).

32. M.C. Georges-Courbot, et al., "Serological Surveys of HIV Antibodies in Central and East Africa," paper persented at the Second International Conference on AIDS in Africa," (Naples, 1987).

33. Merlin, et al., "Evaluation of Prevalence."

34. Georges-Courbot, et al., "Serological Surveys in Central and East Africa."

35. L. Gurtler, et al., "Prevalence of HIV-1 in Selected Populations and Areas of Malawi," paper presented at the Second International Conference on AIDS in Africa (Naples, 1987).

36. B. Bottiger, et al., "Prevalence of HIV and HTLV-IV Infections in Angola," *ibid.*

37. Georges-Courbot, et al., "Serological Surveys in Central and East Africa."

38. J.P. Durand, et al., "Aids in Cameroon," poster presented at the Second International Conference on AIDS (Paris, 1986).

39. E. Delaporte, et al., "Prevalence Rates of Antibodies to HIV 1 and HIV 2 in Population Samples from Gabon," paper presented at the Second International Conference on AIDS in Africa (Naples, 1987).

40.   Souleymane M'Boup, et al., "HIV and Related Viruses in Senegal," *ibid.*

41.   Lasana Sangare, et al., "HIV and Related Human Retroviruses Seroprevalences in Ouagadougou, Burkina-Faso," *ibid.*

42.   G. Leonard, et al., "Prevalence of HIV and STLV-II Related Human T-Lymphotropic Retrovirus (HTLV-IV) in Several Populations in Ivory Coast, West Africa," paper presented at the Third International Conference on AIDS (Washington D.C., 1987).

43.   N. Clumeck, et al., "Seroepidemiological Studies of HTLV-III Antibody Prevalence among Selected Groups of Heterosexual Africans," *Journal of American Medical Association*, CCLIV (1985), 2599-2602.

44.   T.C. Quinn, et al., "AIDS in Africa: An Epidemologic Paradigm," *Science*, CCXXXIV (1986), 955-963.

45.   Myron Essex, personal communication (Oct. 1987).

46.   Phyllis J. Kanki, et al., "Human T-Lymphotropic Virus Type 4 and the Human Immunodeficiency Virus in Wast Africa," *Science*, CCXXXIV (1987), 827-831.

47.   Mann, et al., "Natural History of Human Immunodeficiency Virus Infection in Zaire," *Lancet*, II (1986), 707-709.

48.   B. Ngaly, et al., "Continuing Studies on the Natural History of HIV Infection in Zaire," paper presented at the Third International Conference on AIDS (Washington, D.C., 1987).

49.   Randy Bulatao, "Initial Investigation of the Demographic Impact of AIDS in one African Country," mimeo, World Bank (1987).

50.   Quinn, et al., "AIDS in Africa;" Melbge et al., "Evidence for Heterosexual Transmission."

51.   *Ibid.*

52.   Henderson, personal communication (Dec. 1987).

53.   Mann, *AIDS: Global Impact*, 4.

54.   Chen, "The AIDS Pandemic."

55. Melbge, et al., "Evidence for Heterosexual Transmission."

56. Jeff Harris, personal communication (June 1987).

57. Kreiss, et al., "AIDS in Nairobi Prostitutes."

58. Leonard, et al., "Prevalence in Ivory Coast."

59. Clumeck, "Seroepidemiological Studies of HTLV-III Antibody Prevalence;" Ryder, personal communication (Oct. 1987).

60. Mann, *AIDS: Global Impact.*

61. Summary memo of National Academy of Sciences Conference on AIDS Modeling (Washington, D.C., 1987).

62. *Ibid.*

63. Bulatao, "Initial Investigation."

64. Summary memo of NAS Conference on AIDS Modeling.

65. Bulatao, "Initial Investigation of the Demographic Impact of AIDS in One African Country."

66. C. Myers, D. Shephard, and N. Causino, unpub. paper in preparation.

67. Bulatao, "Initial Investigation of the Demographic Impact of AIDS in One African Country," mimeo, World Bank (1987).

68. Panos Institute, "AIDS and the Third World" (London, 1987).

69. J.P. Gouteux, et al., "Le Coût du Traitement Individuel de la Trypansomiase a T.B. Gambiense dans le Foyer du Niari (Congo)," *Médecine Tropicale*, XLVII (1987), 61-63.

70. World Bank, *Financing Health Services,* App. Tables.

71. Mann, et al., "Human Immunodeficiency Virus Seroprevalence in Pediatric Patients 2 to 14 Years of Age at Mama Yemo Hospital, Kinshasa, Zaire," *Pediatrics,* LXXVIII (1986), 673-677.

72. Henderson, personal communication (Dec. 1987).

73. "World Contraceptive Use," *Population Newsletter,* XLII/XLIII (1987), 1-5.

74. Henderson, personal communication (Dec. 1987).

7: Friends and Foes:
American Policy in North Africa

LISA ANDERSON

The Reagan administration came into office committed to, as the campaign rhetoric went, "making America strong again." In practice, this meant aggressively opposing real and apparent Soviet ambitions throughout the world and actively intervening in the Third World to prevent harm to American interests or prestige. Both for political reasons—because the appearance of weakness in the face of hostage-takers in the Middle East had contributed to the defeat of President Carter—and out of ideological conviction—because the new administration believed that the Soviet Union was the backer and beneficiary of anti-American violence—the Carter administration's emphasis on support for human rights was replaced by a campaign against terrorism. This shift was particularly apparent in policy towards the Middle East and, by extension, North Africa. Because the countries of North Africa are overwhelmingly Muslim and Arabic-speaking and because they border the Mediterranean, United States policy in the region has reflected policy in the Middle East as much as in sub-Saharan Africa. Thus the Administration's initial concerns in North Africa were, as in the Middle East, the extension of a "strategic consensus" to oppose Soviet ambitions and the ending of what was called "state-sponsored terrorism."

Both these notions were tangential to the interests and concerns of the countries of North Africa, as gradually became apparent during the administration's ensuing two terms. From the outset, Reagan policy in North Africa was preoccupied with Libya. The repudiation of Carter's focus on regional agendas in the Third World in favor of emphasis on the superpower rivalry meant that the global revolutionary ambition of Libya's Colonel Mu'ammar al-Qaddafi, which had been interpreted largely as a regional problem, was transformed into a major international confrontation. Unfortunately, this policy accorded Libya and its regime unmerited attention and highlighted the United States' relative neglect of the equally strategic and more populous countries to the west.

The 1984 Moroccan-Libyan Treaty of Union, the 1985 Israeli bombing of Tunisia, the gradual thawing of the administration's initial coolness towards Algeria, the growing recognition of Syrian and Iranian responsibility for sponsorship of terrorism after the American bombing of Libya in 1986, all marked shifts in American expectations and policies which, taken together, constituted an abandonment of the administrations's early ideological perspectives and commitments. Although many observers felt the change came too late, particularly since it coincided with a loss of momentum occasioned by the president's medical and political problems in 1986 and 1987—his cancer and prostate surgery and the blossoming of the Iran-Contra scandal— much of the damage done to American standing in northern Africa during first term of the Reagan administration was repaired during the later years.

The attention to Libya in this survey reflects its weight in recent United States policy rather than its intrinsic importance. Indeed, the populations of Morocco and Algeria, at about 22 million each, and even those of Tunisia and Chad, at seven and five million respectively, dwarf Libya's three and a half million. Libya has the least diversified economy in the region: with less than half the cultivated land of much smaller Tunisia, for example, Libya relies almost entirely on oil exports. Only in per capita income, estimated at $7,500 in 1985, does Libya loom large; Algeria, also a hydrocarbon exporter, was next at $2,230 dollars while Tunisians disposed of $1,220 and Moroccans of $610 a year per person.[1]

North Africa: The Regional Context

The conventional wisdom in Washington for the last 20 years or so has been that Morocco and Tunisia are American "friends" while Algeria and Libya are not.[2] This reflects the fact that the American frame of reference for the region is provided by the Arab-Israeli conflict and the superpower rivalry. That North Africa is not simply a backwater of the Middle East or an arena of United States-Soviet competition is not immediately apparent in most official American discussions of the region.

Indeed, in both academic and policy circles in the United States, North Africa is usually seen as an extension of the Middle East. From this perspective, Morocco and Tunisia are ordinarily identified with the "moderate Arab" camp on issues involving the Arab-Israeli conflict: both King Hassan, who acceded to the throne in Morocco in 1961 and Habib Bourguiba, president of Tunisia from independence in 1956 until he was deposed as senile in November 1987, were longstanding advocates of a negotiated settlement with Israel. The governments of Algeria and Libya, by contrast, have been outspoken advocates of the Palestinian cause and were charter members of the "radical" Steadfastness and Confrontation Front.

In fact, however, the policy differences among the North Africans on Arab-Israeli affairs are often rhetorical rather than substantive. None of the governments backed the Israeli-Egyptian Camp David agreements of 1979, universally regarding them as a separate peace damaging to Palestinian and Arab interests. It was "moderate" Tunis which became the headquarters of the Arab League when it was withdrawn from Cairo after the signing of the Camp David accords, and of the Palestine Liberation Organization (PLO) when it was evacuated from Beirut after the Israeli invasion of Lebanon in 1982. Perhaps more importantly, although Morocco has hosted discreet meetings of Arab and Israeli officials and Libya has provided funding and training sites to Palestinian guerrillas, by and large the North African contribution to Arab-Israeli causes of any persuasion has been marginal.

The regimes of Morocco and Tunisia are also considered sympathetic to the United States in the superpower rivalry, while those of Algeria and Libya are thought to be Soviet clients. Certainly this is reflected in the arms trade: although Morocco has received Soviet weaponry, its principal suppliers are the United States and France, as are Tunisia's, while Algeria and Libya are reliant on the Soviet Union for military hardware. Moving beyond purely military trade, however, the picture becomes much more complicated: the Soviets buy eight times what the United States does in the Moroccan marketplace and are heavily involved in the important phosphate and fishing sectors there, while the United States shares with France the preeminent foreign position in the Algerian economy; in fact the United States is Algeria's largest trading partner, and was until recently Libya's as well.

Regional politics are more directly determined by historical rivalries among the countries than by conflicts outside the area. Algerian opposition to Moroccan claims to the Western Sahara, for example, not only reflects the ideological differences of the two regimes—Algeria's revolutionary Islamic socialism contrasts sharply with Morocco's laissez-faire monarchy—but also the longstanding rivalry over which of the two countries will dominate northwestern Africa. Similarly, Tunisia walks a thin line between its two petroleum-rich neighbors, courted and threatened by each in turn.

As a consequence, North Africa is not susceptible to a simple inclusive approach on the part of outside powers—the diversity of the four countries is simply too great to permit their being approached as a single unit—but neither can policy be reduced to a series of independent bilateral relationships. As the Carter administration recognized, the provision of military hardware to Morocco for use in the Western Sahara inevitably dismays Algeria, a country which can be of considerable aid to the United States in its dealings with the Third World. The hard-won lessons of the 1970s were quickly forgotten by the Reagan administration, however, only to be laboriously learned again.

Libyan-American relations, for example, were difficult throughout all four of the American administrations which span Mu'ammar al-Qaddafi's tenure in Libya, but they became increasingly strained during the campaign which led to Ronald Reagan's election. Qaddafi came to power in September 1969 espousing non-alignment and, while his opposition to communism remained unshaken in the ensuing decade, he came to believe that what he viewed as Western imperialism—including the existence of Israel—was the greater threat to international equity and national independence. By his own admission, he was a revolutionary and, in stark contrast to the revolutionary Algerian regime, which worked within the international system to change it, Qaddafi prided himself on being considered an outlaw in a world where, as he saw it, the law itself was unjust.

Moreover, the revolution of which Qaddafi was founder and philosopher was designed for export. Here again the contrast with Algeria is instructive. Algeria's socialism was a conventional developmental version, designed to provide a guide for domestic policy which fosters both equity and growth. If it succeeded, it would constitute a model for other Third World nations, but it was not for export as such. Qaddafi's ambitions were much greater. What success his revolution enjoyed in Libya, however, was largely due to acquiescence born in egalitarian distribution of high oil revenues; the political and economic mismanagement revealed by the oil glut of the 1980s seriously eroded the regime's popular support at home. By the 1980s, moreover, few other regimes in the Arab world or Africa were surprised or sorry to see opposition to Qaddafi on the rise. His regime was widely, if privately, considered a meddlesome anachronism by other Arab governments: his calls for Arab unity and international revolution rang false to the many regimes he had tried to subvert.

Nor were the sources of domestic dissatisfaction with Qaddafi's regime far to seek. The deleterious effects of the revolution's radical economic policies on domestic production had been exacerbated by the investment and consumption cutbacks occasioned by the world oil glut and Libya's declining oil revenues. Revolutionary policies designed to ensure the equality of all Libyans discouraged private investment and created a substantial black market; bureaucratic inefficiency contributed to the uncertainty. None of this was helped by the world oil glut. Earnings plummeted from $22 billion in 1980 to $5 billion in 1986. Foreign exchange reserves dipped from $13 billion in 1980 to $2.7 billion in early 1986.[3]

The economic and political crises facing the Libyan regime were far and away the most severe in North Africa, but the end of the 1970s saw challenges in the other three countries as well. In 1978 Algeria weathered the death of Colonel Houari Boumediene, who had led the country since 1965, and the selection of Chadli Benjedid as his replacement marked the country's first peaceful succession since independence in 1962. Benjedid soon put his own stamp on Algerian policy, abolishing exit visa requirements for foreign travel, encouraging limited private enterprise, and relaxing political restrictions. That these were not an unqualified success was suggested by the growing Islamic challenge to government policy.

By Tunisian and Moroccan standards, however, Algeria's Islamic protest looked tame. In 1980 and 1981 what may have been the worst drought of the century in the western Maghrib hit Morocco particularly hard; in 1981 and 1984 rioting broke out in Casablanca after the IMF sponsored the lifting of subsidies on bread and other consumer goods. In Tunisia rioting in 1978 and again in 1984—the second round also in response to IMF sanctioned consumer price increases—contributed to the fall of two governments as the aging President Bourguiba refused to relinquish the reins of power and instead sacrificed his prime ministers.[4] Both Morocco and Tunisia were attempting what may have been the impossible: political liberalization combined with unemployment rates estimated at about 25 percent of the labor force in both countries. One of the results was the growing strength of Islamic protest movements in both countries.

United States Policy in North Africa: The 1970s

While it was not a source of major international tensions, neither was North Africa without problems for the United States during the 1970s as the Nixon, Ford, and Carter administrations found themselves required to respond to Qaddafi's growing opposition to American influence. In the early days the United States attempted to cooperate with the new regime but Qaddafi proved unmoved from his anti-imperialist position by apparent American flexibility and, by 1972, American diplomatic representation in Libya had been reduced to the level of a chargé d'affaires. Qaddafi participated enthusiastically in the oil boycott of the United States which followed the 1973 Arab-Israel war and nationalized all or part of several United States oil companies.

Through the second half of the 1970s relations remained strained. The United States accused Libya of supporting international terrorist groups, and the Libyan government accused the United States of supporting imperialism and terrorism in its backing of Israel and the Camp David peace process. In December 1979, soon after the taking of American hostages in Iran, a government-backed mob sacked and burned the American Embassy in Tripoli and by May 1980 the United States had pulled out its last diplomats from Libya. Throughout the 1970s the expressions of mutual hostility were diluted, however, by ambiguous signals from both sides. Libya enjoyed cordial relations in the American private sector, awarding lucrative contracts to American firms and sending as much as 40 percent of its oil exports to the United States, a figure which constituted 15 percent of American oil imports.

Apart from Qaddafi's growing but still somewhat limited capacity for mischief, the principal American concern in North Africa during the 1970s arose from the dispute over the Western Sahara. In 1974, when Spain pulled out of its colonial territories on the Atlantic coast south of Morocco, the International Court of Justice granted joint administrative control to Mauritania and Morocco while leaving open the question of sovereignty. Under considerable pressure from Morocco, Mauritania abandoned its claims in 1979, leaving Morocco occupying most of the territory and fighting a sporadic but very costly war to maintain its positions. The United States was caught between fidelity to the principle of self-determination, demanded by the liberation movement known as Polisario in the name of the perhaps 150,000 Sahrawis, and support for a friendly government which claimed the region as sovereign territory. Complicating the equation was steadfast Algerian support for Polisario, less reliable but more worrisome Libyan aid to Polisario, and a Moroccan king who staked the reputation and longevity of both his person and his regime on a successful conclusion to the conflict.

In the later years of the Carter administration, United States policy in the Western Sahara dispute was influenced by the administration's dilemmas in Iran. Concerned that American policy had contributed to the fall of the Shah and grateful to King Hassan for his willingness to host the Shah in exile, the administration lifted its unspoken embargo on shipments of military equipment which could be used in the Western Sahara in 1978. This was not quite the "tilt" toward Morocco it would become during the early Reagan administration, however, since Carter recognized and warmly appreciated services rendered by Algeria in negotiating the release of the American hostages in Iran. Tunisia alone seemed to be an island of tranquility for the United States. Successful development projects were pushing the country over the income cap for further United States aid and the longevity and apparent stability of the regime obscured the profound political and economic problems which would become apparent in the 1980s.

United States Relations with North Africa: The Reagan administration

Within days of coming into office—virtually hours after Algeria's successful efforts to gain the release of the United States hostages in Iran had borne fruit—the Reagan administration announced new arms sales to Morocco. In doing so, the new administration not only insulted the Algerians, it also announced the tenor of the new administration's policy in the region. President Carter's emphasis on human rights was abandoned in favor of opposition to Soviet influence and what was known as international terrorism. Although Algeria was initially regarded as a radical Soviet client state—hence the willingness to be rude to the Algerian government—it was Qaddafi who was singled out for special attention as a symbol of everything abhorrent in international affairs.

Libya has relatively close ties with the Soviet Union: when President Reagan took office it was estimated that the Libyans had spent $12 billion on military equipment from the USSR, a figure which would soar to $20 billion within five years. Qaddafi's support of revolutions and national liberation movements around the world constituted, if not terrorism strictly defined, certainly an effort to undermine the Western-inspired international order. Moreover, insofar as Qaddafi's revolutionary policies constituted a threat to pro-Western governments in Africa and the Arab world, and to Western interests more generally, American opposition to his government was to have illustrated the administration's reliability as a friend and ally, something on which the Republicans had faulted the Carter administration in Iran.

With the much-publicized expulsion of Libyan diplomats from the United States in May 1981, Libya and the world were put on notice that Qaddafi's revolutionary ambitions would not be tolerated. The longstanding tacit United States agreement not to challenge Qaddafi's claim of the Gulf of Sirte as territorial waters was soon abandoned and, in August 1981, United States naval maneuvers there precipitated a dogfight in which two Libyan aircraft were shot down. The publicizing of Libyan transgressions against "international norms of behavior" continued throughout the fall to culminate in the December announcement of a "hit squad" allegedly sent by Libya to assassinate President Reagan.[5] The United States cancelled all passports for travel to Libya, requested all Americans leave the country and, in March 1982, announced the embargo of oil imports from Libya and the banning of high technology exports. High Libyan prices and a glut on the world oil market had already reduced Libyan exports to the United States to less than 20 percent of Libyan production and one percent of American consumption; the embargo's effect was largely symbolic.

Partly as a result, American efforts during the first Reagan term to win the cooperation of the European allies in sanctions against the Libyan regime were largely unavailing. The Europeans felt that the United States, much less dependent upon Libyan oil exports or on its labor and commodity markets, was needlessly provoking a regime with which they had no choice but to deal. Moreover, the administration's failure to impose a full-scale economic embargo and fully to enforce its ban on travel to Libya—between 500 and 2,000 Americans continued to work there—lent a hollow ring to the government's rhetoric.

The replacement of Secretary of State Alexander Haig by the lower-key George Shultz removed Libyan-American relations from the front pages of the newspapers for several months. By February 1983, however, Secretary

Shultz was claiming that an American show of force had put Qaddafi "back in his box where he belongs" after he allegedly threatened the Sudan, and in August Libyan incursions into Chad in support of ex-President Goukouni Oueddei brought American AWACs to the Sudan and, following strong American pressure, French paratroopers to the aid of the then President Hissene Habre. An earlier Libyan effort to support Oueddei when he was president in 1980 had provoked considerable dismay in Africa, and Qaddafi had pulled out in hopes of assuming the chairmanship of the Organization of African Unity (OAU). After two years of failed efforts to convene a quorum in Tripoli, however, the position was denied to him in June 1983, leaving little incentive to continue his forbearance in Chad. African opposition to Qaddafi's assumption of the chairmanship had been orchestrated by Morocco, which objected to Qaddafi's support of the Polisario in the Western Sahara, and was strongly supported by United States diplomacy.

During this period, the OAU was also the forum for several attempts to resolve the dispute over the Western Sahara. The Polisario had established a government-in-exile, the Saharan Arab Democratic Republic (SADR), in 1975 and by 1982 it was gaining support for full admission to the OAU. The prospect of SADR's admission halted what had appeared to be moves towards a settlement of the dispute the year before when Morocco had agreed to a vaguely-worded resolution calling for a cease-fire and referendum on the future of the territory. In the same meeting in which Qaddafi lost his bid for the chairmanship, SADR withdrew its demand for admission; Morocco had won what proved to be a temporary victory.

Within a year it became apparent that King Hassan and Colonel Qaddafi had quietly recognized that they shared common interests in African affairs and that they had agreed not to oppose each other's ambitions in the Sahara. Qaddafi suspended aid to Polisario and King Hassan pointedly failed to condemn Libya's return to Chad. This political marriage was consummated in the summer of 1984 in the Treaty of Oujda, which committed the two signatories to creation of an "Arab-African Union." In November, after the OAU lost patience with what the majority saw as Moroccan intransigence, and seated a SADR delegation, Morocco withdrew from the organization.

The Treaty of Oujda came as a surprise to administration officials and it contributed to the removal of Ambassador Joseph Vernier Reed, a flamboyant political appointee and enthusiast of the Reagan administration's early warm embrace of King Hassan. The personal relationship he had cultivated with the king did not extend as far as had been hoped and the willingness of the king, an American "ally," to unify if only rhetorically with the despised Qaddafi, was seen as a profound betrayal in Washington.[6] Although the treaty came to very little in practice—promises of employment for Moroccans in Libya went largely unfulfilled and the king abrogated the agreement in the summer of 1986 after Qaddafi criticized his meetings with Israeli Prime Minister Shimon Peres—it did have the salutary effect of forcing a re-evaluation of United States policy in North Africa.

Relations with Algeria had already begun to thaw; Vice President George Bush became the highest ranking American ever to visit Algeria in September 1983. Although disputes on gas prices limited Algerian exports to the United States, agricultural aid agreements were signed and in the aftermath of the Treaty of Oujda, President Chadli Benjedid made an official and well-publicized visit to Washington in April 1985. Although United States officials attributed the warmth of his reception to their view that, as one observer put it, Algeria had "adopted more reserved and responsible positions on Middle East issues," [7] in fact, the presidential visit was widely interpreted as signalling annoyance with Morocco.

The Reagan administration's approach to Tunisia during the first term reflected its preoccupation with Libya. Concerns that Tunisia was threatened by Libya were exacerbated in 1981 by an abortive attack designed to spark an uprising which was launched from Algeria on the southern town of Gafsa by a handful of Tunisian dissidents trained in Libya. Although Tunisia's 28,000 man military had been kept small and minimally equipped for decades while Bourguiba argued the money was better spent on social services and education, he seemed to bow to United States pressure to respond to the Libyan threat, and United States military aid shot up to $100 million a year. Many Tunisians began to worry that the United States was purposely or inadvertently fostering an authoritarian solution to the perennial succession crisis, rekindled by one of Bourguiba's recurrent health problems in 1984.

By that year United States AID had reversed its earlier decision to withdraw its development programs, partly in light of the food riots of early that year, and the overheated military assistance slowed, but the perception lingered of an American policy which encouraged the Tunisian government to use an exaggerated Libyan threat to justify internal repression. The activities of Ambassador Peter Sebastian in, for example, hosting well-publicized and controversial dinner-discussions on Tunisia's future, at which the right wing of the political élite was prominently represented, did little to alleviate fears that the United States was prepared to interfere in domestic Tunisian politics to support the "forces of stability" over those of democracy.

By the beginning of the second term, Reagan administration officials had significantly moderated their insistance on superpower relations as the litmus test of loyalty in northern Africa. The administration had cultivated better, though still correct, relations with Algeria and had achieved a more realistic, though still sympathetic, assessment of the national interests and government priorities of Morocco. Relations with Tunisia and Libya, however, were still burdened by administration misconceptions which grew out of the United States policy-makers' preoccupation with the Middle East and with terriorism.

Many observers inside Tunisia and out felt that the United States took Tunisia's stability and fidelity too much for granted. Although it had been partly at American urging that Tunisia agreed to provide a site for the headquarters of PLO after it was removed from Beirut in 1982, the administration appeared oblivious to the domestic and regional dangers this posed for the Tunisian government. The Tunisian regime was concerned that Palestinian irredentism would inflame the discontent which roiled under the surface in Tunisia, as it had in Lebanon, and worried that the PLO's presence invited problems not only for Tunisia's Jewish community but for the government's longstanding arms-length policy toward the Arab-Israeli dispute.

As it turned out, these fears were somewhat misplaced but by no means groundless: in the fall of 1985, Israeli war planes bombed the PLO headquarters outside Tunis. President Reagan not only failed to condemn the attack but argued that Israel had a right to strike back at terrorism. Secretary Shultz was somewhat more critical of Israel and expressed regret for the Tunisian casualties, but the United States abstained on a UN resolution condeming Israel and the Tunisian government found itself hard pressed to explain its unusually close ties with the United States to an increasingly skeptical public.

Within several years, American policy-makers appeared to have recognized the unfortunate profile the United States had aquired in Tunisia and to be working to correct it, although inability to get Congressional approval left a new and highly regarded ambassador, Robert Pelletreau, unable to take up his post for a number of critical months. Nonetheless, Bourguiba's crackdown on Islamic protest leaders during the spring of 1987 was not endorsed and United States policymakers showed a stronger interest in freedom of speech, assembly, and press.

This left the United States in a good position to welcome the deposition of President Bourguiba when it came in November 1987. After apparently consulting with other government officials and leaders of the recognized opposition groups, as well as informing selected foreign governments, the newly appointed prime minister, Zine el-Abdine Ben Ali, invoked the Tunisian constitution's provision for the removal of a permaneantly incapacitated president on the grounds that Bourguiba was senile. The move was heralded both within and outside Tunisia as a regrettable but necessary step since jockeying for position at the succession and Bourguiba's own erratic and often senseless policies had paralyzed the regime at a time when growing economic and social problems demanded serious attention.

Although Ben Ali, a general and longtime head of domestic security, obviously had the support of the Tunisian military, his attention to the legal niceties reflected the strength of Tunisia's civilian institutions and boded well for the stability of the new government. In the immediate aftermath of the change, Ben Ali reversed some of Bourguiba's more militantly secularist policies in an apparent effort to move Tunisia back into the mainstream of the modern Islamic world and to defuse the radical Islamic protest movements while simultaneously promising to pursue the moves to political pluralism that had stalled in recent years. That he would be able to walk this tightrope was an open question but he appeared to be a good candidate to win popular support. For the United States, where Ben Ali had spent time in military training programs and with whose representatives he enjoyed cordial relations, his appearance in power seemed to be a lucky and positive development.

In the early years of the administration's second term, Libya was also treated as something of a caricature, albeit of course unfriendly, and it was not until late in the term that this started to change. Qaddafi continued to be portrayed by both United States government officials and the American mass media as a genuinely dangerous opponent to American interests. In 1984, the State Department described administration policies as a response to Libya's "unacceptable activities," including its "illegal occupation of northern Chad... support for international terrorism... [and] subversion of governments friendly to the United States." [8] American condemnation did not dampen Qaddafi's enthusiasm; in fact, he was usually happy to bask in the publicity. In January 1986, he told a Western reporter that he

believed his personal prestige was enhanced by Reagan's attention.[9] Both
the United States administration and the Qaddafi regime found their confrontation a useful device for symbolizing their respective international
commitments and for reinforcing their domestic standing.

Although the administration had been preoccupied with terrorism from
the outset, the determination to do something decisive was markedly
strengthened in June 1985 when a TWA passenger plane was hijacked in
Beirut. One American was killed and 39 others held for 17 days in an ordeal
which was televised in excruciating and—to the administration—humiliating
detail. During the following July top administration officials met and agreed
that while Iran and Syria had probably been more heavily involved in recent
acts of terrorism, including the Beirut hijacking, Libya was the more visible
and more vulnerable symbol of hostility to the United States. It was in this
atmosphere that the CIA drew up a plan—which became public in news leaks
the following November—to topple the Qaddafi regime.

It was apparent, however, that the administration could not win unanimous
support for this policy even within its own councils. As the year ended, the
United States charged that Libya had supported the group that carried out
bomb attacks at the Rome and Vienna airports in which five Americans were
killed, although American officials conceded that the evidence was cir-
cumstantial and the Europeans refused to go along with the American call
for further sanctions against Libya. Although all remaining commercial ties
were declared severed, a dozen American companies, including four oil companies, were given exemptions ostensibly designed to prevent the Libyan
government from reaping windfall profits in a sudden exodus. These companies did not end their involvement in Libya until June 30, 1986, well after
the United States had resorted to military action. The ambiguity the exemptions introduced into the policy of unrelieved hostility to Qaddafi was com-
pounded in early January 1986 by the visit to Tripoli of the United States
ambassador to the Vatican, William A. Wilson. The State Department—
which had been unaware of the ambassador's trip—denied that he had been
authorized to speak for the United States government but, since he owed
his position to his longstanding friendship with President Reagan, Wilson
was not reprimanded—he stayed on in Rome until May—and it looked as
though the White House was pursuing several mutually contradictory policies
towards Qaddafi.

At the end of March the United States began naval exercises in the Gulf
of Sirte, deliberately crossing the latitude that Qaddafi claimed marked

Libyan territorial waters. Ostensibly to demonstrate the American commitment to freedom of navigation (the boundary claimed by Libya is not
recognized internationally), the exercises were designed to lure Qaddafi into
a foreign entanglement which would spark dissident army factions to launch
a coup against the regime. It was unsuccessful. After an exchange of gunfire
on March 22, the United States sank two Libyan patrol boats—perhaps 40
Libyan sailors were lost—and bombed a missile site. There were no reports
of unrest in Libya and the Americans completed their naval exercises
peacefully.

The end of weeks of tension about United States policy towards Libya
was finally announced during the evening news on April 14. Nine days earlier,
on April 5, a discotheque in Berlin frequented by American soldiers had been
blown up; one American and one Turk were killed and 200 people wounded.
The United States once again pointed the finger at Libya, and despite considerable European skepticism, administration spokesmen were adamant that
the evidence of Libyan involvement was irrefutable. On April 14, 16 United
States Air Force F-111 bombers flew from England under cover of darkness
to attack three targets near Tripoli, including the military barracks at Bab
al-Aziziyyah where Qaddafi was known to stay.

Simuiltaneously 15 A-6 and A-7 aircraft from Navy carriers in the Mediterranean attacked military facilities near Benghazi. One American F-111 with
two crewmen aboard was lost in the operation. At least a hundred Libyan
civilians were killed—including, it was said, Qaddafi's adopted infant
daughter—and numerous more wounded—including two of Qaddafi's sons.
Qaddafi himself escaped the attack on his barracks uninjured, although he
was reportedly shaken by the American attempt on his life.

Reagan administration hostility towards Libya had a variety of purposes,
only some of which were served by the raid and the attendant publicity. At
the level of domestic emotional and symbolic politics to which the administration was particularly attuned, the military raid reflected outrage and frustration at the absence of international controls on terrorism and an attempt
at retaliation for the dozen or so American lives lost to terrorists. Doubts
that the significant loss of civilian life in Libya caused by the attack
constituted the "proportional" response for which President Reagan had
said he was looking, or that the "return address" for retaliation was the
correct one, did not diminish popular support for the raid at home. The
domestic groundwork had been laid in the preceding years—Reagan himself

had characterized Qaddafi in terms ranging from "mad dog" to "flaky"—
and the popularity of the attack reflected the popularity of the president.

The administration also found some satisfaction in the fact that the Europeans, who had been slow to join earlier American efforts to isolate Libya,
took steps during the spring and summer of 1986 to expel Libyan diplomats,
restrict Libyan students, and otherwise express their displeasure with the Qaddafi government. Most of these moves were symbolic, born less of conviction that the United States' approach was appropriate than fear that failure
to impose sanctions would prompt even more dangerous unilateral action
on the part of the United States, such as destruction of Libyan oil fields.
After the United States imposed its initial embargo on imports of Libyan
crude oil in 1981, the proportion of Libyan oil going to Europe had risen
from 55 percent to 90 percent in 1984, and the Europeans were eager to see
Libyan production remain high so Libya would be able to settle its debts
to European contractors. European reluctance to go along with United States
sanctions also reflected the fact, however, that loopholes in the American
provisions permitted American oil and construction firms to maintain a
substantial and profitable position in the Libyan economy, including stakes
in operations accounting for 45 percent of the country's total oil output, well
into 1986.

The raid was also the culmination of American efforts to destabilize the
Libyan regime and in this, it was an obvious failure. The attack had been
intended to spark a military rebellion against Qaddafi or otherwise to lead
to his demise; administration officials coyly claimed that they could not have
been making an attempt on the Libyan ruler's life because American law
forbids assassination of foreign leaders, although they did concede that they
would not have been sorry to see him go. Within a month of the attack the
administration also conceded that there had been no lessening of either
terrorist activity in general or Libyan plots specifically in the aftermath of
the raid. In October a former State Department official wrote, for example,
that Libya had been implicated in a rocket attack on a British airbase in
Cyprus and an attempt to blow up the American Embassy in Togo in August
and may also have been involved in the September hijacking of a Pan-Am
plane in Pakistan and attack on a synagogue in Istanbul in which 40 people
were killed.[10]

If Qaddafi had not been dissuaded from his revolutionary activity, the
eagerness on the part of the administration to publicize evidence of Libyan
complicity in anti-American activities around the world diminished

dramatically in the year following the raid. Thus by the first anniversary of the bombing most Americans had the impression that Qaddafi's campaign against the United States was no longer active; in fact it was as much a new discretion on the part of his former publicists in the administration as reticence on his part which had lowered Qaddafi's profile. Indeed, during the fall, American claims about the role of Libya in international terrorism in general had come under suspicion as news reports revealed that the administration had undertaken a "disinformation campaign," deliberately planting false stories about Libya and American policy in the international press. At the same time, the news reports of the Libyan role as sponsor of terrorism were eclipsed by fresh evidence of Syrian and Iranian involvement in terrorist activities. The British severed diplomatic relations with Syria after the conviction in October of a Syrian-backed Palestinian for having plotted to blow up an El Al passenger flight, while the Reagan administration acknowledged in November that it had been shipping arms to Iran for 18 months in an effort to win the freedom of American hostages held by pro-Iranian groups in Lebanon.

Moreover, and predictably, administration discretion proved more embarrassing to Libya than had the earlier attention. During the spring of 1987 Goukouni Oueddei defected from the Libyan camp in Chad and his loyalists joined Hissene Habre's troops. During the summer, bereft of local allies and scouts, the Libyan troops stationed in Chad were routed by what was widely portrayed as a band of rag-tag Chadian soldiers. The United States and France downplayed their logistical support of the Chadians, and the Libyan military regime, which lost considerable advanced Soviet matériel, also lost much of what little remaining prestige it enjoyed at home and abroad.

The American Position in North Africa: the 1990s

In the waning days of the Reagan administration, it was apparent that few of the goals that had been announced by the administration at the outset or, more generally, that could be construed as forwarding American interests in North Africa, had been accomplished. The Soviet Union's position in the region was essentially unchanged, although it appeared more likely as time went on that Libyan isolation from the West might permit the Soviets to solidify their position in that country. The moderation of unqualified American support for the increasingly unpopular regime in Tunisia appeared to have come in time to prevent serious problems for the American position in the immediate future, but the question remained open. The complexity of the superpowers' positions in Algeria and Morocco—the unwillingness of either of the North African regimes to be restricted to one or another superpower camp—remained the order of the day despite the administration's early embrace of King Hassan and snub of Chadli Benjedid. There was little evidence that North Africa constituted a significant source of support for terrorism, or that American policy had changed what support there was. Moreover, in wisely if belatedly returning to the style and substance of earlier administrations' policies, the Reagan policymakers had to give lie to their own declarations of American reliability, projecting instead an image of early myopia and subsequent inconsistency.

Nonetheless, the Reagan administration is to be credited with having come to appreciate the fact that American interests in the region, and the policies by which those interests are furthered, must be more carefully weighed than they had originally thought if United States credibility is to be maintained. Containing Soviet influence and discouraging any government on the southern Mediterranean coast from granting the Soviets naval bases or basing rights is more effectively accomplished by calm persuasion than frantic confrontation. Similarly, access for private American business to commodities and markets in North Africa is more effectively secured by adherence to the principles of free trade than by measures which, while symbolizing American outrage, close markets to American companies in favor of European and even Soviet competitors.

Over the long run, the most effective guarantee of a sympathetic hearing for American interests in North Africa is to accord such a hearing to the countries of the region themselves. The assumption that they can be fit to an ideological template born of the superpower rivalry is not only erroneous, it is insulting, since it suggests they have no agendas of their own. To court friendship and discourage opposition by attending to the specific concerns of the countries themselves is not easy. Not only will the United States and each of the countries of the region not always see eye to eye but the concerns and interests of each country are not necessarily identical to those of the regime in each country, and it is the regime with whom the American government must deal in the first instance. Nonetheless, sympathy, understanding, or support of United States policies elsewhere—notably in the contiguous regions of Europe, Africa, and the Middle East—will be shaped in large measure by the intelligence with which the policies are formulated and presented. As both Morocco and Libya demonstrated in recent years, these are not regimes which can be bought, however much they may present their aid requests to Washington or Moscow in terms of quid pro quos.

It must therefore be borne in mind that the United States has interests in Libya, Tunisia, Algeria, and Morocco that should and will outlive any leader or regime. It is very likely, for example, that before the 1990s are very far along, the international orientation of the Tunisian government will move away from Bourguiba's infatuation with the West. This is independent of anything the United States may do, although United States policy may still influence the degree of alienation from the West in Tunisia or, for that matter, the extent of reliance on the West in a future Libyan government. In both cases, the possibility of short-term advantage in, for example, supporting pro-American but repressive policies in Tunisia or a pro-American but unscrupulous opposition to Qaddafi, must be balanced against the long-term interest of the United States in stable regimes free of undue Soviet influence and open to American economic and political interests.

Policy disagreements, even severe ones, do not require that the United States undertake to change regimes here any more than in Eastern Europe. In cases, like that of Libya under Qaddafi, where the regime explicitly repudiates the rules of conventional international conduct and diplomacy, this affront to the international community should be addressed by the international community in concert; the United States need not—and in fact, cannot—take sole responsibility for maintaining discipline in world affairs. Indeed, respect for international law is at least in part ensured by example. No American government which cynically exploits principles of freedom of navigation to justify provoking a foreign government into a military confrontation, or whose attitude towards American laws on assassinating foreign leaders borders on contempt, can credibly claim outrage at the flouting of international law by other governments.

United States policy should and could reflect more faithfully the long term American interests in North Africa. Such a perspective reveals three particularly important issues for the future:

(1) The equitable and locally satisfactory settlement of the conflict over the Western Sahara. This dilemma pits United States support of a friendly regime in strategically important Morocco against the principle of national self-determination and the OAU's declaration of the sanctity of colonial borders and it raises the still distant specter of Soviet influence on the Atlantic

coast. Although the United States cannot now intervene directly to speed a resolution of the conflict, greater consultation with the OAU members involved in the conflict and in the mediation efforts may be appropriate. The United States, through both its actual and potential aid programs and its demonstrated commitment to the monarchy's stability, has more leverage here than has been exercised.

(2) Coordination of American security policy in the region with European allies, for whom this region is vitally important. The economic and military power of the United States has permitted not only unilateral actions against the regime in Libya in recent years but three or four fold increases in military aid to regimes like those of Chad and Tunisia. This go-it-alone approach to security issues in the region is not only unnecessarily expensive, it is not apparent that it is in the best interest of either the countries in question or the United States. Since they are closer to the scene and have greater immediate interests, the European allies should be asked to take a more active role in assessing needs and coordinating provision of both military aid and military sanctions. Ill-considered arms transfers policies, of which American deliveries to Tunisia in the early 1980s are probably a case, may prove more destabilizing than useful to the regimes and therefore to the region, while unified military action against the Qaddafi regime would have very likely been both more popular in Europe and the Arab world and more effective.

(3) The economic stability and prosperity of the peoples of the region. Far from being merely a faint hope to which everyone must pay lip service, or serving solely to enhance American trade opportunities (which is, of course, not insignificant in itself), this is the ultimate guarantor of political stability and political responsibility in international and domestic affairs. The principal political platform of the Islamic fundamentalist groups across North Africa is their severe and justified criticism of the economic development records and plans of the governments. High unemployment, growing income disparities, burgeoning populations, over-reliance on tourism, all provide fertile ground for protest movements which couch their complaints in the Islamic idiom of social justice and moral responsibility. The United States obviously cannot ensure economic development. It can, however, accord some of the real and rhetorical attention lavished in recent years on countering terrorism to programs and institutions, including the IMF and the World

Bank, which do support efforts to enhance the lives and prospects of the peoples of the region.

To accomplish these goals is not a realistic aim of a single American administration, but certain concrete steps would provide an auspicious beginning. Thus the next administration should continue the current studied indifference to Qaddafi while closely monitoring the activities of the regime. Insofar as terrorism, in Spain, Peru, and Japan, as well as the Middle East and North Africa, is a real concern and not merely a public relations issue, its solution cannot be unilateral, and the new administration should therefore focus its attention on coordinating intelligence with our allies and cooperating with international police and enforcement agencies. The collapse of the Qaddafi government, should it come during the next administration, will not necessarily provide great opportunities for renewed United States influence in Libya, since there is likely to be a period of marked instability in Libya after Qaddafi's demise. What opportunities do arise to renew diplomatic relations, revive educational and commercial exchanges, or provide technical expertise, however, should be welcomed.

While Tunisia is by no means out of the woods, the recent change in government appears to have brought that government back from the brink of very serious political problems and provided an opportunity to address the country's social and economic dilemmas. Here a new American president should be prepared to lend moral and material support to such efforts and to moves toward greater civil liberties and political pluralism despite what will inevitably be a less enthusiastic embrace of Western causes in foreign affairs.

The Western Sahara conflict is an enormous drain on the Moroccan economy at a time when it can ill-afford it. Both the Polisario and the king should be encouraged to examine other avenues to resolution of the dispute and the king should be urged, by word and by aid allocations, to stake his legitimacy and longevity on social reform and economic development, not military prowess.

Finally, the new administration should resist the temptation to view North Africa through lens focused on the superpower rivalry or the Arab-Israeli dispute. The Moroccan king should not be able to win American attention or favor merely by inviting the Israeli prime minister to visit any more than should Qaddafi merit American military attacks for his opposition to Israel and his professed willingness to join the Warsaw Pact. The possibility that these countries could be of assistance in furthering a resolution of the Arab-

Israeli dispute must be kept open, as must all possibilities, however remote, but these countries are not now—nor should they be encouraged to become—involved in the conflict and they are not likely to be part of its resolution. To ask them to play such a role is to impose burdens on already overburdened regimes, and it should be American policy to decrease rather than increase the problems of these countries.

Notes

1. These data are from *The World Atlas, 1987.* The per capita income figures for Algeria and Libya are significantly lower than they were in the late 1970s, due to the glut on the world oil market and the subsequent fall in prices and revenues to producing countries.
2. Among the recent general works on American policy in North Africa, see P. Edward Haley, *Qaddafi and the United States Since 1969* (New York, 1984), Richard B. Parker, *North Africa: Regional Tensions and Strategic Concerns* (New York, 1984), and the special issue on "North Africa in Transition" in *Arab-American Affairs,* VI (1983), 24-101.
3. *The Financial Times* (London), 9 January 1986.
4. See "Insurrection in North Africa," *Merip Reports,* 127 (October 1984).
5. According to allegations made during the Iran-Contra investigations, it was the Iranian arms dealer Manucher Ghorbanifar who was the origin of the still-unsubstantiated story that Libyan hit squads had been sent to assassinate the president.
6. See Richard Parker, "Appointment in Oujda," *Foreign Affairs,* LXIII (1985), 1095-1110.
7. John Damis, "United States Relations with North Africa," *Current History,* LXXXIV (1985), 196.
8. United States Department of State, "The Libyan Problem," Special Report, 111 (October 1983).
9. Robert Fiske in The *Times* (London), January 15, 1986.
10. Lillian Craig Harris, "America's Libya Policy Has Failed," *Middle East International,* 285 (October 10, 1986).

8: Gorbachev's Africa Policy

MARK N. KATZ

Even more than previous presidents, Ronald Reagan has feared that Soviet influence in Africa will spread to the detriment of American security interests. His administration has worried that the USSR could become the dominant superpower on the continent. Should this occur, several American interests would be threatened, including access to the sea lanes around the Cape of Good Hope and through the Red Sea, as well as access to strategic minerals in southern Africa. The Pentagon also fears that Soviet dominance in Africa could lead to the loss of American military facilities on the continent that could be instrumental in supporting United States military forces in the Persian Gulf or other regions. More ominously, the acquisition of military bases in Africa by the USSR could facilitate Soviet military intervention elsewhere.

To what extent the growth of Soviet influence in Africa would harm American interests is, of course, debatable. But are the Soviets likely to succeed in spreading their influence significantly in Africa? In looking at the Soviet record during the 1970s, the Reagan administration concluded that Moscow indeed sought to become the dominant superpower on the continent, and had made considerable progress in achieving this goal. During this time, avowedly Marxist governments came to power in Ethiopia, Angola,

Mozambique, and Guinea-Bissau. Although not Marxist, Mu'ammar al-Qaddafi of Libya moved closer to the USSR. Cuban military intervention (with Soviet assistance) defeated a South African- and American-backed effort to destroy the MPLA in Angola. Soviet and Cuban military intervention also helped Marxist Ethiopia drive Somali forces out of the Ogaden. Although Moscow lost two important friends during the 1970s (Egypt and Somalia), the fact that the USSR and its allies were willing militarily to intervene in Angola and the Horn gave rise to fears that they would do so again elsewhere in Africa.

From the perspective of the late-1980s, however, the Soviets have not significantly expanded their influence in Africa since the mid-1970s. Marxist-Leninist governments have not come to power outside Ethiopia and the former Portuguese empire. Indeed, the commitment of these regimes to Marxism-Leninism and a pro-Soviet foreign policy orientation is open to question. Mozambique and Guinea-Bissau have improved their ties with the West over the past decade and have not permitted the Soviets to obtain predominant influence in their countries. Angola and Ethiopia have remained firm Soviet allies, but their foundering economies and inability to defeat insurgent movements have imposed substantial economic and military burdens on the USSR and Cuba. Finally, the Soviets and Cubans have not undertaken any additional military interventions in Africa.

Many in the West feared that the Soviets would be able to sponsor Marxist revolutions in neighboring countries from their "footholds" in Angola and Ethiopia. This has not happened at all. Angola and Ethiopia have not provided an attractive model for other African nations to emulate. The poverty of these two nations has demonstrated that Marxism-Leninism and Soviet aid are no cure for Africa's economic ills. In the Horn of Africa, the very fact that the USSR backs Addis Ababa has hurt Moscow's prospects for substantially improving relations with Ethiopia's regional rivals, Somalia and the Sudan. The Soviets themselves did very little to help Libya avoid defeat in its efforts to dominate Chad. Far from being predominant, Soviet influence in Africa at present appears very limited indeed.

What about the future? Will the Soviets continue to enjoy only limited influence or will they be able dramatically to expand their presence in Africa? According to one noted analyst of Soviet-African relations, David Albright, Moscow currently has four operational goals with regard to the continent: (1) to win local acceptance of a Soviet presence (including military); (2) to gain a voice over Africa's affairs; (3) to undermine Western influence; and (4) to limit Chinese influence.[1]

Just because they may have these goals, however, does not necessarily mean that the Soviets will achieve them. This depends on the opportunities for, and the obstacles to, the expansion of Soviet influence that exist in Africa. What are these opportunities and obstacles? A useful way to examine this question is to look at it from the Soviet point of view. This can offer an interesting perspective on the extent to which Moscow sees American foreign policy toward Africa as helping or hindering the USSR to achieve its aims.

Space will not allow a full discussion of Soviet views on this subject in previous decades. What follows is an examination of Soviet statements since Mikhail Gorbachev came to power in 1985 about Africa and American policy toward Africa. While there is a limit to what can be deduced from these statements, they can serve as a useful indication of what expectations Soviet analysts and commentators have with regard to Africa in the near and medium term.

Economic Issues

Soviet leaders, including Gorbachev, have accused America and the West of being the root cause of Africa's economic problems. American transnational corporations have taken billions of dollars in profits out of Africa. Africa's burden of debt to America and the West has grown tremendously. The International Monetary Fund and the World Bank (both of which, Moscow claims, are controlled by the United States) have imposed onerous demands on African states as a condition for receiving new loans. These conditions, which worsen the lot of the people, are aimed at allowing transnational corporations to exploit Africa all the more easily. Secretary of State George Shultz's call for African governments to reorient their economies from the socialist to the capitalist model of development had the same goal. But, Moscow claims, the experience of the Ivory Coast, Kenya, Nigeria, and Liberia have all shown that capitalism has failed to bring about economic development.[2]

The Soviets want to encourage antagonism between the United States and African states over economic issues. Above all, the Soviets sought to discourage African states from increasing economic cooperation with the United States which could weaken their ties to Moscow. They fear that

African leaders may well become convinced that the USSR has little relevance to their pursuit of economic development.

The Soviets appeared particularly defensive about American and Western charges that the USSR did little to aid Ethiopia during the food crisis of 1984-85. Moscow claimed that it actually gave substantial food assistance during this period. The United States only gave food assistance, Moscow asserted, because it feared that American corporations would lose business otherwise (as if United States corporations had much business with Ethiopia to protect before the famine). The Soviet purpose was to defend the USSR's aid record and to discredit the American famine relief effort.[3]

Southern Africa

Soviet scholars have devoted substantial attention to discussing the relationship between the United States and the Republic of South Africa during the Gorbachev era. According to the Soviets, the United States government actively supports Pretoria in maintaining apartheid internally, illegally retains control of Namibia, and attacks neighboring states (especially Angola and Mozambique).

The Reagan administration's policy of "constructive engagement" toward South Africa has come under particular criticism from Moscow. The Soviets insist that this policy amounted to a de facto American alliance with Pretoria. The United States, according to Soviet analysts, is unconcerned with the injustice of the apartheid system, but wants only to protect the sea lanes and the "enormous profits" of American corporations. Through constructive engagement, the United States government claimed that it sought to engage Pretoria in a dialogue leading to the peaceful dismantling of apartheid and transition to black majority rule. But in reality, say the Soviets, the United States government used constructive engagement to divide the Frontline states and the "anti-racist" forces inside South Africa.[4]

America's true support for Pretoria is demonstrated, according to Moscow, through the repeated American (and British) veto of U.N. Security Council resolutions imposing economic sanctions on South Africa. The American position that economic sanctions would hurt the blacks of South Africa and neighboring countries is dismissed as an excuse to continue siding with Pretoria. *New Times* once cited Archbishop Desmond Tutu's criticism of the Reagan administration's argument against imposing sanctions against South Africa since this would only hurt the black majority; such concerns, according to Tutu, did not stop Washington from imposing sanctions on Poland or Nicaragua, even those that hurt the people there. In fact, the Soviets claim, the United States actually gives military assistance to Pretoria, both directly and indirectly, via Israel.[5]

The Soviets have recognized that the United States government, especially Congress, has been critical of Pretoria and has also imposed certain economic sanctions such as banning South African Airways from the United States and limiting visas for South African businessmen. Moscow strongly argues, though, that these are only minor sanctions that will not bring about the end of apartheid. These moves were undertaken primarily to appease black voters in America. Although Congress is more critical of Pretoria than the Reagan administration, the Soviets insist it is only willing to impose symbolic sanctions; 20 percent of United States Senators, *New Times* claimed, have investments in South Africa which they do not wish to damage.[6]

Moscow has taken special efforts to convince the black population of South Africa that United States Congressional actions against Pretoria are not serious. The Soviets give particular emphasis to this message in Radio Moscow's Zulu language broadcasts. Moscow may do so in order to persuade the Zulu that the United States is their enemy and that a pro-American peaceful path to political change in South Africa is fruitless. The Soviet goal may be to undercut popular support for Chief M. Gatsha Buthelezi's Inkatha movement (the main basis of support for which is the Zulu population) and to increase Zulu support for the more confrontationist African National Congress (ANC).[7]

The Soviets extol the virtues of the ANC. In 1987, though, Moscow revealed its nervousness about ANC contacts with the Reagan administration through warning that seeking Washington's recognition by isolating itself from the South African Communist Party would result in the ANC being weakened to the point that it could not head the revolutionary struggle— which is what the United States really wanted.[8]

Moscow also seeks to persuade black Africans (especially in South Africa) that the United States opposes black majority rule and that achieving it peacefully, as the United States advocates, is impossible. This does not necessarily mean that the USSR actively supports or soon expects violent revolution in South Africa. What the Soviets do want, though, is to influence opposition groups and the black population generally to be anti-American as well as anti-Pretoria. If this occurs, Moscow may ultimately hope to increase the prospects for any future black government of South Africa being anti-American and pro-Soviet.

With regard to Namibia, Soviet commentators blame the United States for its continued domination by South Africa. According to Moscow, South Africa has been able to retain control of Namibia only because the United States has repeatedly vetoed U.N. Security Council resolutions imposing sanctions on Pretoria for not withdrawing and yielding power to SWAPO. American calls for Cuba to withdraw from Angola at the same time as South Africa withdraws from Namibia are considered illegitimate. South Africa is illegally occupying Namibia while sovereign Angola has the right to allow soldiers in from any country it chooses. One article likened this demand to Angola insisting that American forces be withdrawn from Britain. The Soviet goal is to rouse African opposition against any link between Namibian independence and the withdrawal of Cuban troops from Angola.[9]

Soviet commentary on UNITA, the Angolan opposition movement, and its leader Jonas Savimbi, has been especially harsh. Moscow claims that Savimbi was a CIA agent working to defeat the MPLA long before the revolution. The fact that UNITA has received South African aid demonstrates that Savimbi is a South African puppet. Moscow especially criticized Congress' lifting of the Clark Amendment banning aid to UNITA in 1985 and the official resumption of United States aid to UNITA in 1986. (Moscow claimed, though, that the CIA had aided UNITA even before the Clark Amendment was rescinded.) According to the Soviets, the fact that UNITA received both United States and South African assistance proved that the United States and South Africa were working together. Both past and present United States aid to UNITA show that the United States seeks to "strangle" Angola. American calls for the MPLA and UNITA to negotiate a peaceful end to the civil war were harshly denounced. According to *New Times,* no civil war exists: the lawful government of Angola is acting against American- and South African-backed terrorists.[10]

In making this argument, Moscow's goal is to portray UNITA as having no independent basis of support within Angola, but only external backing from the United States and South Africa. The Soviets also seek to blame all of Angola's economic and other problems on UNITA, the United States, and South Africa while characterizing the MPLA and its socialist backers as popular in Angola and having done nothing at all to give rise to domestic opposition. The Soviets are particularly concerned that the black African as well as global audience believe this and that they do nothing to help UNITA or hurt the MPLA.

The Soviets are also concerned that the MPLA government retain a negative view of the United States so that Luanda does not seek to increase its cooperation with Washington to the detriment of Moscow and Havana.

With regard to Mozambique, Soviet commentators seem mainly concerned with instilling fear in the FRELIMO government that the United States is supporting the South African-backed RENAMO opposition. *New Times* noted in October 1985 that although President Reagan received FRELIMO leader Samora Machel at the White House, the United States gave visas to three RENAMO leaders and a bill was introduced in Congress to give RENAMO $5 million (Moscow neglected to mention that the bill was never enacted). In October 1987, TASS criticized Vice President Bush for having met with RENAMO's foreign secretary. According to the Soviets, the United States was helping South Africa violate the Nkomati accord. Through this campaign, Moscow hoped to convince the FRELIMO government to abandon its policy of improving relations with the United States and rely exclusively on the USSR and its socialist allies instead.[11]

Since Gorbachev came to power, South Africa has conducted several military strikes against Zambia, Zimbabwe, Botswana, and Lesotho as well as Angola and Mozambique. Soviet analysts insisted that the United States supported these actions since, they argued, South Africa would not dare to undertake them without American approval. According to *Asia and Africa Today,* fighting in Zimbabwe's Matabeleland was not due to inter-ethnic conflict, as "imperialist" propaganda claimed, but to United States-supported actions by South Africa. By accusing the United States of sponsoring South African military operations, Moscow sought to foster black African hostility toward the United States of a kind that could lead to worsening relations with Washington and improved ones with Moscow.[12]

The Horn of Africa

The Soviets have not accused the United States of supporting the Eritrean, Tigrayan, or other rebel groups fighting the government in Addis Ababa. Soviet analysts denounced as "lies" American claims that the Ethiopian government was forcibly evacuating tens of thousands of people from parts of the country. Moscow insisted that these relocations were part of Addis Ababa's famine relief efforts, which the United States was said to oppose. Moscow also accused the United States of taking advantage of famine in Kenya; Washington supposedly only gave food aid in exchange for greatly expanded access to military facilities in the country. In addition, Moscow portrayed the Somali government as the victim of United States efforts to expand its network of military bases. The Soviets applauded Somalia for entering talks with Ethiopia aimed at reducing tension between the two. The United States was said to oppose this since good Somali-Ethiopian relations would damage American plans to militarize the region.[13]

Before the overthrow of the pro-American leader Gaafar Nimeri, there were demonstrations in Khartoum over the ending of food subsidies. Moscow claimed that these demonstrations were actually anti-American in character because the lifting of these subsidies had been mandated by the United States-controlled IMF. After Nimeri's overthrow, Soviet analysts emphasized that Washington was "angry" with the new government for improving relations with Libya and Ethiopia. Moscow also gave much attention to the trial in Khartoum of former government officials who participated in the airlift of Falashas (Ethiopian Jews) from Ethiopia to Israel via the Sudan. According to Moscow, the Falashas were forcibly transported to Israel at the instigation of the CIA.[14]

The Soviets sought generally to foster resentment against the United States among the people of the Horn. The Soviets also portrayed the non-communist governments of the region as victims of American imperialism rather than as active collaborators with it. Moscow hoped that all of them would rely less on the United States and more on the USSR.

Libya

From late 1985 through April 1986, Moscow claimed many times that the United States military buildup near the Gulf of Sidra was in preparation for military intervention against Libya. The Soviets vociferously condemned both the United States attack on two Libyan missile sites in March 1986 and the larger attack in April 1986. According to Moscow, these attacks were unjustified. American claims that Libya supported terrorism were dismissed as completely false. In the Soviet view, the main reson for the American attack was to punish Libya for its independent, anti-American, anti-Israeli, pro-Palestinian, and pro-Soviet foreign policy.[15]

Although Moscow repeatedly predicted that the United States would attack Libya for about five months preceding the American raid, the Soviets did not foretell new raids on Libya afterward. Instead, the Soviets have warned that the United States might launch a similar raid on other Arab states, including ones in North Africa which opposed Washington's Middle East policy.[16]

Soviet commentators denounced the United States for attempting to do from the south what it failed to do from the north by giving military assistance to Chad in its rout of Libyan forces during 1987. Moscow called for the withdrawal of American and French military personnel from Chad. Moscow very definitely saw the government of Hissene Habre as the collaborator of United States imperialism. Moscow warned that the United States sought to establish a military base in Chad from which to destabilize neighboring African countries.[17]

Other African Issues

The Soviets criticized the visit of then Israeli Prime Minister Shimon Peres to Morocco in July 1986 as being a United States-Israeli attempt to lure other nations into the Camp David process. Moscow, however, did not criticize King Hassan for having received Peres, but warned that, as Egypt supposedly demonstrated, the United States gave little aid to countries participating in the American-sponsored peace process. In the statements surveyed for this study, there was no Soviet commentary about Polisario or the conflict in the Western Sahara. *Asia and Africa Today* did warn, however, that the NATO countries were attempting to "whip up particularist sentiment" among the Berbers of Morocco (and of Algeria). Moscow sought to improve its relations with Rabat while weakening Morocco's ties to the United States through encouraging doubts and fears about American intentions. The Soviets had no desire to worsen relations with Morocco through issuing favorable commentary about Polisario.[18]

Moscow accused the United States, with Israeli help, of setting up a military base in Zaire from which to threaten neighboring countries. Private American citizens were involved in abortive coup attempts in Liberia and Ghana. In both cases, Soviet analysts intimated that the United States government was actually behind these plots. The Soviets undoubtedly intended to promote fears in these as well as other West African governments that the United States was actively seeking to overthrow them. Moscow contrasted the United States government's lament for the downfall of Nigeria's democratic government with Soviet support for the "popular" military regime of General Ibrahim Babangida. The Soviets also applauded Nigeria's refusal to accept United States-inspired IMF conditions for new loans. Generally, the Soviets sought to encourage all black African governments to regard the United States as hostile and the USSR as friendly.[19]

Conclusion

In reviewing these Soviet views, it is evident that Moscow currently sees several opportunities for the expansion of its influence in Africa. Among the most important obstacles to increased Soviet influence are found in the economic realm. This is due to growing African disillusionment with the socialist model of economic development. Indeed, it is difficult to convince Africans of the virtues of central planning when the USSR and other socialist countries are themselves relying less on it and experimenting more with market mechanisms. More significantly, the Soviets feel themselves powerless to halt what they see as a growing trend for African states to look more toward the West for economic leadership. Moscow has also been worried that African states will see Soviet economic assistance as less generous and effective than aid from the West. Moscow itself, however, did little to enhance its image in this regard when it gave substantially less in famine relief to its own ally, Ethiopia, than did the West.

On the other hand, the Soviets see Africa's growing indebtedness as an issue that could bring about serious strains in American relations with Africa. This is an issue, however, over which the Soviet exercise little leverage. They are not willing or able to lend money (especially hard currency) in amounts sufficient to allow African states to escape from dependence on Western banks. The Soviets would undoubtedly be happy to see American-African relations worsen over this issue, but they cannot do anything themselves to exacerbate them. Thus, if the debt issue provides an opportunity for the expansion of Soviet influence in Africa, it is not one that Moscow can actively exploit.

In southern Africa, the Soviets clearly see the Reagan administration's policy of constructive engagement with Pretoria as something that is unpopular with black South Africans and with black African governments generally. Moscow understands that repeated American vetoes of U.N. Security Council resolutions imposing sanctions on South Africa are similarly unpopular. The Soviets have sought to exploit these American policies as well as the lack of United States government support for black opposition groups in South Africa and Namibia to improve Soviet standing in the region. The Soviets hope that American actions will persuade black Africans that America and the West oppose black majority rule in South Africa and that the Soviet Union is the only superpower supporting this transformation.

Although most black Africans want the United States to abandon constructive engagement and cease vetoing U.N. sanctions against Pretoria, Moscow actually wants Washington to continue these policies. Through their continuation, the Soviets hope to see American influence in southern Africa diminish and Soviet influence there increase. Moscow appeared genuinely frightened that even the minor sanctions against Pretoria and the few Reagan administration contacts with the African National Congress would encourage black South Africans to regard the United States as a friend rather than an enemy. The Soviets seem to fear that greater American sanctions against South Africa as well as expanded United States government contacts with black opposition movements (including the ANC) would not only limit the growth of Soviet influence with the black opposition, but could even serve to reduce it.

Similarly, the Reagan administration's renewal of military assistance to UNITA serves Soviet interests insofar as (1) the insurgency is containable with Soviet and Cuban help, and (2) American aid to UNITA alienates the MPLA. South Africa, of course, is the main supporter of UNITA. American insistence that South African withdrawal from Namibia be linked to a Cuban withdrawal from Angola also serves Soviet interests. The MPLA feels too insecure to send Cuban forces home unless the South Africans depart from Namibia first. Indeed, the continuation of the insurgency as well as American and South African aid to UNITA has helped the USSR strengthen its influence in Angola.

If there were no insurgency, the MPLA might have concluded long ago that it had little interest in relying exclusively on the USSR and Cuba but might have turned instead to the West for economic assistance . One reason why the African Party for the Independence of Guinea and Cape Verde (PAIGC) did not invite a strong Soviet presence into Guinea-Bissau may have been that it did not face a Western-backed opposition movement. Even FRELIMO, which is fighting a South African-backed opposition movement, has sought to limit Soviet and Cuban influence in Mozambique and to improve relations with the United States and the West instead. Moscow has attempted to convince FRELIMO that the United States actually does support RENAMO, in the hope that Mozambique will abandon its courtship of Washington and turn to Moscow instead. If the United States ever did support RENAMO, as some Republican presidential candidates have advocated, FRELIMO may conclude that it must do just that. American support for RENAMO could enhance Soviet influence in Mozambique just as American support for UNITA has helped Moscow retain influence in Angola.

In the Horn of Africa, Moscow has attempted to exploit the Sudanese disaffection over American support for the deposed leader Nimeiri, the Somali leadership's unhappiness over the level of American aid, and concerns in

Somalia and Kenya regarding the presence of American military facilities. But if this unhappiness with American foreign policy represents an opportunity for the Soviets to gain influence in the Horn, the main obstacle faced by the USSR is its own unwillingness to provide significant economic assistance to those countries or to reduce support to Ethiopia, whose aid to Sudanese and Somali opposition groups provide Khartoum and Mogadishu with a strong incentive to retain close ties with Washington. More than anywhere else in Africa, changes in Soviet foreign policy (as opposed to the continuation of current Amerian policies) could serve to enhance Moscow's influence in the Horn. The Kremlin, however, is unwilling to risk losing influence in Ethiopia for the uncertain prospect of gaining any in Somalia and the Sudan—two countries in which they have lost influence before.

The most benign American policy toward Libya might not help Washington improve relations with Qaddafi. A hostile American policy, however, only provides the Soviets with more opportunity to increase their influence in Libya. The Soviets have hoped that American hostility toward Libya would be perceived by other North African states as hostility toward them as well. Libya's neighbors, however, have little reason to love Qaddafi. Recognizing this, Moscow has prudently dissociated itself from Libya's adventures in Chad so as not to increase North African apprehensions about the Soviet Union. Although Moscow would like to persuade them otherwise, most governments in North, Central, and West Africa have little reason to fear or hate the United States so much that they would be willing to allow the USSR predominant influence in their countries.

Even if the Soviets seek to gain influence in Africa at the expense of the United States and threaten other American interests from Africa, the Soviets themselves recognize that there are serious obstacles to achieving their goals any time soon. To the extent that there are opportunities for the expansion of Soviet influence, these result, in Moscow's view, from counter-productive American foreign policies, especially toward southern Africa. These policies, however, are ones that America can change and thereby undercut existing opportunities for the expansion of Soviet influence in southern Africa and the continent as a whole.

Notes

1. David E. Albright, *Soviet Policy Toward Africa Revisited* (Washington, D.C., 1987), 4-8.
2. See Kim Gerasimov, "Taking Up a Point,"*New Times,* 20 (May 1985), 31; "The 27th CPSU Congress on the Main Tendencies in the Contemporary World," *Asia and Africa Today,* 3 (May-June 1986), 2-3; Amath Dansokho, "The Destiny of Capitalism and the Prospect Before the Developing World," *World Marxist Review,* 1 (January 1987), 30-37.
3. S. Belenchuk, "Providing Enough Food," *Asia and Africa Today,* 3 (May-June 1985), 11-13.
4. See, for example, Y. Bochkaryov, "Crimes of Apartheid Continue," *New Times,* 15 (April 1985), 15; Anatoli Gromyko, "Racism and Colonialism in Africa Must Be Ended!" *Asia and Africa Today,* 4 (July-August 1986), 6-8.
5. Y. Bochkaryov, "Bankruptcy of the Apartheid Regime," *New Times,* 33 (August 1985), 18-21; Moscow World Service in English, 2 August 1985 in Foreign Broadcast Information Service, *Daily Report: Soviet Union* (hereinafter cited as *FBIS: SU*), 5 August 1985, A2; M. Pavlov, "The Stubbornness of Racists," *Asia and Africa Today,* 6 (November-December 1985), 21; Moscow TASS in English, 6 April 1986 in *FBIS:SU,* 7 April 1986, CC8-9.
6. "U.S.A.-South Africa: The Same Root," *New Times,* 35 (September 1986), 7-8. See also Moscow in English to Southern Africa, 24 July 1986 in *FBIS: SU,* 25 July 1986, A2-3; Moscow in Zulu to Southern Africa, 27 July 1986 in FBIS: SU, 5 August 1986, J1-2.
7. Moscow in Zulu to Southern Africa, 22 July 1985 in *FBIS: SU,* 25 July 1985, J2; Moscow in Zulu to Southern Africa, 22 November 1985 in *FBIS: SU,* 25 November 1985, J1-2; Moscow in Zulu to Southern Africa, 9 December 1985 in *FBIS: SU,* 16 December 1985, J2.
8. "Apartheid Regime in Deep Crisis," *New Times,* 2 (January 1987), 21; Joe Slovo, "Cracks in the Racist Power Bloc," *World Marxist Review,* 6 (June 1987), 13-21.
9. "Who Is Blocking a Namibia Settlement?" *Asia and Africa Today,* 1 (January-February 1986), 64. See also Moscow TASS in English, 15 February 1986 in *FBIS: SU*, 19 February 1986, J5.

10. Boris Vasilyev, "Dirty Deeds of the 'Black Cock,' " *Asia and Africa Today,* 3 (May-June 1985), 19-21; Moscow TASS in English, 14 July 1985 in *FBIS: SU,* 15 July 1987, J1; Leonid Fituni, "Equitable and Effective Cooperation," *Asia and Africa Today,* 6 (November-December 1985), 50-52.

11. "Only 'On the Face of It?' " *New Times,* 41 (October 1985), 16; Moscow TASS in English, 14 October 1987 in *FBIS: SU,* 15 October 1987, 32.

12. A. Zhigunov and I. Nikolayevsky, "Zimbabwe: To Turn Back Is Impossible," *Asia and Africa Today,* 1 (January-February 1986), 44-48. See also "Lesotho: New Regime," *New Times,* 5 (February 1986), 9-10.

13. Moscow TASS in English, 4 May 1985 in *FBIS: SU,* 6 May 1985, J1; Vera Burenina, "Some Trends in Socio-Economic Development," *Asia and Africa Today,* 1 (January-February 1986), 78-80; Moscow International Service in Somali, 24 June 1987 in *FBIS: SU,* 25 June 1987, F1.

14. Skuratov, "The Disturbances in Sudan," *New Times,* 15 (April 1985), 15; Moscow TASS in English, 24 November 1985 in *FBIS: SU,* 25 November 1985, H3.

15. See, for example, Dmitry Volsky, "Spring of Terrorism in the Mechanism of Tension," *New Times,* 50 (December 1985), 10-11; Moscow TASS in English, 6 January 1986 in *FBIS: SU,* 6 January 1986, H4-5; Moscow TASS in English, 25 March 1986 in *FBIS: SU,* 25 March 1986, A1; and Moscow TASS in English, 15 April 1986 in *FBIS: SU,* 15 April 1986, A2-3.

16. Moscow TASS in English, 24 April 1986 in *FBIS: SU,* 25 April 1986, H2.

17. Moscow International Service in Arabic, 10 May 1987 in *FBIS: SU,* 15 May 1987, H2; Moscow International Service in Arabic, 8 September 1987 in *FBIS: SU,* 15 September 1987, 21.

18. Zaza Menteshashvili, "The Berbers," *Asia and Africa Today,* 2 (March-April 1986), 79-83; Moscow International Service in Arabic, 24 July 1986 in *FBIS: SU,* 25 July 1986, H1; "By the Rule of Contraries," *New Times,* 31 (August 1986), 8-9.

19. Moscow TASS in English, 4 April 1985 in *FBIS: SU,* 5 April 1985, J2; Valdimir Novikov, "Twenty-Five Years of Independence: A Thorny

Path," *Asia and Africa Today,* 5 (September-October 1985), 64-66; "The Nobistor Mystery," *New Times,* 44 (November 1986), 16-17; Moscow TASS in English, 22 May 1987 in *FBIS: SU,* 26 May 1987, J2.

9: Security, Ideology and Development on Africa's Horn:

UNITED STATES POLICY
—REAGAN AND THE FUTURE

DAVID D. LAITIN

The human tragedy that takes place on Africa's Horn appears to be a story "told by an idiot." Due to British perfidy, both Ethiopia and Somalia felt they had a legitimate claim on the Ogaden desert. On this issue, there has been a virtual state of war between Ethiopia and Somalia since Somalia received its independence in 1960. Both countries have constructed armies at the expense of factories; the wars have created refugees who remain without hope and survive on the hand-outs from international humanitarian agencies. Both countries are led by soldiers who came to power through a coup d'état, and who have only the barest claim to legitimacy. Ideological programs are espoused by these leaders for purposes of procuring military supplies rather than fostering growth. The human rights of political opponents are not only denied; their lives are under threat. Civil war is rampant throughout Ethiopia; it is festering in Somalia. Economic development under these circumstances is not possible; the World Bank reports declining GNP per capita in both countries.

International politics in the Horn has both reflected this tragedy and added its own pathos as well. Ethiopia from the 1940s had been a client of the United States; Somalia played the two superpowers off against each other, getting economic and police support from the West, and military support from the East. But it became a client of the Soviet Union in the early 1970s. By 1978, in an incredible *pas de deux*, the Soviets became the protectors and military suppliers of Ethiopia, while the United States found itself the reluctant patron of Somalia. Military and economic aid have flowed into this region, considered strategically useful by both superpowers, yet this aid has bought neither firm friends nor stable economies.

The Reagan administration heaped scorn on its predecessor for its inconsistent policies that only exacerbated tensions and weakened the United States position in the world. Although Africa's Horn was not of primary focus for his administration, Reagan often cited Ethiopia as a case where the United States had too easily given in to Soviet adventurism. Given the complexity of the situation in the Horn, however, this condemnation was not warranted. In fact, the Carter administration can be credited with ameliorating the arms build-up in the Horn.

And despite the heroic pronouncements, the Reagan policy in the Horn was more prudent and nuanced than the way it was publicly portrayed. There was more continuity with the Carter policy than is generally recognized. Because of this prudence, American influence in this region has been enhanced. In consequence, there are in the coming decade new opportunities for America to bring an end to the human tragedy by helping to fashion a regional peace that could have positive consequences for economic development. The new administration should seize these opportunities.

The Reagan Policy in the Horn

Months after Reagan's inauguration, in testimony before the House Africa Subcommittee, Lannon Walker, deputy Assistant Secretary for African Affairs, signaled a change in priorities in regard to the Horn. The Carter administration had taken a "regional" perspective in regard to the Ethiopian-Somali war of 1977-78. From the viewpoint of the Organization of African Unity (an organization that United Nations Ambassador Andrew Young took most seriously, and he had considerable influence on President Carter), the territorial integrity of Ethiopia (and therefore the boundaries that Somalia considered illegitimate) was of greater import than the self-determination of the peoples who lived in the Ogaden (who, presumably, would favor incorporation into the Somali state). Because of this, when the Soviets began to give military support to Ethiopia in the wake of the Somali invasion of 1977, Carter was reluctant to answer Somalia's call for equal American aid. Carter insisted that the Somalis pull all troops out of Ethiopia before he would release any military supplies. Without significant external support, Somali troops fell to the massively aided Ethiopian army.

After the Soviet invasion of Afghanistan, Carter's policies in Africa began to reflect more globalist concerns. He therefore pursued the idea of an American facility in Berbera even though he was reluctant to identify with Somalia's policies. But Walker emphasized globalism even more, and thereby signaled the Reagan administration's determination to differentiate itself from Carter. Not Somali aggression but Soviet expansion was the key issue in the Horn. Reagan would follow a policy that reduced Soviet influence in the world and eliminated Cuban troops giving support to other Soviet clients. He opened his testimony by saying that "We have two overriding objectives in the Horn. One has to do with Soviet-Cuban presence and the other with our own access to facilities." [1]

To be sure, the Reagan policy in regard to the Horn was not fully hammered out until July, 1982.[2] But that same globalist perspective was articulated by Assistant Secretary for African Affairs Chester Crocker in 1985. In a talk before the Washington World Affairs Council, Secretary Crocker enumerated American interests in the Horn: "safeguarding shipping lanes... access to air fields and harbors for our military forces... halt Libyan adventurism... avoid the isolation of Egypt... prevent radical pressures on Saudi Arabia." He emphasized that "we must be clear about... Soviet objectives," which include "the narrow Straits of Bab el Mandeb [as] a potential chokepoint against Western Europe... a foothold in Africa whence it can destabilize governments across the continent." [3] It is clear that the Reagan administration, unlike Carter's, emphasized global (and Cold War) objectives within the context of a regional conflict.

Despite this rhetoric, the continuity from Carter to Reagan was more striking than any changes.[4] In four key orientations, Reagan's policies had a Carteresque ring:

1. The Reagan Administration did not shower Somalia, the anti-Communist rival to Ethiopia, with military aid.

Under Carter, United States relations with Somalia were cautious. Somali President Siyaad Bane insisted that Somalia was a true bastion against communism and pleaded with America to supply him with the necessary weapons to fulfill that role. Carter officials were unimpressed. In March, 1978, Assistant Secretary for Africa Richard Moose needed extended discussions with Siyaad in Mogadishu before he could get Somalia's commitment that it would not use American arms to invade the Ogaden. He got that assurance on 23 April; but in June, American intelligence reported that Somali troops and arms were helping guerrillas inside Ethiopia. Thus it was not until August, 1980 that a serious agreement was signed, in which Somalia was promised $65 million over a three year period in credits and grants for the purchase of arms; in return, the United States would get use of naval and air facilities at Berbera and Mogadishu. This was far less than Siyaad hoped for, and the nature of the military package would have made it impossible for Somalia to launch a serious attack against Ethiopian positions in the Ogaden.

The Reagan administration was more eager to supply arms to the Somalis. Yet worry by Kenya, which feared Somali hopes to "redeem" its Somali-populated northeastern province, and opposition in Congress, induced Reagan to stick with the Carter aid formula. The Reagan administration considered greater support to Somalia when relations between Ethiopia and Somalia deteriorated in 1982. Ethiopia and Libya were at that time supporting two groups of dissident Somalis seeking to overthrow the Siyaad regime. The Somalis nonetheless took the offensive in June, and their army went 100 kilometers inside Ethiopia to attack a garrison in Shilabo. In July, the Ethiopians responded by attacking and occupying the Somali village of Balenbale, and in August a Somali dissident group with Ethiopian backing took Goldogob, another village in Somalia. The Somalis went to Washington with urgent appeals for help, and Reagan responded on July 15 with a $5.5 million airlift of recoiless rifles, small arms, and ammunition—materiel that had already been scheduled for sea shipment. This was followed by an extra $10 million package of armored personnel carriers mounted with TOW anti-tank missiles. The United States also authorized Italy to transfer to Somalia many United States tanks of Korean war vintage; Egypt and Saudi Arabia would supplement the package. American chargé d'affaires to Ethiopia David Korn wrote that these publicly announced transfers stopped the Ethiopians from further action.[5]

Perhaps so. But it is also the case that the military aid in no way matched the Soviet military package to Ethiopia. The Reagan administration was engaged in symbolic support of Somalia's boundary. Its military aid to Somalia could in no way be interpreted as a threat to Ethiopia. It has refused to provide the tanks and fighter aircraft the Somalis have requested, and the Somali army remains incapable of recapturing two villages occupied by Ethiopian troops.[6]

Finally, and perhaps most significantly, the United States central command, whose responsibilities lie within southwest Asia, and which from time to time uses facilities in Berbera and Mogadishu, has kept its joint military activities with Somali forces in the semi-annual Bright Star operations at a low level. Despite Somalia's claim to be anti-Communist, the Reagan administration, like its predecessor, has kept its new friend at arm's length.

2. The Reagan administration gave little or no support to insurgent groups within Ethiopia.

Unlike Reagan administration efforts in Nicaragua, Angola, and Afghanistan, in Ethiopia there was no cultivation of an anti-Marxist opposition. To be sure, there are rumors and speculations to the contrary. A report in the *New Statesman* claimed that the CIA was "busy at a variety of covert operations to topple the Ethiopian regime," but no evidence was provided. The more reliable *Africa Confidential* reported that the Reagan administration was giving support to the right wing Ethiopian Peoples Democratic Alliance and to the Marxist Tigray Peoples Liberation Front. Both groups denied receiving any United States aid, although the former group claimed it would welcome American support. Since the alleged amount of aid was under $1 million, even if the story were true, it hardly represented a serious effort to destabilize the Mengistu regime.[7]

In any event, David Korn reported that as of July 1982, those in the Reagan administration who sought to help the Ethiopian rebels lost out, and an internal agreement was reached to eschew aid to Mengistu's internal enemies.[8]

3. The Reagan administration, in its negotiations with Ethiopian officials, was willing to tolerate "Marxism" and Cuban troops, but not the violation of human rights.

Despite the large numbers of Cuban troops in Ethiopia, the consistent espousal of Marxist doctrine, and the tête-à-têtes between Mengistu and Colonel Qaddafi—the three grossest affronts to Reagan's world view—Reagan administration negotiations with Ethiopia did not require a turn around on these issues; rather it required a better human rights record.

The Reagan administration pressed for more normal relations with Ethiopia in late 1982. It sent one of its highest officials in the Bureau of African Affairs, Princeton Lyman, to consult privately with Mengistu in April, 1983. (Lyman was not received.[9]) No preconditions were asked of the Ethiopians. Lyman was prepared to normalize relations with Ethiopia despite its

Marxist rhetoric, its housing of Cuban troops, and its agreements with Libya.

Meanwhile, Reagan officials put pressure on Ethiopia at every opportunity to face up to its egregious record in regard to human rights. In a statement before the House Subcommittee on Africa, Secretary Crocker did not mention Marxism, Cuban troops, or Libya as roadblocks to better relations. But he was eloquent in condemning Ethiopia's human rights record:

> Ethiopia remains bereft of the most basic legal, political and social freedoms. This deplorable human rights situation exists because Chairman Mengistu and a small group of associates wield ultimate power through intimidation and arbitrary arrest, and maintain complete control over all aspects of Ethiopian life. There is no free press, no independent means of political participation and no independent judiciary... The United States government uses every opportunity to forcefully express our opposition to such practices.[10]

Similarly, in a statement before the Senate Committee on Foreign Relations, Ted Morse of the Agency for International Development emphasized that the United States was seeking a consensus of all donors of food aid to Ethiopia to refuse to provide aid to resettlement camps. Peasants from drought-ravaged areas were compelled to travel to these camps, which often separated family members. The United States, he said, would not condone such a policy by helping those camps survive.[11]

To be sure, these statements were provoked by Congressional promptings on the human rights situation. But these two Reagan officials did not use their opportunity to lecture on the evils of Marxism-Leninism. Nor did they mention Cuban troops. Rather, they accepted the premise that the main obstacle to better relations with Ethiopia was disregard for human rights. Indeed, this was the very issue that led Carter to hold back military supplies to Ethiopia, and which helped to cement the Ethiopian-Soviet alliance.

4. The Reagan administration has been exceedingly generous in providing food aid for famine relief without making any political demands.

The United States supplied more than half of all the relief food to Ethiopia in 1985, the crucial year of the famine. The Department of State's Bureau of Public Affairs justified this action in the following way:

> Regardless of ideological differences with the Provisional Military Government of Socialist Ethiopia, the United States responded generously to the suffering of the Ethiopian people. As a result of American time, effort, and money, both from

government and private sources, many lives were saved; about
6 million of the estimated 7.9 million Ethiopians at risk from starvation have received food.[12]

A more realistic analysis would suggest that the Reagan administration was
dragged into this policy by a Democratic opposition in Congress that
highlighted the problem, and by a general public horrified by human
suffering. Delay, there was. Once the decision was made, however, an inter-
agency task force, which included the Department of Defense, coordinated
effectively to mobilize resources for disaster relief. As Jack Shepherd points
out, "After two years of delays in sending emergency food aid, and after
being pushed by Congress and the press into action, a new, less dogmatic
and more pragmatic policy is emerging." [13]

The point remains that the Reagan administration in the Horn was guided
more by pragmatism than ideology. Food aid was given unconditionally, and
there is general agreement that the United States has reaped no short term
political benefits for its generosity. Accommodating itself to the realities of
the region, rather than trying to fit the region into preconceived categories
concerning Marxism, Cuban troops, and Soviet friendship treaties, served
American interests well. The United States maintained access to a useful facility
for which it has paid only a small cost. It has not unnecessarily alienated
Kenya, which fears Somali aggression. And it has to its credit the historical
record of helping to mitigate the effects of an ecological disaster in Ethiopia.[14]

Reagan's chief of mission to Ethiopia concluded his survey of Reagan's
policies in the Horn by arguing that the Carter policy was a "failure" which
"set the stage for the more ambitious policy of the Reagan administration...
Reagan permitted, after much internal debate, Boeing to sell airplanes to
Ethiopian airlines in 1983; that same year an educational and cultural
affairs program was re-established at the American Embassy. And Reagan
was quick to support famine relief, the U.S. being the largest donor of food."
It "wisely rejected the idea of trying to bring pressure on Ethiopia through
aid to the insurgencies..." In 1985, a settlement on United States private
property was reached. "Through all these steps, the United States sought
to show the Ethiopian government and people that it valued its ties with
them." [15]

Korn is correct to praise the Reagan policy in the Horn. There has been
little fighting on the Somali-Ethiopian border in large part because the United
States did not fuel the arm's race. Somalia has provided access to Berbera
for United States troops, but the United States is not closely identified with
the present regime. Opposition groups are therefore not calling for the

expulsion of the United States from its favored position. Meanwhile, the Soviet Union is in a quagmire amid the Ethiopian civil wars. All evidence suggests that opponents to Mengistu, if they could capture power, would ride a popular wave if they broke relations with the Soviets. The United States thus is well positioned as an influential agent in the Horn; it has few real enemies there. Although Korn is correct about the assessment, the record suggests that Reagan's Horn policy, in contrast to his policies in southern Africa, represented a continuation of the policies of Carter. Indeed, this is the reason why the Reagan administration achieved in the Horn, unlike southern Africa, moderate success.

The Horn: The 1990s and Beyond

The new American administration, in large part due to the moderate successes of United States policies in the Horn, will not only face new problems, but will have greater opportunity for creative action.

Somalia: Political Succession and Economic Stagnation

The regime headed by Mahammad Siyaad Barre, which came to power by virtue of a coup d'état in 1969, is in its final stages. Siyaad was an extremely popular leader in his first decade of rule. He helped unify the country, and will forever be credited with the resolution of a "script war" that enabled Somalia to rely on its own language for education and administration. In the early 1970s, Somalia achieved moderate economic successes; but by the mid-1970s, the parastatal sector created by Siyaad's socialist government fell to graft and inefficiency. Siyaad was beginning to lose support. But he led the country into a popular war to "redeem" the Ogaden. It almost brought victory; it took massive Soviet aid to defeat the Somalis.

Military defeat and economic decline brought challenges to Siyaad. Most important, Somalia was faced by a colossal influx of refugees from the Ogaden. All attention in government circles was focused for many years on relations with international relief agencies and the organization of survival camps. The society almost collapsed under the weight of this migration, which increased the population of Somalia by a third.

But the Somali president also began to face challenges to his right to rule. Siyaad responded to opposition by surrounding himself with his most loyal supporters, and these were generally those from within his own clan. Oppositional organization had no opportunities other than clan solidarity, since citizens were not free to organize publicly to challenge the president.

By the early 1980s, clan warfare became endemic. Two major opposition clans each formed political/military organizations to challenge Siyaad's rule. Each made alliances with Ethiopia for safe havens enabling them to stage guerrilla actions against the Somali regime. They have been funded by Ethiopia and for a time by Libya. Meanwhile, Siyaad has had to rely on American military aid to repel these dissident forces. American aid therefore was being used to help a dictator fight off his internal enemies.

Presently President Siyaad, barely recovered from a near fatal automobile accident in May 1986 and suffering from diabetes and old age, can only observe ruefully his supporters and enemies fighting for power. His supporters are divided. His prime minister, Mahammad Samantar, heads the "constitutionalist" wing that hopes his second place in the present hierarchy of power would assure him the right to succession. Siyaad initially relied heavily on General Samantar, not only because he was highly competent, but also because he does not command a clan following of great worth. He was therefore, in terms of traditional tribal reckoning, a minimal threat to the president. These constitutionalists are being challenged by the "dynasts": those clansmen of Siyaad who have attained great wealth and power with their wagons hitched to Siyaad. The dynasts are divided among themselves. Siyaad's son Colonel Masleh has gained great wealth in recent years; his half brother, Abdurahman, who is foreign minister, is also maneuvering for power; and former Minister of Defense Omar Haji, another Siyaad clansman, also has supporters among the dynasts.[16]

Despite all this political intrigue, the Somali economy has recovered from the worst excesses of parastatal inefficiency. In 1981, the Somali government reached an agreement with the International Monetary Fund that led to two consecutive stand-by agreements. Somalia's staggering $333.1 million balance-of-payments deficit of 1980 was then covered. These IMF funds also helped get Somalia out of arrears in its payment of interest on its foreign debt to the West. To meet the IMF's demands, the Somali government was compelled to devalue its shilling by 50 percent and to decrease state involvement in the economy.

World Bank and IMF officials publicly praise the progress in Somalia's economy. There has been some growth in agriculture, now that the government is paying reasonable prices for agricultural products.[17] And there have been some reductions in the public payroll. But there have been economic set-backs as well. Somalia lost the hold it had on Saudi imports of live animals, and much of the IMF money has gone to cover the resultant great losses in Somalia's largest export sector. Also, the Somali government has put great hope in an irrigation mega-project near Bardheere, but Western monies have been very slow coming.

In the next few years, United States foreign policy officials will deal with the politics of presidential succession in Somalia, and with a growing disillusionment about the pay-offs for complicity with IMF nostrums.

Ethiopia: Civil War and Soviet Dilemmas

Ethiopia has long been a multi-national empire dominated by the Amharas, who have been feudal lords and aggressive state builders. The Amharic emperors, allied with the ancient Ethio-Christian church, had formed a hegemonic bloc in Ethiopia for centuries. After World War II, Ethiopian Emperor Haile Selassie tried to construct a unitary state. This strategy backfired on him, and he unwittingly unleashed several "national liberation" movements that resented Amharic domination. In Eritrea, the nation has been defined by the common history of Italian colonialism; but Tigray, Oromo, and Somali nationalism has been based on common language, social structure, and territory.

With Selassie's fall in 1974, there was initial hope for a political solution that recognized Ethiopia's territorial integrity as well as its cultural diversity. But with the brutal capture of the revolution by Colonel Mengistu Haile Mariam, Ethiopia's answer to national liberation movements is to send troops and armed peasants to put the rebellions down by force. The country has been in open civil war for a decade.

The "national question" puts Ethiopia's Soviet patrons in a dilemma. On the one hand, the Soviets value their alliance with Ethiopia, a country that espouses Marxism-Leninism and houses the Organization of African Unity. On the other hand, the Eritrean and Tigray movements also have socialist orientations, and had received support from the Soviets before the revolution began. Cuban troops have therefore not been deployed to help Mengistu fight his civil wars. The Soviets have tried to loan their model of national republics to Ethiopia; but the new constitution in Ethiopia ignores those Soviet lessons.[18]

The economic situation in Ethiopia presents a second Soviet dilemma. The Soviet Union is in no position to remedy the famine. It has provided support for the resettlement program, which is considered to be a long term solution. But although technically a reasonable policy, resettlement under present circumstances is not only inhumane, but it is also so badly administered as to assure failure. With famine being Ethiopia's principal problem, Soviet aid is increasingly irrelevant.

Third, the Soviets face a political dilemma in Ethiopia. On the one hand, Mengistu has presided over a social revolution that eliminated aristocratic and religious elites, and in which land was redistributed to the peasants. He has identified with the international communist cause. On the other hand, although he (reluctantly and after much prodding) established the "Workers' Party of Ethiopia," the government is still made up of the soldiers from Mengistu's original junta. A stream of recent defections from Ethiopia should make clear to the Soviets that Mengistu's legitimacy is uncertain. As of this writing, it does not appear that Secretary Gorbachev's reforms have altered Soviet visions or goals in Ethiopia. At best, perhaps the Soviet Union has become more cautious in offering advice to Mengistu. But caution is not an answer for deep policy dilemmas. Given those dilemmas, the prospects for long term Soviet influence in Ethiopia appear to be slim.

Opportunities in the 1990s

For the United States to cultivate long-term good relations with the states on the Horn, there needs to be (a) a regional peace in which both states and individuals maintain dignity and receive justice; (b) political solutions to domestic political crises so that armed rebellion disappears; and (c) economic development so that victims of famine and poverty do not overwhelm the capacity of their governments to provide relief. By no means can the United States achieve these goals alone. But it is possible, given the good will the United States has achieved over the past decade, to work towards the fulfillment of these goals.

A Regional Peace

In January 1986, a Siyaad-Mengistu summit signaled an era of regional détente. A joint committee to develop a peace plan met that May. An outline of a possible peace was drawn: Somalia would give up the idea of redeeming the Ogaden and would cease providing support to the Western Somali Liberation Front; Ethiopia would grant the Ogaden region administrative autonomy and the leadership of the Western Somali Liberation Front would be incorporated in the new government.

These talks represent an historic opportunity because the outlined solution does promote dignity and justice. To be sure, negotiating seas have not been smooth. In early 1987, the *Indian Ocean Newsletter* reported rather large military build-ups on the Ethio-Somali border. Negotiations are only sporadic now. But the United States should be ready to support the proposed solution should the opportunity again arise. As we have learned in Zimbabwe, a powerful outside actor can help "midwife" solutions between groups divided by language and history, but unfortunately sharing the same territory. Affirmative policies inducing negotiation are already in practice in the Horn. Italy, which has made some of its development aid contingent on good-faith negotiations on the regional issue, is using its power to a good cause. And Chevron too has made clear to the Somali government that regional peace would make the exploitation of oil reserves economically feasible. Future United States aid policies should always be tied to a regional politics that promotes peace and justice.

Domestic Justice

In Ethiopia, there can be no immediate changes in United States policy. The United States has no influence on the course of the civil wars. As long as the massive Soviet presence dominates politics in Addis Ababa, Ethiopia will accept food donations but not political advice from the Americans. No advice should be offered. The United States should continue supplying famine relief despite the lack of acknowledgement by Ethiopian authorities and their inhumane policies that often keep the food from those most affected by the drought. Perhaps the only initiative that should be undertaken is the development of informal ties with the leadership of the liberation fronts. If the Soviet Union is evicted from Ethiopia, the United States should be clear about the political accommodations that would be necessary before the United States identified with the Ethiopian government. The United States should have a political strategy for Ethiopia's possible reincorporation into the Western orbit.

In Somalia, a more long-term political and economic strategy is overdue. Already the United States has begun to dissociate itself from the Siyaad regime. For 1987, the American military package was cut in half by Congress from the previous year, and the Reagan administration acquiesced. This is wise, in large part because those weapons were too often used by Somali troops to attack dissident Somali armies. United States advisors were not vigilant enough to monitor the purposes for which their airlifted materiel were put.

Meanwhile, the Somali constitutionalists, the dynasts, and the dissident groups are each building ruling coalitions that will necessarily alienate and dominate clan outsiders. Unless American officials use their presence and influence in Mogadishu to induce competing groups to incorporate broader constituencies in their programs, America will become a hostage in the post-Siyaad civil war (choosing the least bad contender and finding itself unwelcome should that contender lose) rather than a commanding presence pressing for a democratic outcome in which all groups would have a stake.

On the economic front, Somalia presents for the United States a special challenge. Liberalization of the grain markets, elimination of parastatal interference in the banana trade, and devaluation of the currency all helped to bring some short-term stabilization. But a longer term solution to Somalia's economic stagnation is a necessary condition for long-term political stability. And, should Somalia experience a degree of economic dynamism, it is clear that many Ethiopians would see that as a model for their larger, and better endowed country.

There is no panacea for a country with a moribund economy in which debt service is higher than expected export earnings. But there are political reasons why it is to the United States' interest to go beyond IMF liberalism to seed a dynamic element in Somalia's economy. This may mean greater support for the Bardheere Dam on the Juba River, even though World Bank officials are unsure whether it would bring a good return on capital. At least some opportunities would open up for private initiative to exploit a new invest-ment opportunity in irrigated land. This may mean providing lines of credit to private Somalis who seek to invest in farming, fishing, or small manufac-turing. More thinking and experimentation is indeed necessary, because the present strategy, which has brought some rectification, will not energize the economy for future growth.

Policy Recommendations for a New United States Administration

This paper has stressed the common foreign policy concerns of the United States that have transcended the ideological differences between Carterites and Reaganites. But a new administration must take into account its ideological goals and its political coalition.

A Republican president might well be surrounded by advisors who believe that the Ethiopian government is merely a pawn of the (reconstructed but still dangerous) Soviet Union. Somalia, an enemy of Ethiopia, must by this logic be a friend of the United States. It will be important for foreign policy advisors to a president with these views to articulate the moderate success achieved in the Horn based on a bipartisan continuity of policy. Ideological passion could lead to costly errors in the Horn. Granting the Somalis their wish list of weapons could easily make the United States slaves to the Somali political agenda. Withholding food aid to Ethiopia unless human rights are better recognized could lead to massive starvation and human degradation. Advisors to a new Republican president should stress continuity.

A Democratic president will be in a better position to take advantage of new opportunities. Upset with Reagan failures in South Africa, Namibia, and Angola, many Democratic foreign policy experts wish to articulate bolder programs for Africa. A forward looking policy for the Horn could fit that agenda.

In light of this, they should advise the president to announce a peace initiative in the Horn as part of a larger program for foreign policy successes in Africa.

Revival of the spirit of January 1986 between the Somali and Ethiopian leaders should be the immediate goal. The state department could collaborate with their Italian counterparts to push for further meetings to fashion a long-term peace. The United States would have to contribute to an aid package that would help to persuade both sides of the notion that peace might be profitable. Something more than IMF stabilization ought to be promised. On the diplomatic front, the United States would have to cultivate links with dissident Somali groups to make sure that any successor government would accept the outlines of a proposed agreement. It could also bring in the Soviet Union, which might be happy to support one less front in Ethiopia's turmoil. Mengistu, too, might be ready to make more substantial concessions to Somali autonomy in the Ogaden if the Somali government recognized the principle of territorial integrity of the Ethiopian state.

A regional peace in the Horn based on justice for all nationalities would not only be better for the people in the region; it would take another potentially explosive situation off the international chessboard. An American administration that plays a role in the development of a peaceful solution in the Horn will contribute to global peace.

ADDENDUM: An historic agreement between Ethiopia and Somalia was signed in April, 1988. Its ten articles call for the renunciation of armed combat, the respect for the territorial integrity of the other state, the withdrawal of troops from the border region, the end of hostile propaganda, the exchange of prisoners of war, and the reestablishment of diplomatic relations. Finally, both countries have agreed to renegotiate in good faith concerning the boundary question.

Notes

1. Statement by Lannon Walker, Acting Assistant Secretary for African Affairs, Foreign Assistance Legislation for Fiscal Year 1982 (part 8), Hearings and Markup, before the Subcommittee on Africa (Washington D.C., 1981), 347. The author acknowledges the help of Ronald Kassimir, Walter Barrows, and conference participants for help in the preparation and revision of this manuscript.
2. David A. Korn, *Ethiopia, The United States and the Soviet Union,* (Carbondale, 1986), 55-57.
3. Chester Crocker, "U.S. Interests in Regional Conflicts in the Horn of Africa," United States Department of State, Bureau of Public Affairs, Washington D.C., Current Policy No. 764.
4. Reagan's Africa policy in Angola, Namibia, and South Africa indeed represented a clear departure from Carter's policies. Ethiopia and the Horn represent an exception.
5. Korn, *Ethiopia,* 75-77.
6. See Anthony Shaw, "Barre's Balancing Act" *Africa Report,* (November-December, 1986), 28. Indeed, after Secretary Crocker emphasized the global security issues in his speech before the World Affairs Council, "U.S. Interests," he went on to contrast the Soviet emphasis on military aid while "we have placed emphasis on economic assistance and development," 2.
7. Claudia Wright, "Holding a Neo-Colony," *New Statesman,* 111 (6 June 1980), 19; *Africa Confidential,* "Ethiopia: EPD What?" (27 Oct. 1980).
8. Korn, *Ethiopia,* 55-57.
9. Ibid., 59-62.
10. "Human Rights and Food Aid in Ethiopia," Hearing before the Subcommittee on Human Rights and International Organizations and the Subcommittee on Africa, October 16, 1985.
11. "Ethiopia Update: Forced Population Removal and Human Rights," Hearing before the Committee on Foreign Relations, United States Senate, March 6, 1986.
12. GIST, "Ethiopian Famine" (December, 1985).

13. "Changing Equations in the Horn," *Africa Report* (November-December, 1985), 25.

14. On unconditionality, see the statement by Secretary Crocker, "U.S. Interests," 4. Both Reagan's diplomatic representative David Korn and political opponent Rep. Howard Wolpe agree as to the failure of the food aid to bring better political relations in the short term. See David Korn, "Ethiopia: Dilemma for the West," *World Today,* 42, 1 (1986), 4. For Wolpe, see "Congressional Study Mission to Israel, Egypt, Sudan, Ethiopia, and Somalia, August 2-20, 1985" Committee on Foreign Affairs, United States House of Representatives.

15. Korn, *Ethiopia,* 182-183.

16. Richard Greenfield, a former political advisor to the Somali government, has outlined the internal battle lines in "An Embattled Barre" *Africa Report* (May-June, 1987), 65-69.

17. See the Report on the "Congressional Study Mission," 13.

18. See M. Lionel Bender "Ethiopian Language Policy 1974-1981" *Anthropological Linguistics,* XXVII (1985), 273-279; "Ethiopia's new Constitution: Cosmetic or 'Power to the People'?" *Africa Now,* 70 (March, 1987), 12-13.

10: U.S. Policy Toward South and Southern Africa

ROBERT I. ROTBERG

The United States seeks a way of intervening effectively in South Africa. Although there may be wholesale disagreement within United States political circles about how best to help South Africa help itself, very few politicians condone apartheid or believe the ending of white minority rule is of indifference to the United States. Successive American presidents have labeled apartheid repugnant, anachronistic, and evil. There is a widespread willingness to act, but little consensus about the efficacy of specific choices within an array of policy options.

Hardly anyone believes that apartheid—the continued political domination of 25 million black South Africans by fewer than five million white ones—will soon be superseded by power sharing, divided authority, varieties of regional autonomy (confederation, consociationalism, or cantonalism), or majority rule. Not even militant Africans expect a revolution to overwhelm the military forces of the hegemonic state immediately, if ever.[1] Likewise, not even the most pollyannish analysts anticipate an outburst of altruism.

The National Party of South Africa has governed South Africa since 1948 and will bend every advantage to continue governing indefinitely. Threatened more from the white right than the white left, and more worried in 1988 about the appeal of oldfashioned, hard-line apartheid than about the menace of African protest, the National Party can hardly be expected to accelerate the transfer of real power from haves to have-nots. Meaningful change seems to Afrikaners to hold more perils than rewards; the dangers of the unknown are palpable. Whites are neither sufficiently frightened, sufficiently beleaguered, sufficiently isolated, nor sufficiently pressured economically to compel concessions, compromises, and the kinds of negotiations which would result in the dismantling of apartheid. White South Africa is still too strong and too secure.

White South Africa, government and citizenry, reposes its confidence in a military force that is the strongest on the African continent and much more than a match for any foreseeable combination of regional or Africa-wide attackers. Indeed, since 1981 South Africa's army and air force have imposed a Bellum Africana on all of southern Africa through cross border raids, mini-invasions, occupations (of southern Angola from 1981-83), and, not least, by arming and funding indigenous proxy forces like the National Union for the Total Independence of Angola (UNITA) and the Resistência Nacional Moçambicana (MNR or Renamo).

Demonstrating an ability to strike boldly and intemperately against its much weaker neighbors, and even into the southern underbelly of Soviet- and Cuban-assisted Angola, South Africa has become the military giant of the region. Using an Israeli military model, it has compelled states as far afield as Zambia, and as comparatively resilient as Zimbabwe, to limit their policy options, end their overt support for the African National Congress (ANC), and generally behave benignly within a sphere of influence that South Africa has successfully claimed as its own. Mozambique, once friendly to the Soviet Union, and a self-proclaimed Marxist state, has been pulled by the dangers of Renamo and the might of South Africa into the orbit of its big neighbor (and toward the West).

Between South Africa and its weaker neighbors there persists an inescapable tension that reflects great and probably enduring disparities of military and economic power. Given the ascendancy of the South African military in the region and given a rail and road system that will continue (under the most favorable circumstances imaginable for the weaker states) for many years to be dominated by South Africa, there is very little that the West realistically can do to alter the balance of power significantly in southern Africa in the near term. Except for Botswana, and possibly Zimbabwe, the nations of the region are desperately fragile and overwhelmingly dependent (except for Angola) on South Africa. Dredging the port of Beira, safeguarding the refurbished rail line from Mutare to Beira, opening the southern rail line from Harare to Maputo, and injecting outside capital into the infrastructure of the region, are palliatives given climbing current account deficits, the massive and chronic paucity of foreign currency, the paucity of working locomotives, and the lack of experienced personnel. Moreover, South Africa's military will retain its ability to harass and disrupt; no policymaker should assume that South African raids need solely to be motivated by real or even imagined anti-insurgency requirements.

South Africa has struck against its neighbors and will continue to strike for political and economic reasons as well as military ones. So, in the same way, UNITA and Renamo will be deployed to undermine the stability of Angola and Mozambique and the region, as well as otherwise promising political and economic developments. United States policymakers should not assume that South Africa wants what may seem axiomatic to Washington—a stable and developing southern Africa. Nor should United States policymakers assume (as the Reagan administration has lamentably done) that South Africa has devised and hews to a single policy for its neighbors. Military, not diplomatic, ideas dominate, and the view of military intelligence often exerts itself over the tactics of conventional forces.[2]

Since the 1960s South Africa has devoted comparatively large portions of its budgets to a large army, a medium-sized air force, and a small coastal navy. The regular army numbers about 80,000, but it is swelled to 250,000 by young white conscripts, who serve 24 months from their eighteenth birthdays (with short deferments for university attendance). Another 250,000 white commandos or reservists are armed, and mobilizable throughout the country on short notice. Ex-conscripts must attend month-long camps every year for 12 years after their service, and are also eligible to be recalled until they are 60. Nearly all white male adults are thus potentially capable of being called up in an emergency. Asians and Coloureds serve in the army and the 9,000-person navy, but not in the airforce, which has 13,000 men. African volunteers serve in the army and in special battalions recruited in Namibia among Namibians for service there only. Only six percent of the total military personnel of South Africa is not white. Thus disaffections, protests, and mutinies should hardly be anticipated. Neither Africa's white rulers, nor Western critics, should expect the collapse of the South African army (as in the Shah's Iran) before a more powerful or more just ideology, or as a result of a great upsurge of left-minded anti-combat sentiment (as in Caetano's Portugal). There is an active anti-conscription movement among whites, largely at universities, but the notion that this movement will undermine South Africa's military might is illusory. Nor among most whites has there been a revulsion against the Namibian border war or the violence in the urban townships. The casualty rate among white soldiers has year after year fallen considerably below the threshold which would trigger protest among an Afrikaner-dominated white population which worries much more about its continued security in troubled times.

Since the UN-sponsored military embargo of South Africa began in the early 1960s, South Africa has steadily increased its capacity to manufacture virtually all of the military equipment—even jet aircraft—which it requires. It suffers from no known shortages of small arms or ammunition, and provides its own armored personnel carriers, tanks, long range cannon, and so on. In 1986, South Africa even obtained mid-air refuelling capability for its air force. Theoretically, South African aircraft can menace middle Africa as far as Bangui and Douala. Weak in avionics, the South African military is otherwise largely selfsufficient. It has stockpiled ample reserves of petroleum. Whether South Africa has the capacity to assemble a nuclear bomb is less important than its ability to strike with impunity against its neighbors with conventional means, and to mobilize a firepower much more massive, and much better trained, than is available to protesters in its townships, the ANC, its neighbors, or any combination of outside forces other than the superpowers. Sanctions have not yet affected the budgets or procurement policies of the South African Defense Force.

In purely military terms, the struggle between black and white South Africa is hardly even. The ANC, the principal guerrilla antagonist of South Africa, has functioned from exile since the arrest and imprisonment of Nelson Mandela and Walter Sisulu and others in 1962. Backed from the early 1970s by the Soviet Union, the East bloc, and others, the ANC since the very late 1970s has been able increasingly to emphasize the vulnerability of South Africa to sabotage. Yet the ANC has not as yet mounted a campaign of terror. It has not attempted to destroy the viability of white life on outlying farms (as happened during the Mau Mau period in Kenya or during the Chimurenga war in Zimbabwe from 1972 to 1979). Its sabotage has been intermittent and seemingly uncoordinated, and unsustained over time. Aircraft have not been hijacked, trains derailed, bridges destroyed, or cities plunged into darkness.

Partly the ANC has followed a long-hallowed policy of minimizing the loss of life; it has not been anxious to unleash a wave of terror for fear of losing its respectability and for fear of massive retaliation. Furthermore, the ANC may number no more than 7,000 to 10,000 activists, by far the largest proportion of whom reside in distant political bases like Lusaka, Zambia, or in training camps in northern Angola.

South Africa has successfully pushed ANC staging points far away from its own borders. No longer can the ANC operate with even comparative impunity from havens in Lesotho, Botswana, Swaziland, Zimbabwe, or Mozambique. As a result, no more than 1,000 ANC operatives in any year are in the field attacking South Africa, although cadres do infiltrate easily and operate within the target country for weeks, if not months. It is a tribute to the persistence and popularity of the ANC that its units still present a definite threat to a regime which has been focused so thoroughly on their extirpation. The ANC will continue to pose a danger to South Africa, and will bore from within, but it is not credible in the near term to think that the ANC can undermine or overwhelm the South African state militarily. To believe otherwise assumes a massive collapse either of South Africa's military capability or of the white will to resist.

The current wave of violence in the townships has endured for more than three years. More than 1,800 Africans have been killed, the larger portion as a result of police or military retaliation. About 10,000 Africans have been wounded. White casualties have been few. About 30,000 Africans have been detained for shorter or longer periods, all without trial. Many of these detained for a year or more have been children. Even successive states of emergency, governmental control of information, censorship and self-censorship, the jailing of protest leaders, and other acts of intimidation failed to break the crescendo of protest until mid-1987. Throughout most of 1986-88, several million Africans successfully withheld their house rents in the white-controlled urban townships for periods of several months to a year. In 1986, but not in 1988, it could be claimed that the government had lost de facto control of the townships (where at least 12 million Africans live). Yet only a limited coalition of black activists—"the Comrades"—could even begin to claim that local authority, and then only temporarily and episodically.

By its very design and nature the protest in the townships was decentralized, uncoordinated, allied principally in spirit to the banned and underground

ANC, and although tied more directly to the United Democratic Front (UDF)—an above-ground pro-ANC amalgam of more than 600 township and national African and other interest groups—it was not beholden directly to the UDF, or directed from any command post. Thus the massive unrest of 1984-87 was based on a mobilization of sentiment, indigenous and local in inspiration but national in scope, which could not have been expected to have been a part of the engine of long-term confrontation. The unrest represented the aspirations of an urban people long aggrieved and finally energized. The lesson of the mid-1980s is, rightly or wrongly, that African protesters feel that they can ultimately achieve majority rule.

White politicians in South Africa largely share a rather different belief. Since the 1987 whites-only election to parliament confirmed both the continued ascendance of the ruling National Party *and* an alarming sympathy among white electors for the Conservative Party, farther to the right, there can be no early expectation of the rapid dismantling of apartheid. The Conservatives campaigned against the reformist designs of the National Party, and won both a surprising 22 seats (previously they held 17) and approximately 26 percent of all white votes and 40 percent of all votes by Afrikaners. Although the National Party gained seats (from 117 to 123), its share of the popular vote fell to 52 percent (from an accustomed 57 percent). Indeed, tellingly, analysts suspect that the National Party relied for its victory on votes cast by English-speaking and other non-Afrikaner South Africans. In 1988, the Conservatives easily won three seats in by-election contests against the National Party, deepening the gloom in ruling circles. No longer can the National Party claim to be the exclusive voice of Afrikanerdom.[3]

Both Conservative and National Party gains were at the expense of the Progressive Federal Party, which lost its mandate as the official opposition. Its total number of seats slid from 26 to 19 (and subsequently fell to 17 with the formation of the National Democratic Movement). Many of its former seats were lost by narrow margins, probably because of the abstention of "liberals" and younger voters. The National Party also won a number of seats from Conservatives by equally slim pluralities, thus strengthening its fear of the popularity of the right. Progressive-leaning ex-National Party Afrikaner independents also won a single seat and frightened the ruling regime in two more constituencies.

Despite the qualified success of the independents, the Progressives suffered a severe loss of legitimacy, as well as a possibly fatal blow to their morale. Since the election, too, dissension within party about the participation of a handful of its members in a meeting with ANC leaders in Senegal, and about the party's official caution in the face of National Party verbal abuse, has deepened its crisis of legitimacy.

The fates of local political parties are of little concern to foreign policy. However, the perceived shift in the inclination of the electorate has important consequences for decision-makers in South Africa and in the West. With the loss of electoral credibility of the parliamentary left, the possibility of a massive leftward realignment of white voters has receded. Western policy officials have often dreamed of a strong, electorate-driven impetus for meaningful reform. Many of the initiatives and constraints of the United States program of constructive engagement were founded on optimistic assessments of the behavior of white voters. Even in South Africa, liberals believed, until election day, 1987, that whites would come to their senses, appraise their options rationally, and begin swinging behind the Progressive Federal Party and breakaway members of the National Party. Those hopes, based as they were on misplaced notions about the true nature of South African politics, are now forlorn. There may come a time when a desperate white electorate votes for the party which favors the end of apartheid and open negotiations with authentic representatives of the African majority. But that time will not be soon. The white electorate, as presently constructed and presently threatened, will not of its own accord opt for the perils of the unknown. Even bold leadership may not be able to persuade electors to recognize the imperative of reconciliation.

In present and foreseeable circumstances, such governmental leadership is in any event conspicuously lacking. Given the perceived threat to the National Party posed by the upsurge of support for the Conservatives, innovative leadership for meaningful reform by the present ruling oligarchy cannot be anticipated. The National Party will be more loath than ever to risk its position as both an Afrikaner and a national institution (in that order). Thus, even if constructive engagement had been founded on a sure appreciation of Afrikanerdom and white politics, anxiety among the ruling élite regarding the appeal of the Conservative message effectively curtails, if it does not decapitate, the existing thrust of National Party reforms. Only a courageous ruler will move assertively forward in the face of determined attack from the right.

President Botha and his colleagues are neither exceptionally brave nor sufficiently sure about the end game of South Africa to risk too much change.

Doing little minimizes risk (and minimizes gain). Since one of the premises of United States policy toward South Africa has long been that the government there would be induced to take positive steps to end apartheid only if it were sufficiently reassured and cajoled (the Reagan administration view) or threatened (the view of the sponsors of the Anti-Apartheid Act of 1986 and similar measures), it is critical that the very weakness of the National Party regime is understood. Paralysis would be too strong a description, but the oligarchy that dominates the National Party believes that its effective options are few. Altering South Africa by exerting far stronger pressure on a weak and uncertain government is therefore difficult. Even the regime of President Botha before 1987 resisted the blandishments of constructive engagement.[4] Politically, as well as emotionally, it then saw few advantages accruing to the party from meaningful change. None is apparent to them now, although Westerners (and some South Africans) argue that the very future of the state, and of a white role in it, will remain in the balance only in the short term.

What constitutes meaningful reform? From the black perspective, the answer is now reasonably specific: only a vast expansion in African political participation at the national level counts. It is too late to substitute political privileges at the local level for enfranchisement alongside whites. Nor will Africans accept being diverted at the national level to a fourth (black) house of parliament with coordinate rather than commensurate power. Africans seek more influence than Coloureds and Asians now can exert through their parallel chambers. Africans want it, most of all, directly, i.e. without separate electoral rolls and the other paraphernalia of neo-apartheid. A further consideration is essential to: political participation within a re-integrated South Africa. African political plans presuppose the demise of separate development, the re-absorption of homelands, and—rhetorically at least—the building of a nation without political divisions based on color.

Americans respond well to the fundamental aspirations of black South Africans. Only a small minority of white South Africans on the left edge of the political spectrum accepts their legitimacy, however, or even the possibility of attaining such goals. Even if they appreciate the necessity of meeting black political demands, white South Africans in power, and the vast bulk of their constituents, believe that there simply must be another way by which to satisfy African expectations. Hence the various pretzel-like twists and turns by which the National Party has attempted to introduce reform without in fact introducing the kinds of improvements which Africans (not whites) would welcome and recognize as acceptable.

In 1987 the ruling party advocated a National Statutory Council, a consultative body to which a minority of blacks would be elected by their fellows and a majority appointed by the state. This plan, discussable a decade ago, is derided even by so called moderate African leaders like Chief M. Gatsha Buthelezi of KwaZulu. If it ever meets, the Council will be composed of urban councillors, homeland leaders, and other Africans who owe their positions to white patronage. Likewise, new Regional Service Councils were supposed to be tertiary governmental bodies on which Africans could serve, representing their localities. But because President Botha gave authority in the councils to appointed white administrators, and in any event limited control of such institutions by blacks, they have not proven an arena in which to test the devolution of authority at the provincial or sub-provincial level. In 1986 and 1987, President Botha's government further prohibited the grant of full multiracial regional autonomy, as proposed by the Natal Indaba process.

The government espouses the protection of *group* rights; the ANC, Africans, and a handful of whites seek to affirm the primacy of *individual* rights. Both sides are in fact arguing about power and the distribution of resources. Whites seek a form of words to justify the continued exclusion of a vast majority from power; Africans merely want that entitlement which many other majorities have obtained since the brutal close of the eighteenth century.

South Africa's white government in recent years has ingeniously explored a variety of formulas by which Africans could be appeased and existing power relations more or less be confirmed. Or to put the same proposition in another, also candid, form, the government has sought to devise plans which would have the appearance of compromise but would continue to enshrine existing power differentials in an enduring manner. The government has wanted "change but no change." [5]

Recognizing the strength of whites and the limited ability of blacks to amass sizable countervailing power, the Reagan administration initially supported these crafty schemes of devolving some power onto Africans, but not in a fully national form, nor in such a way that a South African-wide authority could be exercised. Given the reality of existing differences of power, there must continue to be some (misplaced) sympathy for these proposals on the part of Americans. Yet such sympathy is and will continue to be inappropriate because those schemes which appeal to whites are immediately suspect to Africans, whatever their merit (which is little). All schemes suffer, moreover, from the serious flaw that they divide the country, and fail to deliver the geographical integrity which Africans have come to demand.

One celestial metaphor which still appeals to whites is that of a constellation of states, with the white sun and its peripheral black homelands and other asteroids orbiting. This is the outline of the confederation of states, too, which is a misnomer since whites actually seek to promote a federal system with a strong, white-dominated central government and a clutch of rural and urban black satrapies. The first category of "solution" assumes a set of white and black "governments," tied together for defense, foreign affairs, fiscal affairs, and so on. But matters close to the heart of whites—education, hospitals, and amenities—would remain in community hands (as they have in Namibia, despite the end of segregation and discrimination). Consociationalism, a second category of solution, was favored for a time, for it describes a complicated method of transferring community control on the Belgian model to a much larger and much more scrambled plural entity like South Africa. It was an ingenious way of keeping Africans from genuinely sharing power.

More recently, whites have been entranced by an adaptation of Swiss cantonalism. South Africa would be divided into 306 "cantons" along the lines of the existing magisterial districts. Most would have black or Coloured majorities, and, presumably, local governments dominated by persons of dark pigmentation. A few cantons would be the homes of whites. Individuals could move back and forth, but could only vote in their original residences. Whites would not be threatened, and education and health would remain local and hence communal concerns. But who would control the ample resources of the nation? Here this severely decentralized solution breaks down, and the old questions of power once again become prominent.

The cantonalism solution is premised on the efficacy of group autonomy as a cleavage- bridging device. It presupposes a confederal South Africa divided into a large number of small cantons with strong local governments and an excessively weak central government. The most recent proponents of this extreme answer to the South African dilemma assume that questions of power would be inconsequential since the cantons would have little power to share with the center. South Africa, as a modern industrial state, would slide into oblivion. But such a proposition conveniently ignores allocation of resources issues which are basic both to modern South Africa and to all nations, especially those bitterly divided by color, history, and conflict.[6]

A third kind of answer to the South African dilemma is partition, but its defects are those ultimately of cantonalism and of any other shortcut which ignores a negotiated resolution of the fundamental problems of control over flowing water, fertile land, harbors, airports, railways, minerals, and the other natural and man-made riches of South Africa. Maasdorp demonstrates that partition is a practical impossibility, and premature. Partitions almost always occur as a result of civil war, and not before.[7]

There are innumerable other ways in which majoritarian power can be diluted. Over-weighted voting proportions for minorities or the linking of the franchise to educational or occupational qualifications (as in the old South) could result in shared power without the submerging of a minority. So would minority vetoes, guaranteed blocs of white-held seats (as in Zimbabwe from 1980 to 1987), and bills of rights without explicit methods of enforcement.[8]

These and other ingenious expedients remain essentially expedients. Given the vast present differences in power between the ruled and the rulers. Africans remain too weak to impose their demands and must keep protesting and fighting. Whites still hold too much power, augmented by police state methods and the selective use of terror, for a shift from the posture of "change but no change" to that of power sharing to be expected. Yet many on both sides want to negotiate and many presume sooner or later that Africans and whites will have no other recourse but to talk about their mutual future. The inescapable conclusion to be drawn from these considerations is that if the country is not to be destroyed, there is no alternative to the forging of a new political system in which all South Africans can participate. What is more, such a system cannot be unilaterally imposed by the present regime "through the barrel of the gun"; it will have to be established through the give and take of negotiations.[9] Outspoken African leaders within and without South Africa call (as they have since 1912) for negotiations. The United States has urged and implored President Botha and his government to bargain with authentic African representatives. Even compromised figures like Chief Buthelezi have demanded similar discussions. But he and more militant Africans, as well as many influential American policymakers, recognize that there can be no bargaining until Nelson Mandela and other ANC leaders are released from prison and the ANC unbanned.

How to move white South Africa to the bargaining table with Africans is the challenge of the late 1980s and early 1990s. Neither military victory nor a collapse of will can confidently be predicted for either whites or blacks. Since the reform initiatives of the National Party have not succeeded and, because of their origin, by definition cannot succeed in satisfying African aspirations, only the kinds of thoroughly open negotiations for which the ANC calls, and President Botha rejects, promise to end the current and continuing violence or hold any realistic hope of creating conditions for the kind of enduring peace and political cooperation that could lead to non-violent change. However, Berger and Godsell argue correctly that it is "too early" for negotiations—that both sides wrongly think that they can "win." [10]

The imposition of economic sanctions has done little to alter South Africa's internal political equation. Although passage of the Anti-Apartheid Act in 1986 prohibited the continued export of iron and steel, citrus and deciduous fruit, diamonds, and coal from South Africa to the United States, and the United States subsequently interpreted a provision of the same act to bar the reprocessing of South African uranium in the United States, through mid-1988, the discernible political impact of the act was difficult to quantify. Economically, all exports to the United States fell by 45 percent, and of the banned products, by 100 percent (a drop of about $300 billion). African jobs must have been lost in at least modest numbers, yet of the products prohibited only coal mining employs substantial African workers, and the United States was never a major buyer of that fuel from South Africa. Indeed, since the Congressional bans were erected against commodities of comparative insignificance in United States-South African trade, it is understandable that the economic result could hardly have proven decisive. Even in those export areas where South Africa's other major trading partners have decreed prohibitions similar to those promulgated in Washington, South Africa has not begun to hurt substantially. Evasion has been apparent, too. France has been buying coal from "Australia" which appears to be South African. Swaziland has been exporting far more fruit than customary. South African sales to Israel have often resulted in new exports of raw materials to third countries.

Ultimately, the most significant economic flaw in the sanctions model is its target. Gold supplies at least 60 and often possibly as much as 70 percent of South Africa's annual foreign exchange earnings. Coal provides another 10 percent, manganese, chromium, platinum, and other minerals a further 10 percent, diamonds 5 percent, and iron and steel and fruit together no more than another 5 percent. Thus prohibiting the import of goods other than gold "punishes" South Africa insignificantly. Gold mining also employs far more African workers (500,000, of whom half are South African) than any other industry.

American sanctions presumably were devised to provide both an economic stick and an equally strong carrot with which to motivate the stubborn mule of South African politics. Congress reasonably assumed that President Botha and his ruling oligarchy would be unwilling to let South Africa suffer economically. Sanctions would be the tough alternative to apartheid which would compel the president and his men to negotiate. But this was another misreading of the realities of South African trade patterns. It failed to appreciate South Africa's limited reliance on commodities other than gold.

It was an even greater misreading of the political realities of that country. Not only are Botha and his cabinet now fearful of the right-wing Conservative Party, but he and they also believe that sanctions can be evaded and, if not, that the world will continue to want South African gold and many other commodities and manufactured goods. If necessary, Botha and company think that South Africa can tighten its collective economic belt. It is not that United States' sanctions have not hit hard enough; it is that there is every evidence that unilateral sanctions alone cannot compel the ruling National Party to alter its political course profoundly. Even multilateral sanctions might not. A total trade boycott could have a more telling impact, but how to impose such a broad-ranging international boycott is the formidable political problem of the age. Then, too, what about sales of gold?

Divestment is the flip side of sanctions. Many influential Americans have long pointed to the potential for political leverage which would flow from the withdrawal of United States companies from South Africa. Multinational firms began selectively selling their businesses in the early 1980s. In 1985 and 1986 the trickle of disaffection became a flood of dismay. Between mid-1985 and mid-1988, 130 United States companies left South Africa. By mid-1988 only 148 American-owned companies remained. Those who fled did so because of South Africa's worsening business climate (profits were smaller than before for several years in a row), continued violence in the townships, and increased pressure at home. Many firms sold their assets and goodwill locally or to European or Japanese multinational mining, manufacturing, or service corporations. A few set up local trusts for their employees and managers. A handful arranged to sell their businesses at bargain prices to white managers and, sometimes, jointly to managers and employees. One or two virtually walked away from their South African markets. Overall, total employment by American-owned firms fell from 85,000 to 45,000. United States' direct investment in South Africa slumped from $2.3 billion in 1982 to $1.3 billion in 1987. Trade between the United States and South Africa fell in 1986-87 from $3 billion annually to $2.3 billion, behind Japan at $3.1 billion. Even so, nearly all of the products of the disinvesting American companies remain freely available in South Africa, either as a result of licensing to new foreign- or locally-owned entities or as a result of third-party offshore exchanges.[11]

Disinvestment has reduced *direct* trade between the United States and South Africa, but so has the general lack of commercial confidence in South Africa. Disinvestment has primarily resulted in the inexpensive transfer of United States' assets to South African whites and foreigners. Africans have lost employment opportunities. Disinvestment has not deprived South Africa, nor even the South African war effort, of valuable goods. Nor has it even driven up the cost to South Africa of any class of commodity. In many respects those goods are being produced within South Africa more cheaply than they were before the wave of disinvestment. It is callous to suggest that South Africa may have benefited from this first major wave of American and a few minor eddies of European disinvestment. But there is little evidence that white South Africa has suffered or that disinvestment has encouraged Botha and the National Party to think more conscientiously about meaningful reform. Indeed, a weakening dollar strengthened gold prices at the same time as sanctions were intended to put added pressure on South Africa. Arguably, macroeconomic trends were more important, and more favorable to South Africa, than sanctions were economically negative.

Gold is the hinge of a case for economic leverage. Because South Africa since 1896 has relied so extensively on demand for the shiny metal to overcome political errors, even calamities, it is reasonable to assume that policy makers should hardly expect easily to alter South African white political behavior and assumptions unless and until the world-wide value of gold, or the saleability of South African refined gold, can be undermined. But even to contemplate such an unthinkable option distresses most conventionally-tutored policy experts. Nevertheless, it is *theoretically* possible to drive the world price of gold down substantially by selling United States (and, better yet, International Monetary Fund) reserves even without the cooperation of France or the Soviet Union. There are substantial direct benefits to the United States (and the Third World) which could flow from such an exercise. And

South African foreign earnings would plummet. The key question is the obvious one: How far would the price of gold have to fall, and for how long, for South Africa's leadership to do the currently unlikely: release Mandela, unban the ANC, and negotiate its future? But the very fact that the unthinkable proposition is the big imponderable lever—the device around which revolves the very question of whether and what kind of economic pressure will compel white South Africa to "see reason" in United States terms—should imply that no instrument other than gold can be sufficient (although some may be necessary) to disrupt the force of white dominance. Since depressing the world price of gold will almost certainly not be entertained by policy makers for psychological and quasi-monetary reasons (for fear of destabilizing world fiscal arrangements), other less direct alternatives will have to be sought.

South Africa is no Grenada. Invasion is also no panacea for decision-makers. This is less a fact because South Africa's military is strong and its ruling minority determined than it is a result of immense distance and a significant Soviet interest in the outcome of the struggle there. Moreover, from a policy viewpoint, most American decision-makers would view it as hazardous to unleash dammed up forces without a firm belief in their ultimate employment for good locally and globally. An American political consensus was much easier to achieve over Grenada than could conceivably be obtained over the far less surgically sure complexity of South Africa.

Over South Africa there is continuing dissensus about the nature of the real interests of the United States. A body of opinion claims that South Africa is strategically critical to the industrial health of the United States. South Africa holds 50 to 60 percent of the free world's reserves of manganese and platinum. It has abundant supplies of chrome and vanadium. The United States purchases 95 percent of its manganese, 90 percent of its platinum, 80 percent of its chromium, and 40 percent of its vanadium from South Africa. In the making and hardening of steel, manganese, chromium, and vanadium are essential. Platinum prevents automobiles from polluting the atmosphere and has valuable applications as a catalyst when petroleum is refined. Why, asks a lobby of influence, antagonize such an important (white) supplier of minerals? Moreover, what if South Africa, and thus the sea route for oil from the Persian Gulf around the Cape of Good Hope to Europe (and in an insignificant way to the United States), fell into the hands of the Soviet Union or its clients? Would the rule of South Africa by blacks mean the disruption of American steelmaking or of the free flow of oil and other goods to and around the Cape? For these and other reasons, why should the United States assist any acceleration of instability in South Africa? Why not leave well enough alone, and anti-communist whites in power?

There are good answers. During the last decade the steel industry of the United States has forcibly slimmed. American mills demand far less manganese and other minerals. Modern methods use fewer tons of South African metals than before. Resource recovery is possible, if still practised more in Japan than in the United States. There are existing free world sources of vanadium in quantity. Platinum is not essential for *strategic* purposes. Chromium is available from Zimbabwe and other suppliers. All, and manganese, exist in quantity under the—as yet—unexploited soils of black Africa. If shortages occur, prices will rise, and mining will begin. Reducing dependence upon South Africa in this way would take time. But price is the decisive variable. If South African minerals became unavailable the United States would purchase supplies—at a stiff price—from the Soviet Union. More significantly, how, other than selling minerals, would a hostile black-run South Africa employ its valuable underground resources? They would surely find their way into international commerce.[12]

Loss of the Cape sea route is unlikely to occur for the same reasons. It is almost inconceivable that a black South African nation would risk hostilities with Europe and the United States by attacking tankers traveling 40 miles or more offshore in international waters. Would a black South Africa be that strong? What would it gain? There is a strong argument, too, against the Soviet Union employing its presumed South African satellite in this way. If a war were wished, the Soviet Union would wisely harass shipping in the Persian gulf, so much closer as it is to air bases in the motherland. Anyway, given what we know about the black struggle for freedom in both Africa and South Africa, and its predelictions so far, it is as likely as not that a Soviet-oriented Marxist state would result from full political participation. Zimbabwe represents a very different outcome than that predicted by those whites who feared the worst.

The interest of the United States in the future of South Africa rests on far stronger foundations. American policymakers have long recognized the volatility of southern Africa, the consequent desirability of avoiding the kinds of local conflicts into which the Soviet Union would inject itself on the side of an oppressed majority, and the possibility that such a regional war could somehow trigger a global conflagration. Avoiding regional war is and should be the predominant aim of United States foreign policy in southern Africa. Additionally, most noticeably during the Carter administration, the United States cared that the brothers and sisters of color of 12 percent of the American population should finally receive just treatment and their rightful share of power. Given the possibility, however problematical, that a South African color conflict could infect the United States, the Carter administration wanted to avoid anything resembling an all-out race war in South Africa.

Both of these concerns are worthy and overriding ones for American policy in the 1990s. There are no sound moral or political arguments against continued United States activity in search of a solution to the dilemmas of a divided South Africa.

South Africa is no longer the monolithic, closed-minded, ruthlessly apartheid society it tried to be in the 1960s. The laws and mores of the total society have altered out of all white recognition since the grim days of Prime Minister Hendrik Verwoerd (1958-1966). But the majority is still relentlessly disenfranchised, aware as never before of its ultimate powerlessness without the vote, and determined in a vigorous and new manner to reclaim all that is the right of a large, underprivileged population. Whites are no longer secure. Nor can they be. Hence the political stalemate which becomes more fixed the more vociferous Africans become. Short of a reversal of the present balance of power, the relevance of African numbers serves to drive whites (as exemplified by results of the recent election) away from compromise. It paralyzes their leaders, especially in the face of potential white political revolts and, conceivably, military antagonisms.

As a consequence of the still unequal forces arrayed within South Africa, there can be no easy or sure ways to persuade its rulers that the West or the United States knows what is best for them or for the future of their country. There are no magical mechanisms by which to compel South Africa's government to drop "change but no change" for meaningful reform, power sharing, full political participation, and the possible dangers of honest and thoroughgoing negotiations. What is obvious, however, is that the policies of the Reagan administration toward South Africa have failed to produce positive results. They failed to bring about reforms desired by Washington, failed to increase the level of African political participation, and have failed to instill any confidence that President Botha's regime really intends to share power with blacks. Constructive engagement also failed in one of its other main aims—the freeing of Namibia from South African control.

The Carter administration, by turns sanctimonious and calculating, unsuccessfully tried to bully the government of South Africa. Over Namibia it achieved an unexpected and major breakthrough—South Africa's agreement to negotiate a satisfactory withdrawal from its lapsed mandate. The ensuring negotiations came to the brink of success on several occasions, but it was never in white South Africa's clear self interest to discard what was, during those brief years, its principal psychological and strategic bargaining chip.[13] Over South Africa's own political development, the Carter administration also succeeded in persuading an admittedly scandal-ridden and thus weakened regime to seek a variety of compromises in the wake of the Soweto uprising and the brutal killing of prominent blacks.

The Reagan administration misunderstood what the Carter administration had achieved and how it had done so. The Reaganites also assumed, since white South Africans had resented being bullied, that the obverse of forceful badgering would work wonders. More flies could be caught with honey than with a swatter. Indeed, white South Africans welcomed constructive engagement, the name given to the resultant policy enunciated by Assistant Secretary of State Chester Crocker.[14] But as much as they liked the honey and the attention, they found endless reasons why they could respond only ineffectually over Namibia and, later, hardly at all over South Africa. Moreover, under the umbrella of constructive engagement, South Africa managed to thrust its military tentacles deep into surrounding black Africa.

The displacement and removal of Africans within South Africa never ceased. Ultimately some discriminatory legislation was weakened and rescinded, but only after the townships of the country had erupted into a violence that surpassed anything yet glimpsed in South Africa. By the time that the black urban lowrise slums had thus become inflamed, and Botha had declared an emergency, constructive engagement had altered governmental behavior little for the better, and forfeited goodwill for the United States among politicized Africans.

In the aftermath of constructive engagement, United States policy toward South Africa must primarily be directed toward regaining its lost leverage and, simultaneously, formulating a winning approach regarding that country's internal crisis. The ultimate question must be how best—and with least bloodshed—to move white and black South Africans to the conference table. Economic methods as heretofore devised are insufficiently powerful. A compelling drop in the world price of white South Africa's golden gift might be enough. So could a combination of as yet untried quasi-economic sanctions like the withdrawal of postal and telecommunication contacts, the cutting off of air travel, and the loss of tourist entry rights to the nations of the West. But the employment of even more creative forms of pressure will impact differentially on classes and language categories of whites. It need not threaten the ability of the National Party to govern or the military to dominate. A series of methods less dramatic and punitive than economic and quasi-economic ones must be sought if white *and* black, Afrikaners and ANC, are to be brought effectively to a bargaining table.

Most conflicts end in negotiations of some kind. In South Africa the object of American foreign policy is the laudable but trying one of moving both sides to negotiate before, rather than after there is a full-scale local civil war. Already, in the post-constructive engagement era, the United States has begun talking with the ANC and thus giving diplomatic credibility both to the ANC and to the United States.[15] By at last conversing with both sides, Washington may soon be able to provide the brokering services it was too partial-appearing to offer before 1987. A new president of the United States ought to want to use the immense power and prestige of his office personally to bring Africans and whites together, possibly in a modern version of a Camp David summit. Before he or she will wish to do so, however, the ingredients of an agreement will be required. Playing a successful brokering rôle will thus depend upon speaking publicly to both sides. Carrying a big stick of some kind will be essential. So will the ability to speak well and softly to white South Africans without fawning, and without limiting the American freedom to speak and act. Pleasing the desire of Congress for dramatic and appealing action at the same time is almost impossible, but necessary.

These are goals of a new policy. What could conceivably make or break the reception of initiatives by the United States is the depth of white ambitions in South Africa. Since white South Africans now look to the United States as their most meaningful long term commercial partner, and since continued minority suzerainty in South Africa is in the medium term desirable only if it means recognizable prosperity for whites, the United States would gain leverage if it reversed its present policy of punitive sanctions and attempted to develop appropriate incentives to appeal to whites. Congress will probably never approve such an innovation, but if the United States renewed South Africa's sugar quota, promised growing markets for coal and steel, resumed the processing of uranium, offered to purchase more fruit, and attempted to maximize South African growth in exchange for serious and open negotiations between whites and blacks, would white South Africans be tempted by an American willingness to organize a bargaining conference? Possibly white South Africans and, especially, their leaders, are insufficiently insecure to be enticed by such economic and political bait. But it is only by thinking the unthinkable that a solution can be advanced for South Africa.

A successful new American policy for South Africa will hardly be new. It will consist of the elements of policy that have proven partially successful in the past: a clear recognition of the self-interest of the United States; an open and determined appreciation of white fears and power equally with black aspirations and numerical superiority. An openness to the arguments of both. A refusal to be captured by the appeals, political, economic, or moral of either. A suspicion of easy, oversimplified solutions and of economic over-determination.

A workable policy will find some new method of appealing to white South African self-interest and of helping black South Africans bridge the chasm between black ambitions and white insecurity. The new president will take a well articulated position against continued intransigence. The United States will also need to provide economic and political incentives for creative constitutional planning by authentic representatives of all South Africans. A mixture of tangible threats and persuasive rewards (greater market shares as well as funds for civil service training) will be necessary. Given a recognition of the limits of United States power, still there ought to be a commitment of prestige and energy on the part of the new American chief executive.

In the region the policy options are much clearer. A strengthened Zimbabwe, Mozambique, Zambia, and Botswana (and also Swaziland and Lesotho) reduces South African economic and military leverage in southern Africa. Substantial economic assistance to all four (or six) countries is critical, particularly in response to the rebuilding and infrastructural needs of war-torn Mozambique. There is much to be done. Those who oppose aid to Mozambique must be reminded of its newly pro-Western status.

Generous assistance regionally will directly further American aims in South Africa. Thus it is also in the self-interest of the United States to recognize Angola, whether or not the Cubans remain. Since the solution to the Namibian problem lies in South Africa and not in Angola, the United States can best hasten Namibian freedom by recognizing the legitimate existence of Angola. Washington also needs to back away from UNITA. A more even-handed policy in Angola will distance the United States from South Africa and also allow Washington to play honest broker within the power struggle of that country. The quickest and surest way to undercut the Soviet relationship with Angola's government, and thus the soundest method of avoiding escalated regional conflict, is a refusal to take sides within Angola itself. The president of the United States needs to provide such clear direction, and be determined to secure the peaceful development of southern Africa and South Africa.

Notes

1. See the helpful arguments in Peter L. Berger and Bobby Godsell, "Fantasies about South Africa," *Commentary,* LXXXIV (1987), 36.

2. See Robert I. Rotberg, "South Africa in its Region—Hegemony and Vulnerability," and "Decision Making and the Military in South Africa," both in Robert I. Rotberg et al, *South Africa and Its Neighbors: Regional Security and Self-Interest* (Lexington, 1985), 1-11, 13-26.

3. Robert I. Rotberg, "Going Beyond Sanctions," *The World and I* (July, 1987), 26.

4. But see the bizarre formulation in Berger and Godsell, "Fantasies," 39.

5. Robert I. Rotberg, "Seven Scenarios for South Africa," *CSIS Africa Notes* (29 October 1985).

6. Leon Louw and Frances Kendall, *South Africa: The Solution* (Bisho, 1986), 129-156: The best published critique of cantonalism is a review of the Louw and Kendall book by Arend Lijphart, the leading modern analyst of consociationalism as it applies to South Africa, in *Publius: The Journal of Federalism,* XVII(1987), 222-224.

7. Gavin Maasdrop, "Forms of Partition," in Robert I. Rotberg and John Barratt (eds.), *Conflict and Compromise in South Africa* (Lexington, 1980), 107-146.

8. Walter Dean Burnham, "Milestones on the Road to Democracy: Electoral Regimes and Their Relevance to South Africa," in ibid., 77-105.

9. Berger and Godsell, "Fantasies," 37.

10. *Ibid.*

11. See the revealing interview, Anthony H. Bloom, "Managing Against Apartheid," *Harvard Business Review* (Nov.-Dec., 1987), 49-56. See also Rotberg, "Sanctions," 28.

12. Michael Shafer, "Mineral Myths," *Foreign Policy,* 47 (Summer, 1982), 154-171; Robert I. Rotberg, *Suffer the Future: Policy Choices in Southern Africa* (Cambridge, Mass., 1980), 100-115; Robert I. Rotberg, "South Africa Under Botha: How Deep a Change?," *Foreign Policy,* 38 (Spring, 1980), 141.

13. Robert I. Rotberg, "Political and Economic Realities in a Time of Settlement," in Rotberg (ed.), *Namibia: Political and Economic Prospects* (Lexington, 1983), 29.

14. Chester A. Crocker, "South Africa: Strategy for Change," *Foreign Affairs,* LIX (1980), 346-351.

15. Two speeches in September 1987, "The Democratic Future of South Africa" by Secretary of State George C. Shultz, in New York, to the Business Council for International Understanding, and "A Democratic Future: The Challenge for South Africans," by Chester Crocker, to a City University of New York conference on "South Africa in Transition," in White Plains, signify and articulate post-constructive engagement policies.

11: Armed Conflict and Competition in Africa

BY KENNETH W. GRUNDY

Militarization is a symptom of a larger malaise in modern Africa. It is one manifest response to those nagging problems that African governments have faced since independence—scarce resources, poor economic performance, governmental weakness and ineptitude, wide and growing dissatisfaction and cynicism, vulnerability to external pressure and manipulation, and domestic instability. This, in turn, leads to wider dissent, greater instability, and more determined use of repressive force. It is not an automatic response. Some African governments have sought other solutions to their perceived problems. But militarization is a common fallback for governments in trouble.

Militarization, expressed as a form of military buildup, can be operationalized by several indicators—armed force levels, military expenditures, arms imports, arms production, wars, and military regimes. We cannot deal with all these indicators here, but a few will serve to illustrate the general point.[1]

The pattern of growth in force levels is marked throughout the continent. Growth from 2.1 armed men per thousand in 1968 to 2.7 in 1976 to 3.1 per thousand in 1984 is significant. This is especially remarkable given the rapid growth in population. It represents a grand total of 1,562,000 troops armed to defend national governments. This does not include rebel and secessionist movements and other revolutionary and irregular forces.[2]

There has, likewise, been a growth in military expenditures, but that is less pronounced, less even, and more heavily concentrated in a few countries, most notably Libya, Lesotho, Ethiopia, Mozambique, and Somalia, all states under immediate military threat. Indeed, if one looked at expenditures in constant prices, African military expenditures actually started to dip. Using constant 1983 prices and exchange rates, in 1975 African states (excluding Egypt) spent $12.5 billion on armed forces. That climbed to $16.7 billion in 1979 and fell to $15.7 billion in 1984. Even so, this represents but 1.8 percent of the world's total military expenditures.[3]

With growing force levels and budgets for the security forces (even in the face of shrinking state economies), it follows that the armed forces frequently expect a more central role in policy making. And the military perspective is often to coerce and demand rather than to negotiate, compromise, and cooperate. As Joseph Schumpeter pointed out in his classic on imperialism, once a military machine, whose job it is to make war and to control people, is entrenched, it is only a matter of time until war gets made.[4]

Weak governments may be propelled toward militarization and militaristic regimes and policies, especially domestically. In the end, the armed forces come to be seen as the government's most responsible policy instrument. In that sense, then, militarization as a process becomes self-fulfilling, contributing to a generalized view that disputes and conflicts of interest can best be addressed by preparing for and using coercion. Falk memorably puts it: "Africa is a playing field without a referee." Military might serves as a surrogate referee to assure that decisions go your way.[5]

Elements of instability frequently flare up into small-scale wars—wars of secession, civil wars, and localized struggles to re-order domestic power distributions. But the process does not end there. The territorial integrity of many African states is suspect. Their boundaries are porous. Segments of their populations are less than loyal to the central government and may, indeed, identify with peoples and governments in neighboring states. In addition, parties to disputes, particularly those not doing well with the given power equation, often seek assistance—locally to broaden the base of coalition, regionally to gain allies and support, and, internationally, to enlist the aid of one or more of the great powers.

Even in the face of the arguments advanced in the preceding paragraphs, it is noteworthy that Africa departs somewhat from this overall global pattern. Simple models and simplistic explanations seldom suffice for African realities. Except for southern Africa, the Horn, and North Africa, and areas touched by North African hegemonies (significant portions of the continent, to be sure), there have been rather low levels of inter-state violence in Africa. Considering the number of states, the degree of ethnic diversity, the fact that Africa's international boundaries were imposed on those states, and the general lack of economic viability for its relatively small state units, Africa has not been deeply troubled by large-scale international warfare.[6]

Nonetheless, there is a persistent inducement to widen intra-state conflicts into inter-state conflicts and inter-state conflicts into conflicts that involve militarily stronger, often global, actors. However one defines intervention, it usually results from a convergence of factors. Some are rooted in the nation where intervention takes place. Some are located in the intervening nation. And some result from the nature of the international system itself. In Africa, opportunities for intervention always exist, or so it seems.[7]

There is a kind of symmetry and natural internationalization built into essentially localized issues or disputes, especially in an era of superpower confrontation and tension. It takes considerable self-restraint for a party losing under the existing arrangements not to seek to redress a negative local balance by widening the parties to, and theater of, warfare. Yet restraint sometimes occurs. In the era of proxy warfare, Cold War actors might be tempted to engage a low cost, low risk proxy to destabilize a presumably hostile government. Similarly, outside parties, which normally might be keen to destabilize or restabilize a potentially explosive situation, may nevertheless decide that the potential gains are not great enough to offset the risks or costs of their involvement. There was a time when Americans referred to a "Vietnam reflex," when the United States, fearful of repeating its costly experience in Southeast Asia, was reluctant to be drawn into widening commitments and ugly wars with ill-defined aims. Might the Soviet Union ever develop an "Afghan reflex"? By definition, closed polities are less sensitive to societal opinion than open ones. But social pressures operate not only as restraints on interventions; they might also operate as stimuli to intervention. Still, the powers may, instead, seek other means to influence the outcome. Or they may avoid direct commitment. Or they may actually seek to find ways to resolve the dispute.

Nonetheless, there is an integral link between the whole process of small and larger wars, and between the process of the resolution of disputes by the use of force. This essay will explore some of those linkages.

1. Force Levels and Budgets

Earlier it was mentioned that there has been a steady rise in armed force levels throughout Africa—in absolute terms as well as in terms of forces per capita. To be sure, not all armed forces have grown either absolutely or at the same rates. Some, such as Nigeria, have been reduced from a high of 320,000 members in 1971 to around 144,000 in 1984. Expressed differently, this is a fall from 5.6 troops per 1,000 people to 1.4 per 1,000 in 1984. Clearly, this reduction is related to the demobilization after the Biafran war for independence. Zaire, likewise, has fallen from 65,000 in 1973 to 23,000 in 1979, a modest decline, but in per capita terms noteworthy. It rose to 60,000 in 1984. Zimbabwe's force levels were reduced from 90,000 in 1980 to 46,000 in 1984. We might have expected to see similar falloffs in military preparedness in Angola and Mozambique had those civil wars been terminated at independence. But the conscious destabilization by South Africa, the economic difficulties, and the assistance Pretoria and other countries supply to proxy forces and dissident challenges to central government regimes in these states provide compelling reasons for maintaining high mobilization.[8]

It should be pointed out that Africa is one of the least mobilized continents. In 1977, for example, where African governments had an average 3.2 troops per 1,000 people, East Asia had 5.3, Europe 12.3 (Warsaw Pact countries were at 15.3), the Middle East had 12.8, and North America had 8.8. Only South Asia had a lower ratio, 2.6 per 1,000. In 1984, Africa (at 3.1 per 1,000) was lower than all regions except South Asia (2.2). The Middle East was up to 16.9, higher than any other region.[9]

Although all African states have not participated in this pattern of military enlargement, those currently engaged in military operations or in areas of high tension have contributed to a pattern of overall growth. Considering that this growth occurred at the time when Africa's population was booming from an annual average growth rate of 2.4 percent in the 1960s from a rate of 3.2 percent today, the absolute process of militarization in some regions of the continent is stunning.[10]

To illustrate the current uneven pattern, in 1984 15 states maintained forces with over five soldiers per 1,000 population. They are: Libya (24.8), Guinea-Bissau (13.1), South Africa (12.3), Mauritania (12.3), Egypt (9.8), Equatorial Guinea (8.8), Congo (8.6), Algeria (7.9). Gabon (7.3), Angola (7.0), Morocco (6.6), Somalia (5.8), Tunisia (5.4), Zimbabwe (5.4), and Guinea (5.3). The anomalies of Gabon, Guinea, Guinea-Bissau, Equatorial Guinea, and Congo, should be noted. All but Guinea are countries with very small populations, and thereby capable of high troop to population ratios with relatively small forces. Higher troop densities tend to cluster in three areas—North Africa (8.8/1,000), the Horn (7.5), and southern Africa. These are admittedly low ratios given the degrees of instability and regime vulnerability, and actual violence, but they clearly reflect the current and immediate past unrest.[11]

Similar patterns of concentration are apparent when one looks at military expenditures. Twenty-one states spend more than ten percent of their central government expenditures on defense. On the basis of recent data provided by the Arms Control and Disarmament Agency, the highest percentages are Libya (40 percent), Mozambique (29.1 percent in 1982) Lesotho (28.5 percent), Somalia (27.5 percent), Ethiopia (25.1 percent), Egypt (25 percent), Angola (25 percent in 1983), and Chad (22 percent). Supplementary evidence suggests that some or all of these percentages may be greatly understated.[12]

Other than the fact that some North African states (especially Algeria and Libya) have high petroleum revenues which tend to reduce the extent to which high military expenditures would otherwise dominate the budget, we still see high regional clusterings of states in which military expenditures dominate state expenditures. The Horn, North Africa, and southern Africa still stand out. (Note Angola and Mozambique, both fighting indigenous movements and trying to defend against external penetrations.) But among a few West African states (Mauritania, Burkino Faso, and Chad) high military expenditures merit comment. Chad has been a target of Libyan interventions and internal violent factional politics for years. Mauritania and Morocco have territorial claims to the Western Sahara. Together they administered the former Spanish colony until Morocco laid claim to all of the Western Sahara and found itself locked into a bitter war with Polisario, an organization of indigenous

Saharawis backed by Algeria. These two hot spots, Chad and Western Sahara, result from the expansionist policies of Libya and Morocco. They fall into the North African fault zones, although spatially they may be regarded as West African.

It would appear from a cursory look at a map that a form of spatial diffusion explains the patterns of military preparedness in Africa. An issue arises, say a territorial dispute between Ethiopia and Somalia over the Ogaden region of Ethiopia. The two countries prepare to fight over it. Eritrean secessionists see an opportunity to achieve independence, greater autonomy, or more political leverage in Ethiopian politics. The Sudan identifies with the Muslim Eritreans. Kenya, fearful of Somali irredentism, makes overtures to Ethiopia. As the dispute widens territorially, the superpowers get involved. The United States had long been identified with Ethiopia. After the overthrow of the Selassie regime by leftist soldiers, the superpower roles are reversed. In the case of the Soviet Union, the levels of military assistance to Ethiopia are greatly expanded. The Sudan itself is fighting a secessionist movement in its south. Ethiopia sees advantage in assisting the rebels. These conflicts are also related to fighting in Uganda and Chad, and so it goes. It is, in a way, a contagion, not easily contained. But there are limits or bounds to the dispute. Boundaries or limits exist in terms of the capacities of the central contestants and of their superpower sponsors to sustain military operations and project power.[13]

Similar scenarios can be sketched in southern Africa and in Western Sahara. Contagious diffusion of warfare spreads from state to state by conscious policy and by proximate spillover. Borders in Africa are permeable and people, refugees, and fighters easily move from country to country. Thus proximity, which itself means shared social and cultural characteristics and problems, contributes to the spread of war. Seldom, however, do the superpowers foresee all of the potential ramifications of their actions before they become engaged.

Insofar as international politics in Africa conforms to a Kautilyan pattern, there is a built-in capacity for widening unrest. The Kautilyan concept of a Circle of States posits a checker-board model of relationships in an unadulterated power political structure. Ideology matters very little. A friend of my friend is my friend—an enemy of my friend is my enemy, and so forth. The result is, with some exceptions, a "locational determinism," a regular alternation of friends and enemies, a checker-board of relationships across the continent. Because of the ethnic overlaps, the territorial claims and counter-claims, neighboring states tend, in this model, to be at loggerheads.[14]

II. Arms Transfers

Of course, this is far too simple. Ideology does matter—especially when great powers are involved and when the issue, as in southern Africa, is either independence, racism, or majority rule. Yet even here there is the potential for choosing allies on the basis of whom one's opponents assist. If the USSR supports Angola, then the United States must be hostile to the Angolan government. If the USSR is cozy with Addis Ababa, the United States may feel obligated to support Ethiopia's opponents. If Soviet military assistance is used by Libya, then Libya's targets (Egypt, Chad, the Sudan) become candidates for American assistance.

In recent years, African arms purchases have tailed off. In that respect, African states followed the overall pattern of constriction in the Third World arms market globally. Generally, arms purchases in sub-Saharan Africa were low until around 1974. In 1977 they took a large leap, nearly 13 times greater than five years earlier. The peak was 1978 and since then there had been a decline. Elsewhere in the Third World the peak was 1982 with a constriction in purchases since. Generally this is attributed to a number of causes not strictly related to levels of tension and violence in the region. Adverse economic conditions (which hit black Africa before and more deeply than North Africa and elsewhere in the Third World, especially because other large purchasers still had significant oil revenues), mounting debt burdens, a "saturation" of military inventories, a need to "absorb" and learn to use effectively expensive, sophisticated weaponry, and—to some extent in North and South Africa—the development of domestic weapons industries, contributed to this fall off in purchases. Weapons purchases of more than $1 billion (1975 constant prices) per year lasted from 1978 to 1982 in North Africa and only from 1977 to 1978 in sub-Saharan Africa.[15]

Obviously the superpowers use military sales and assistance as instruments of their foreign policies, although it may not always be clear in the case of the United States that there is effective policy coordination. The powers want to further their political and economic interests and to prevent loss of influence in regions of perceived strategic importance. Yet Neuman has found that the superpowers have, by and large, been cautious and notably restrained in their resupply of their partners and proxies in order to avoid a too rapid escalation of local conflicts that might affect the superpowers adversely. Superpower commitments can be moderated in light of their global concerns and responsibilities and their desires to retain control over the quality if not the quantity of the arms trade.[16]

The sources of these weapons still are largely the industrialized West and the socialist bloc countries. But patterns are shifting. From 1973 to 1980, the USSR and the United States together filled 66 percent of all Third World orders. The four major European producers (France, the United Kingdom, Germany, and Italy) supplied 25 percent of the purchases. From 1981 to 1985, the United States-USSR share had fallen to 58.6 percent and the European suppliers added up to 27.6 percent. More recent figures will reflect further reductions in the United States and USSR shares, and a growth in European sales. Second tier producers, especially from the Third World itself, are capturing larger market shares. Today's arms market is very competitive, a buyer's market in which sellers are offering long-term credit, often at concessionary interest rates, and often with the connivance of the manufacturers' governments.

Looked at more precisely, we can see that the United States really had but a small share of the African arms market before 1980.

The purchasers of American arms tend to have other suppliers, too. Between 1966 and 1975 only 3 of 16 purchasers bought over 50 percent of their weapons from the United States. In 1976-80, of the 11 purchasers, only 2 bought over 50 percent from the United States. In the latest period, just 3 of 12 were in the 50 percent or above category. In contrast, the USSR had more purchasers (15, 22, and 19 in these 3 periods) and over half of the governments made over 50 percent of their purchases from the USSR. In fact, between 1976 and 1980, only 4 got less than 50 percent from the USSR. The potential for political leverage is apparent.[17]

While the process of militarization in the 1970s carried on apace, it became clear that force levels and military spending created significant gaps between the most and the least armed African states. In a continent which is the venue of several major wars and military confrontations, and of numerous minor conflicts, these imbalances have created a heightened sense of vulnerability. Moreover, external powers have intervened (usually after requests from particular governments), if not directly by supplying personnel, then by massive injections of military hardware and logistical and intelligence support.

France, Cuba, the Soviet Union, and some east European socialist states still maintain contingents of forces in Africa. South Africa, ideologically and

Table 1
Major Arms Suppliers to Africa, 1966-1985

Suppliers	Value	% Total	No. Recipients
1966-1975			
USSR	$1,086 million	34.5	15
France	741	23.5	24
U.S.	361	11.5	15
U.K.	219	7.0	11
W. Germany	109	3.5	16
1976-1980			
USSR	$11,300 million	52.6	22
France	2,400	11.2	21
W. Germany	1,400	6.5	17
Italy	1,200	5.6	12
U.S.	825	3.8	11
1981-1985			
USSR	$13,875 million	50.4	19
France	2,700	9.8	24
Italy	1,500	5.5	13
U.S.	1,350	4.9	12
Czechoslovakia	915	3.3	5
U.K.	890	3.2	13
W. Germany	880	3.2	10

Source: U.S. Arms Control and Disarmament Agency, *World Military Expenditures and Arms Transfers 1966-1975,* ACDA Publication 90 (Washington, D.C.: ACDA, December 1976), Table V, 77; *World Military Ex penditures and Arms Transfers 1971-1980,* ACDA Publication 115 (March 1983), Table III, 117; and *World Military Expenditures and Arms Transfers 1986,* ACDA Publication 127 (April, 1987), Table III, 143-44.

Note: *Data include all African countries except Egypt. Values are current dollar figures.*

politically if not geographically an outside power, is engaged beyond its borders, fighting in Namibia and elsewhere on the fringes of Pretoria's realm. The United States, less directly through aid and military assistance to governments and covert and open help to proxy forces, is entangled in African military affairs. In the early 1980s, Washington negotiated facilities for its rapid deployment forces with Egypt, Liberia, Kenya, Morocco, and Somalia.

To be sure, the increased military spending of the 1970s levelled off at the end of that decade and actually declined in the straitened economic circumstances of the early 1980s. Nonetheless, the continent is still a major zone of contention and potentially an explosive region of warfare. But the country-by-country and regional variations are significant.

The rising levels of preparedness and firepower are noteworthy. By the mid-1960s only one country, South Africa, had high-performance combat aircraft and missile systems. By the early 1980s, however, nearly every country had at least a token armored force. More than a third had new or nearly new jet combat aircraft and two-thirds were equipped with some kind of missile system. Still, material capabilities are uneven. Only six states—Algeria, Ethiopia, Libya, Morocco, Nigeria, and South Africa—possess an all-around conventional military capability and even among these the differences between, say, South Africa and Libya are considerable.[18]

Another 7 to 10 countries have a sub-regional military capability, that is, they can defend themselves and marginally project their power beyond their borders. The remaining countries have military establishments to symbolize their sovereignty and to protect the governments from low level civil unrest and threats to internal security. The rest is guesswork.

Particularly problematic is the ability of the social, economic, and bureaucratic fabric of society to sustain protracted and intensive military operations. In that regard, for some states, military preparedness may be but a veneer covering a less than solid substance.

III. Patterns of Warfare and External Involvement

What is remarkable about such wide disparities in military capability is that with some important exceptions, these governments have not used their military muscle to bully weaker neighbors or to unify separate state entities. The conquest state was a creature of another era in African history.

Certainly several governments with large military establishments have taken a direct political and military role in neighboring countries. At present only

Libya, South Africa, and Morocco deploy major troop contingents beyond their borders in territorial or hegemonial campaigns. Ethiopia, Somalia, Algeria, Tanzania, Zimbabwe, and Mauritania, and, earlier, Rhodesia and Zaire have fought beyond their borders. Assistance to factions in civil strife is a common form of intervention. The provision of sanctuary, diplomatic assistance, and training facilities and other aid to guerrilla forces and refugee movements is common. In other instances, foreign troops are used to bolster established governments.

Indeed, the supply of troops and military equipment by African governments to other friendly African governments is becoming a convenient foreign policy tool. Tanzania has made its forces available to back rebellion in Uganda and a standing government in Mozambique. Libya supplies high performance aircraft to the Sudan. Morocco assists Zaire to put down provincial unrest and foreign incursion. Zimbabwe pledges to assist Mozambique against South African-instigated banditry. Nigeria, Guinea, and Ghana earlier on assisted African states in need. Increasingly, African governments with regional and continental aspirations engage in active foreign policies and utilize their armed forces to implement those policies. Military assistance from one African state to another seems less bedevilled by ideological concepts, and certainly less by simplistic East-West notions. It offsets the need for outright military invasion, seizure of territory, the overthrow of governments, and direct destabilization of civil order. Another more benign form of military force projection is the supply of troops to United Nations and Organization of African Unity peacekeeping contingents.

As the military capabilities of African states have grown, so have armed conflicts between them become more frequent, more intense, and more conventional. The patterns of the 1960s were predicated on token shows of force or irregular, often guerrilla-type wars. Wars for independence and majority rule, and civil wars and secessionist wars aimed at already independent black governments, tended to be irregular and sporadic. They usually followed a pattern of protracted guerrilla warfare. Only the Biafran and Katangan wars of secession, the Somali-Ethiopian fighting, and, at its closing stages, the Algerian war of independence, assumed the proportions and character of conventional warfare.[19]

In the late 1970s, however, guerrilla struggle seemed to lose its appeal. Before Reagan, the United States was not a keen advocate of protracted guerrilla warfare. In the mid- and late-1970s, the basis of Soviet intervention shifted from support for guerrilla movements to the provision of military hardware and assistance to governments. Guerrillas still gained their support, but a new emphasis was established. Except for the on-going wars in Zimbabwe and Namibia, wars in Africa became marked by a scale, concentration of firepower, and destructiveness that demanded higher levels of preparedness, mobilization, more sophisticated weaponry, and a necessity to employ force openly. Thus Libya projected force throughout northern Africa, and the Ethiopian-Somalian war, the Tanzanian war in Uganda, the South African invasion of Angola in 1975-76, Angola's running war with UNITA, and South Africa's numerous cross-border strikes were well-planned, modern, high-performance operations, if on a small scale. Defense against these aggressions were also conventional. Even the Polisario war for independence showed hints of a relatively conventional undertaking.[20]

Interestingly, the campaigns by proxy forces (UNITA in Angola and MNR in Mozambique), the secessionist struggles in Eritrea and other parts of Ethiopia and southern Sudan, and the actions of Ndebele dissidents in Zimbabwe, have more of the improvisational character of guerrilla operations. The extensive use of tanks, armored vehicles, radio equipment, aircraft, and ordnance with high firepower, has changed the nature of warfare in Africa. In the process, it has inflated the importance of foreign intervention. Technologically-advanced materiel is what foreign states can supply efficiently.

Knowing this tendency and the demands for sophisticated weaponry, foreign powers try to exploit African conflicts for their own ends. Thus the war for greater autonomy in Eritrea, an ethnic, religious, and even economic struggle for social and political change, may begin to take on Cold War characteristics.

Although extensive external military intervention goes far back into African history, a modern watershed came in the five years between 1974 and 1979. During that spell the Portuguese colonial empire was ended, the liberation struggle in Zimbabwe gained its final momentum, the Haile Selassie regime fell in Ethiopia and the new Marxist regime there confronted Somalian arms in the Ogaden and Eritrean nationalism on the coast, and the post-independence instability in Mozambique and Angola spilled beyond their borders and also provided outsiders with opportunities to help or hinder the consolidation of national power. These contests led to further foreign involvement in the military affairs of the continent.

Most particularly, the socialist bloc got deeply drawn into Africa for the first time. Cuba provides troops in large numbers for Angola and Ethiopia. The USSR provides logistical support, advisors, and massive shipments of arms. Other eastern European countries also send military assistance. In that neither the Angolan nor the Ethiopian governments were able to stabilize themselves in power without protracted fighting, the socialist bloc probably found these theaters more costly than they at first planned. United States intelligence sources estimate that, in 1986 alone, Moscow sent $1 billion worth of arms to Angola, and in the last decade sent as much as $4 billion. The Soviet Union did demonstrate its undoubted capacity to project military power far beyond the confines of the socialist bloc and the traditional venues of communist power. Amidst problems with governments and their enemies, the socialist bloc has not withdrawn its support.[21]

What is more, the continuing socialist presence in Africa has provided cause for American involvement in support of neighboring governments and dissident parties opposed to Addis and Luanda, if not Maputo. The French, as well, have responded to Chad's several requests for assistance against Libya. Yet France has been wary of getting too involved. It wants to keep Chadians on the front lines and to avoid alienating other French-speaking African governments by providing Colonel Mu'ammar al-Qaddafi with evidence to support his charges of neocolonialism.

While Americans (particularly those in Washington today) are inclined to focus on the Soviet military presence in southern Africa as the dominant feature of foreign intervention, and there is no question that 35,000 Cuban, 2,000 Soviet, and 2,500 East German military personnel have a profound effect on the security of the Luanda government and the politics of the region, the fact is that those states close to South Africa regard Pretoria as the major external threat. The sheer size of the SADF and its diverse ancillary formations in Namibia, and its indispensible support for proxy groups (sometimes in direct contradiction of international agreements solemnly undertaken by its government), cause alarm in nearby capitals. What is more, South Africa has frequently used its forces beyond its borders with little regard for international law and practice.

Now South Africa's capability to project power further afield is enhanced. In November 1986 it was announced that Israel had supplied two converted

Boeing 707 in-flight refuelling tankers to the SADF. This enables the South African air force to strike at any African city up to the equator and beyond. The range of South Africa's Cheetah and Mirage combat aircraft now exceeds 2,000 kilometers.

Angola stands ready to make good on its 1984 offer to implement a Cuban withdrawal from the southern part of the country if Washington would agree to stop supporting UNITA and to press South Africa to withdraw its forces from Angolan border regions. In exchange, Angola would deploy the Cubans north of the Benguela railway, fully 375 miles north of the Namibian border, clearly posing little threat to either South Africa or the UNITA base at Jamba.

Partly as a response to Soviet involvement and the breakdown of détente, partly in an effort to play a more active mediatory role, and partly as an adjunct to American policy in the Middle East, the Persian Gulf, and the Indian Ocean, the United States has become more militarily and diplomatically ambitious in Africa. The military thrust is toward the Horn and Egypt, which have been included in the command responsibilities of the rapid deployment force. In 1984 that force was reorganized as the United States Central Command (USCENTCOM). Facilities for this force have been negotiated with Morocco, Egypt, Liberia, Somalia, and Kenya to complement its more extensive facilities in Diego Garçia and Oman.

In addition, the United States has begun to compete with the USSR as a major supplier of arms to African states. Egypt is the chief recipient, but Morocco, the Sudan, Kenya, and Somalia are also major buyers. In southern Africa, the policy of "constructive engagement," especially during its efflorescent period in the early 1980s, meant that South Africa could more easily purchase "gray" area and "dual-use" equipment. Restrictions were relaxed for transfering military and policing technologies to South Africa, not always using official channels. America's role in encouraging South Africa to insist on Cuban troop withdrawal from Angola first, before settlement in Namibia, contributed to militarizing the region into the 1990s. The "Reagan Doctrine," which asserts that the United States will support insurgencies against what are regarded as pro-Soviet regimes in the Third World, provides the rationale for assistance to UNITA and possibly to Renamo in the future. The decision to assist UNITA represents an admission that the diplomacy of "constructive engagement" failed (in the field and in Washington), was never fully activated, or was, in fact, a mask for the tilt toward South Africa.[22]

Where Soviet involvement tends to be overt and extensive, American involvement (other than arms sales and military training) seems to lean toward the covert. Soviet ideology is at ease with intervention. The use of force is justified by history. Liberal tradition in the United States, however, tends to undermine interventionary behavior. Hoffman, 20 years ago, pointed to an American turn of mind that to this day is reflected in American policy toward the Contras in Central America, the Afghan rebels, and UNITA in Angola. "American intervention will be," he wrote, "so to speak, ashamed of itself. Not only will it hide behind the fig-leaf of alleged noninterference, but it will be emasculated by the piecemeal, technical process by which it is undertaken. Once again pragmatism becomes a refuge: expert assistance, administrative advice, and some secret shenanigans express the limit of our daring." The policy of aid to the Contras brings out a good deal of this sense of indecision and ambiguity, as does the tendency towards covert operations rather than unsure public ones.[23]

Although Africa has become an important cockpit of military confrontation for the superpowers, and although the various regions of Africa have been incorporated into the strategic planning in Washington and Moscow, the fact remains for both superpowers that other global regions take precedence in planning, deployment, and risk-taking. In official statements the Soviet Union, for example, rejects the idea that conflict in southern Africa is a manifestation of superpower rivalry. According to Viktor Goncharov, a Soviet Africanist, "For some people in the USA it serves as a pretext for interference in the region, giving financial and military aid to bandit forces in Angola." Goncharov says that, in fact, the United States and the USSR have minimal interests in the region. To be sure, Goncharov does not speak for the Party. Members of the Party hierarchy and military leaders likely feel differently.[24]

American analysts at the Harare conference on regional security in 1987 agreed. They argued that in terms of strictly military and economic strategic thinking, the southern African region ranked "lowest" of all areas of the world for the United States. Nonetheless, with the revelations of secret, independent, or "private" foreign policies being conducted by those outside the normal operational machinery of government, one can almost assume that clandestine assistance to UNITA, to South Africa, and possibly to other forces involved in southern Africa and the Horn, is or has been a reality.

Interests are one thing; perceptions of interest are another. Internal problems and external rivalries, in Africa as elsewhere, are sometimes made ideological and geopolitical. That combination is explosive. Powers act upon them until perceptions become self-confirming and local conflict thereby takes on global or regional importance.

Conclusion and Recommendations

The conditions for warfare, civil and international, are widespread in Africa. Wars might erupt, anywhere, anytime. If the great powers could resolve to stay out of the conflicts, there is every hope that such wars might be settled or resolved, or that they might vanish out of exhaustion or debilitating economic and social suffering. The OAU also is keen to have Africans resolve their own disputes. The superpowers express a lack of vital interest in Africa, and yet they still want to play a role in the outcome of most major disputes there.

The Soviet Union's involvement in Ethiopia and Angola in the mid-1970s was a representation of Moscow's claim to parity with the United States as a global power. Until then, although the USSR was a nuclear force the equal of the United States, there was a feeling in Moscow that the United States did not regard the USSR as an equal as a global power. As early as 1970, Leonid Brezhnev declared: "At the present time, no questions of any importance in the world can be decided without our participation, without taking into consideration our economic and military might."[25]

Soviet policy in the Horn and southern Africa was the embodiment of the claim that the "correlation of forces" in the world had shifted in the Soviets' favor. The Carter administration was, at first, prepared to accept the claims to parity by Moscow. But, later in the administration, it looked as if the president was ready to challenge the implications of Soviet policy in implementing parity. The Reagan administration, at least verbally, rejected the Soviet claims and declared the United States' determination to resist sharing top billing with the USSR. Thus Africa, from the mid-1970s, was turned into an arena of Cold War competition. The effect has been to prolong and enlarge disputes, to escalate and intensify fighting, and to make resolution more important and yet more difficult. Each superpower has coalition partners or political favorites (sometimes movements, sometimes governments) scattered around the continent. Thus virtually any inter-state or major civil war can become a Cold War contest.

Yet it is not simply a matter of the superpowers imposing themselves on hapless Africans. African politicians and movements actively search for help. They forge relationships with other African governments. Complex linkages of support and obligation are developed. Patron-client relationships emerge on an international scale. A state that is a client of a great power may be, itself, a patron of a lesser power. African clients of non-African states may be prepared to do favors for their patron by assisting militarily other African governments, thereby cultivating a clientelist relationship.

The USSR, the United States, and other African governments are only too ready to be of assistance—for a price. Bernard Magubane notes that: "The political economy in Africa can only be understood in terms of the relation of various African countries to the international power structure and the social classes this power structure reproduced within the dominated formations." While this may be too mechanistic and exceptions can be found (e.g. USSR support for Amin in Uganda), a similar assertion may be made about warfare in Africa.[26]

Conflict in Africa draws the militarily powerful states like blood attracts sharks. And they are drawn to support those partners with whom they tend to share ideological and class interests. The capacity of aggrieved and weakened groups to organize transnational networks to support their causes and their demands carries with it the capacity to broaden wars and to make settlement difficult. As Brown argues so cogently:

> Finding ways of allowing underrepresented groups and movements to prosecute their demands in international forums, negotiating arenas, and adjudicatory bodies—giving them hope to obtain redress without having to resort to violence and terrorism—may well be as important a challenge to contemporary statesmanship as the direct mitigation of conflict between the superpowers.[27]

Despite all the tendencies described in the body of this chapter, localized purely African wars have a tendency to burn themselves out. Limited resources, problems of logistics, pressure from the OAU and other governments, lack of popular support for the war, costly ramifications, such as refugees and governmental instability, opportunity costs with regard to more important issues on the state agenda, all lead to efforts to terminate the wars. Governments unable to resolve disputes tend to fall.

It is the Cold War and the involvement of the external powers, including African governments, that raise the intensity and extensity of the wars. And this makes resolution very difficult. Thus, timing is all important. If a war should break out at the time when détente between the United States and the USSR is flourishing, or at a time when the superpowers are already deeply committed to costly military campaigns elsewhere, a local war is more likely to remain exclusively an African undertaking. If, however, the superpowers are ready to support and encourage the various parties, or if one or more of the actors identify already with one or the other superpower, a symmetry of sorts sucks in both superpowers.

At present, only West and Equatorial Africa seem remote from superpower commitments of this sort. So it may be too late, barring a reestablishment of détente, or a Soviet preoccupation with domestic economic affairs or bloc political affairs, to keep Africa's wars separate from the East-West conflict.

It is in the interest of the United States to do all that it can to reduce the levels of violence and warfare in Africa. United States policy should seek to help African economies to grow and develop in order to become viable markets for trade, investment, and reliable sources of raw materials. Monies and skills diverted to military activity jeopardize the basic economic and social goals of state. Moreover, wars disrupt economic and social activity and add immeasurably to the social costs of survival. It follows that, by devising effective programs to stimulate economic growth and development in Africa, the United States may help reduce the vulnerability of African states to violent revolution and civil unrest. Such policies might also reduce the likelihood for foreign intervention and military competition.

Compared to the Soviet Union and some West European states, the United States has not been a major source of weapons for Africa, except for a few countries. Nor have United States military forces been directly involved in Africa, except for instructional and advisory roles. There have been some roles for the CIA and secret specialized forces, but covert and overt military assistance does not come easily to a people that purports to favor peaceful and popular resolution of international and domestic conflict.

In contrast, the Soviet Union has few successes in Africa independent of regimes that have been afforded large-scale military assistance and sales. Moscow's strong suit in Africa, insofar as it has one, is military support. That is not the United States's strong suit. The United States, therefore, would benefit by trying to alter the choice of foreign policy "weapons." It is important that while the United States should back off from applying Cold War interpretations to all foreign policy as well as domestic foreign issues, the military dimension is one where there is a confluence of aims. A reduction of regional tension and fighting has both a practical and a Cold War advantage for most African governments and for the United States.

It would make sense for the United States to try to persuade other arms suppliers to reduce their levels of arms trade with Africa. Such a proposal represents a reinstitution of a policy put forward early in the administration of Jimmy Carter. From 1977 to 1979 the United States tried to negotiate an agreement with the Soviet Union to limit arms transfers to the Third World. Africa was to be central to that scheme. But the Soviet Union preferred to emphasize limiting flows to the Middle East, and it insisted that other European weapons-manufacturing states be included in an arrangement. The Europeans were reluctant to cooperate. The United States wanted to avoid Soviet input into Middle East policy, and the African leaders, themselves, were opposed to outsiders establishing policy in Africa against their wishes. So the Carter plan got nowhere. The idea didn't work then, but it just might work in the next decade. Now that the USSR is preoccupied with domestic economic and political issues, and with Afghanistan and eastern Europe, the timing might be right.

It is important for us to back off from applying East-West or Cold War interpretations to all foreign policy issues in Africa whenever possible. Since the military dimension of policy tends to draw in the great powers, a deemphasis of military activity would make sense for the United States.

There is no inherent reason why we must always regard Soviet foreign policy in Africa as a zero-sum game with the United States. It is worth the effort to try to figure out where our interests coincide with those of the Soviet Union, and to try to work with them to resolve outstanding grievances and disputes. White minority rule in South Africa may provide opportunities for such a policy overlap. Pretoria seeks to encourage a rigid, ideological split, and to polarize contestants along a pro-communist/anti-communist axis. They do this to force the West to assist them in their struggle against majority rule. The United States cannot benefit from such a characterization of that struggle.

Existing African international organizations, especially the Organization of African Unity, are keen to maintain and assist South Africa's black neighbors, and to help them gain their economic independence from South Africa. American cooperation in such an enterprise would facilitate United States relations with all of Africa and would, presumably, reduce the tension and potential for violent actions. Moreover, the commitment of the United States (perhaps along with the USSR, although this is not imperative) to the economic well-being of the Front Line States might deter South Africa from striking out preemptively or without provocation across its borders.

The OAU seems anxious to mediate in a number of intra-African conflicts. The Libya-Chad border claims, the fighting in the Western Sahara, and the southern Sudanese secession provide the OAU with opportunities to enhance its stature and to provide a vehicle for resolution peacefully. African states need help and encouragement in finding ways for aggrieved parties and unrepresented groups and movements to pursue their demands peacefully. The United States also benefits when they seek redress without resorting to violence and terrorism. The Carter administration played such a role in the Zimbabwean settlement from 1978 to 1980. It could do so again. The United States should assist the OAU in any way it can to resolve these conflicts.

In the long run, an economic and conciliatory role is for the United States less costly than military involvement. And it is less likely to precipitate Soviet military incursion, a response that has proven to be effective in competing with the United States.

Notes

1. See Andrew L. Ross, "Dimensions of Militarization in the Third World," *Armed Forces and Society,* XIII (1987), 561-78. For excellent background, see: William J. Foltz and Henry S. Bienen (eds.), *Arms and the African: Military Influences on Africa's International Relations* (New Haven, 1985), 171-93.
2. 1968 data from: U.S. Arms Control and Disarmament Agency (ACDA), *World Military Expenditures and Arms Transfers, 1968-1977* (Washington, D.C., 1979), 70. 1984 data from: ACDA, *World Military Expenditures and Arms Transfers, 1986* (Washington, D.C., 1987), 60. Figures do not include Egypt.
3. ACDA, *Expenditures, 1986,* Table I.
4. Joseph Schumpeter, *Imperialism and Social Classes: Two Essays* (New York, 1955), 64-65.
5. Pamela S. Falk, "Cuba in Africa," *Foreign Affairs,* LV (1987), 1077.
6. Saadia Touval, *The Boundary Politics of Independent Africa* (Cambridge, Mass., 1972). A summary of African conflicts from 1975-1980 lists 29 conflicts. All but 11 are in the regions mentioned as exceptions above. Only two of these, the Chadian civil war and the Uganda-Tanzanian war, were major violent clashes. Amadu Sesay, "The OAU and Continental Order" in Timothy M. Shaw and 'Sola Ojo (eds.), *Africa and the International Political System* (Washington, D.C., 1982), 178-85.
7. See James N. Rosenau, "Foreign Intervention as Adaptive Behavior," in John Norton Moore (ed.), *Law and Civil War in the Modern World* (Baltimore, 1974), 129-51.
8. ACDA, *Military Expenditures, 1968-1977,* Table I; ACDA, *Military Expenditures, 1986,* Table I. See also Chapter 10.
9. ACDA, *Military Expenditures, 1986,* 60-61.
10. See Fred T. Sai, "Population and Health: Africa's Most Basic Resource and Development Problem," in Robert J. Berg and Jennifer Seymour Whitaker (eds.), *Strategies for Development* (Berkeley, 1986), 129-52.
11. Data from ACDA, *Military Expenditures, 1986,* Table I. Data on South Africa are from my own calculations, which include larger numbers of ready reserves. A discussion of the utility of the concept "region"

appears in Kenneth W. Grundy, "The Impact of Region on Contemporary African Politics," in Gwendolen M. Carter and Patrick O'Meara (eds.), *African Independence: The First Twenty-five Years* (Bloomington, 1985), 97-125.

12. ACDA, *Military Expenditures, 1986,* Table I.

13. On the Horn, see Paul Watson, "Arms and Aggression in the Horn of Africa," *Journal of International Affairs,* XL (1986), 159-76; Robert F. Gorman, *Political Conflict in the Horn of Africa* (New York, 1981); the survey by Bernard Schechterman, "Horn of Africa Liberation Movements," *Middle East Review,* XIX (1986), 47-60. For the application of the concept of contagion to military coup attempts see David L. Huff and James M. Lutz, "The Contagion of Political Unrest in Independent Black Africa," *Economic Geography,* L (1974), 352-67; Stuart Hill and Donald Rothchild, "The Contagion of Political Conflict in Africa and the World," *Journal of Conflict Resolution,* XXX (1986), 716-35.

14. George Modelski, "Kautilya: Foreign Policy and International System in the Ancient Hindu World," *American Political Science Review,* LVIII (1964), 549-60.

15. Michael Klare, "The Arms Trade and the Third World: Changing Patterns in the 1980s," paper presented to the conference on Militarisation in the Third World, Queen's University, Kingston, Ontario, January 15-17, 1987; Marek Thee (ed.), *Arms and Disarmament: SIPRI Findings* (Oxford, 1986), 46-47.

16. Stephanie G. Neuman, "The Arms Trade in Recent Wars: The Role of the Superpowers," *Journal of International Affairs,* XL (1986), 77-97. See also Noel Koch, "U.S. Security Assistance to the Third World: 'Time for a Reappraisal'," 43-57; Rejan Menon, "Soviet Arms Transfers to the Third World: Characteristics and Consequences," 59-79, both in the same issue.

17. Joseph P. Smaldone, "Foreign Arms and African Armies: Exploring the Limits of Soviet and American Influence," paper presented at the annual meeting of the African Studies Association, Boston, December 7-10, 1983, Tables 2 and 3.

18. Robin Luckham, "Militarization and Conflict in Africa," in Thee, *Arms and Disarmament,* 280.

19. Kenneth W. Grundy, *Guerrilla Struggle in Africa: An Analysis and Preview* (New York, 1971).

20. J. Bowyer Bell, *The Myth of the Guerrilla: Revolutionary Theory and Malpractice* (New York, 1971).

21. Falk, "Cuba in Africa"; *Washington Post,* July 9, 1987, A37.

22. Signe Landgren, *Embargo Disimplemented: A Case Study of South Africa's Military Industry* (Oxford, 1987); Michael T. Klare, "Evading and Embargo: Illicit U.S. Arms Transfers to South Africa," *Journal of International Affairs,* XXXV (1981), 15-18; Thomas Conrad, "South Africa Circumvents Embargo," *Bulletin of the Atomic Scientists* (1986), 8-13.

23. The quotation is from Stanley Hoffman, *Gulliver's Troubles, or the Setting of American Foreign Policy* (New York, 1968), 203-04.

24. "Soviet Policy in Southern Africa," *Work in Progress,* 48 (July 1987), 3-7.

25. Brezhnev is quoted in Morris Rothenberg, *The USSR and Africa: New Dimensions of Soviet Global Power* (Miami, 1980), 6.

26. Bernard Magubane, "The Evolution of the Class Structure in Africa," in Peter C.W. Gutkind and Immanuel Wallerstein (eds.), *The Political Economy of Contemporary Africa* (Beverly Hills, 1976), 185.

27. Seyom Brown, *The Causes and Prevention of War* (New York, 1987), 229.

12: Africa's Ethnic Conflicts and Their Implications for United States Policy

BY DONALD ROTHCHILD

It is misleading to assert, as so many impressionistic observers have been inclined to do, that politicized ethnicity necessarily leads to intense conflicts in Africa. Such generalizations obscure the fact that in many socially pluralistic countries Africans have successfully kept intergroup conflicts at manageable levels, developing norms, conventions, customs, and codes of procedures which have the effect of promoting political exchange and reciprocity among competing group interests. In the Ivory Coast, Cameroon, Kenya, Zambia, and elsewhere, ethnic representatives have been included in the central cabinet and the high party executive committee, where they have negotiated informally over the share of state-controlled posts and fiscal resources to be allocated to their constituencies.[1] Clearly, in situations where the state has emerged as an effective conflict mediator, interacting on a regular basis with the intermediaries of ethnic groups and the spokesmen for other economic and social interests, the result has been to keep conflict within the political system. As a result of this process, largely negotiable demands have been channeled along predetermined lines and ethnic interests have been accorded a degree of legitimacy and autonomy. Conflicts do emerge, but within the established state system. And by remaining an essentially domestic concern, they make interventions by external actors unwarranted and inappropriate.

The important subject of state mediation and its contribution to regularized state-society relations will not be dealt with here in a direct manner. Rather this chapter will focus on those more unique types of interactions which lead to the internationalization of conflicts having an ethnic dimension. It will begin by focusing upon the brittleness of the domestic norms of intergroup reciprocity in contemporary Africa since such weaknesses create the conditions in which intense conflict and political instability become manifest. Such deep-seated conflicts all too often cannot be contained within the state system or even the surrounding region, but spill over into the world at large. In a global environment information quickly traverses state lines and all conflicts are potential subjects for great power contention; not surprisingly, therefore, countries such as the United States frequently become drawn into the fray, indirectly or directly, as a consequence of élite perceptions of national interest, of public shock over the consequences of violence, or of identification with the cause of one of the political actors. After examining the internationalization process, it is but a short step to the main thrust of the chapter: that is, the ways Africa's ethnic conflicts have had an impact on United States policy, and the manner of the American response. Finally, the conclusion discusses some operating guidelines for appropriate United States actions in these kinds of conflict situations.

Old Connections Under Strain

Regularized patterns of political relations among state, ethnic, and other interest group representatives within a single- or no-party structure are under increasing strain in Africa. These informal relationships involve a complicated web of reciprocities among élites at the top of the political system. In the case of the ethnic intermediaries, each lives a precarious political existence, for he must negotiate on a continuous basis both with political factions at the local level, and with state élites and other interest representatives at the political center. The intermediary's long-term survival depends on an ability to deliver on the informal bargains struck at the local level and the political center: that is, he or she must encourage minimal compliance with state regulations on the part of his or her constituents, and ensure that the state allocates a "fair" share of public posts and resources to his or her constituents.

Various reasons can be advanced to explain the intermediary's increasing difficulties in meeting the dual claims of élites at the center and constituents at home. First, and most obviously, Africa's economic recession makes it more difficult than ever to allocate resources on a fair or proportional basis. The structure of state institutions acts to complicate the distributive process. Because the state tends to be overcentralized and overexpanded, it often consumes the bulk of the resources extracted from the productive sectors of the economy. The consequence is to leave the state with little additional surplus for development, especially in the rural hinterland. Where central government resources are insufficient to meet reasonable claims, governments with limited capabilities may take advantage of the lower demands put forward by the relatively disadvantaged ethnoregional and class interests in the rural areas to direct scarce resources to the more favored or productive parts of the country. The resulting economic desperation can heighten political inequity and frustration in the already disadvantaged areas.

Second, where the political institutions of the state lack the fiscal and skilled manpower resources required to implement their programs, the resulting frustration and disappointment may lead to heightened competition among the various élite representatives. As resources shrink, highly politicized élites press their demands on the state more insistently than ever. All too frequently, this leads to a decline in élite cohesion at the political center, complicating the process of political negotiations and exchanges. Alternatively, a process of "disengagement" has become commonplace. As Naomi Chazan points out, "[t]he whittling away of the preeminence of state institutions perforce redirects attention away from the central arena to other, usually sub-national, units of socioeconomic and political exchange." The strengthening of the informal economy compensates, in part, for the decline in state capacity. To the extent that various social units can cope on their own, securing only the barest support from the state, they are inclined to look inward, creating their own self-sustaining opportunities, and to establish only minimal linkages outward to the authorities at the political center.[2]

Third, in terms of social norms and relationships, the understood rules of the game have, with the passage of time, become enfeebled in certain countries. The élites that came to power at independence, with their shared memories of a common struggle, have often been succeeded by new leaders who do not necessarily share in the same informal practices of reciprocity. The result may well be to undercut the older system of consensus politics, making moderation and political exchange among élites more difficult to sustain. As Manfred Halpern puts it, connections are in the process of breaking down, forcing people in many parts of the world to live with "incoherence" as a way of life. This process was painfully evident in General Idi Amin's Uganda and in Chad in the early 1980s, where the breakdown of the state, above all, involved a collapse of the rules regulating societal interactions. The frail connections among élites and among the groups they represent have weakened noticeably, causing many people to play down their cross-cutting attachments and to retreat to the safety of their communal "containers." Paradoxically, then, at the very point that some people were reaching out for broadened cultural and social opportunities, accepting new meanings and the reality of multiple identities, they found themselves forced by the prevailing societal incoherence back into their old parochial connections.[3]

What all this means, in certain situations at least, is a decline in the persistent and recurrent relations among state leaders and the representatives of various social groups. Societal incoherence leads some members of the public to retreat from modern sector competition; they therefore seek out economic activities in the informal sector and accept the narrow community focus that such modes of production encourage. Such tendencies underscore just how aloof state institutions have become and how incapable they are of regulating societal activities, especially in the hinterland areas. Moreover, the increasing fragility of intergroup norms and relationships promotes cleavages among sections which may become the source of aggravated tensions over time. In such circumstances, inhibitions to effective governance and the expansion of domestic conflicts across state lines frequently become apparent for all to see.

The Internationalization of Ethnic and Nationality Conflicts

Where conflicts having an ethnic dimension become intense, a shift in the nature of collective demands and in the style of state-societal politics occurs. Quite obviously, a change takes place in the nature of group demands and in the way these demands are articulated. Elite intermediaries shift their approach from making negotiable claims for distributable resources within the political system to more broad-based claims for territory, or the preservation of group identity within or outside the political system.

Indicative of the kind of politics involved here are the repeated demands made by African ethnic or nationality leaders for the self-determination of a people or a territorial sub-unit. In contrast to the calls for more balanced civil service appointments, inclusion in the ruling coalition, or greater use of the proportionality principle in making fiscal allocations, the demands for self-determination (i.e., the right of a culturally distinct people to enter into autonomous political and social relations with other autonomous peoples and state officials) are often inelastic, uncompromising, and not easily negotiated within the framework of the state. In black-led Africa (Biafra, Eritrea, Katanga, Western Sahara), the spokesmen for communal interests usually advance their claims to self-determination in territorial-specific terms. The concept of ethnoregionalism is utilized to embrace both the subjective of peoplehood and the objective of territoriality. The subjective concerns of the group reinforce the objective interests of a political sub-unit (often multi-ethnic in composition), making for powerful symbolic and substantive claims which cannot be dismissed lightly by ruling élites at the political center. In those situations where legal adjustments and political concessions prove insufficient to mollify the ethnoregional claim for autonomy and control, it seems possible to anticipate increasingly intense conflicts, even wars, between the state and social groups. These, in turn, can be expected to weaken further the norms and understandings linking élites together in the contemporary African polities.[4]

In white-dominated South Africa, self-determination takes on a racial dimension. Although the social boundaries tend to be wider in a racially stratified society such as South Africa or colonial Rhodesia than in the ethnically stratified societies of black Africa, the two forms of stratification nonetheless share many characteristics and can be regarded, for our purposes, as congruent with one another. In South Africa, self-determination generally lacks the aspect of territoriality associated with black Africa's sub-regional struggles. It involves, in essence, a bitter struggle for power between a white minority identity group, presided over by an Afrikaner-led machine, and a black identity group which is denied self-determination—i.e., the full and equal rights of citizenry. The conflict is less one of legitimate interests, which are negotiable within an accepted political order, than one over which set of organizing principles will prevail.

The demand for ethnic or national self-determination, with the basic challenge that this poses to the state and its set of organizing principles, is not without its effects on the style of politics that will emerge in the country affected. Whether or not the call for ethnic or national self-determination will actually lead to high conflict depends upon the context in which the demand is advanced. Such factors as the history of group interactions, the memories that groups hold, and the way in which state leaders respond to legitimate ethnoregional claims, obviously have an effect on the intensity of conflict. Where state leaders react insensitively or display repressive tendencies, they will more than likely provoke adamant resistance in the periphery and possibly, as in South Africa, become the source of escalating conflict over time. Moreover, where the demand for self-determination in black-led Africa is perceived in an "externalist" sense (that is, those peoples calling for self-determination view group relations in threatening terms and consequently opt for separate statehood as the only reliable guarantee of group survival), the struggle is likely to be protracted and possibly lead to military encounters, as in Biafra, the Sudan, and Eritrea.[5]

Africa has surely had its share of totalist perceptions and intransigent conflicts. For many Eritreans and Southern Sudanese, the necessity for sovereign statehood lies precisely in their situation of presumed powerlessness as numerical minorities. Emphasizing the menacing element in intergroup relations, minority spokesmen perceive any concessions to the state as opening the way to new demands by the regime in power at the political center. These separatist leaders resist proposed "internalist" compromises (that is, those viewing group relations as conflict-prone but allowing for negotiation and compromise within the existing state structure on such issues as regional autonomy, proportionality, and inclusion in the dominant coalition). Those perceiving the conflict in essentialist terms are likely to view such compromises as insufficient, leading them to insist instead on absolute formulas providing for sovereign statehood. As in other parts of the world—Sri Lanka, Lebanon, Spain, and Northern Ireland—the results of such intense conflicts are not only destructive of life and property but also of the intricate web of reciprocities and relations that are the basis for genuine community.

All this is not without significance for countries outside the African continent. Thus a global superpower, particularly one with a relatively open foreign policy process such as the United States, often finds that it has little choice but to become involved, at least in a minimal way, in many of the world's conflicts. Certainly, this is by no means inevitable, as the ethnic conflicts in Burundi and Zanzibar made quite clear. In these cases, where such factors as territorial change, strategic centrality, or East-West competition were not critical, American policymakers avoided direct engagement, despite the fact that glaring human rights abuses occurred.

Why, then, did American officials become actively engaged in the ethnically (or racially) related disputes of Biafra, the Sudan, Rhodesia (now Zimbabwe), and South Africa? In part, this reflects domestic group demands. Concerned American citizens, shocked over the widespread starvation and lack of basic medical supplies that affected Biafra at the time of the Nigerian civil war, pressed their government to take swift action to ease the suffering. Moreover, as a state embracing many nations, the United States has citizens from all corners of the globe. Hence every major conflict having an ethnic or nationality dimension in Africa or elsewhere is likely to have its local champions and to result in a new flow of immigrants to North American shores. A limited number of educated and skilled Biafrans, Asians from eastern Africa, Eritreans, and whites from South Africa have repeated a precedent set by others through the years. The pressures these ethnic compatriots exert on American policymakers over time, either in defense of their beleaguered kinsmen still residing in their countries of origin or in opposition to an oppressive regime there (for example, the Eritreans or the Southern Sudanese), may possibly come to prove quite compelling in the future.

On the South African issue, pressure has mounted from churches, universities, human rights groups, and black American organizations—making accommodative approaches such as the Reagan administration's foreign policy of "constructive engagement" unacceptable, and some limited diplomatic and economic sanctions inevitable. The consequences of democracy, as the South African case shows, are to open wide the channels of communication to public influences. America's educated élite, fresh with memories of its own country's history of racial arrogance, has recoiled strongly, as it should, from all manifestations of apartheid and insisted on a course aimed at increasing the costs of Pretoria's defiant posture. Its multi-ethnic character has led it to become more embroiled in this conflict than any other ethnically-related dispute on the African continent. The same phenomenon of public influence on a sectional conflict overseas has been apparent with respect to the Northern Ireland and Cyprus conflicts. Therefore, despite the misgivings expressed by professional diplomats, United States political leaders find that when their domestic public becomes aroused they cannot remain aloof for long from African or other ethnic and nationality disputes. As they respond to various public appeals, they find themselves drawn, indirectly or directly, into internal political struggles and wars which might be viewed by detached observers as lying outside their country's vital interests.

In addition to these domestic urgings, the inclination to become involved in Africa's ethnic and nationality conflicts arises from a number of diplomatic and strategic concerns: the global orientation of American policymakers in the post-World War II era and their apparent preference for supporting the territorial integrity of African states (the Congo, the Sudan). What seems apparent when examining Africa's most intense conflicts having an ethnic or nationality dimension (in Biafra, Eritrea, the Ogaden, Southern Sudan, Katanga, Western Sahara, Rhodesia-Zimbabwe, Namibia, Angola, and South Africa) is that they all have become internationalized at some stage of the dispute. External powers may become enmeshed in the internal ethnic and nationality disputes of other countries, either through commission or omission. Thus foreign states have at times given critically important diplomatic and financial support as well as equipment and supplies to self-determination movements, providing them with indispensable safe sanctuaries, publicity, recognition, protection, and advocacy of their causes at international forums, and even active military intervention on their behalf. On the other hand, by extending diplomatic, economic, and military support to regimes in power (for example, Haile Selassie's Ethiopia, Morocco, and, until recently, South Africa), they have increased the ruling governments' capacity for prolonged struggle or repression of dissent. Either way, African and other civil conflicts have tended over time to spill over into the international arena, complicating international alliances and leading to contradictions in terms of foreign policy objectives.

Here the case of the United States affords an insight into the ways in which a distant North American power has become entwined with Africa's domestic disputes. In Eritrea, where the United States maintained important military facilities as well as a close working relationship with the Selassie government, American officials, seeking to establish a policy on the disposition of this former Italian colony, did not flinch from emphasizing United States strategic interests as against the values of Eritrean self-determination. Former Secretary of State Dean Acheson, in a telegram to the American Consul in Asmara in April 1950, described the United States position on Eritrea as "favor[ing] union eastern part with Ethiopia and Western Province with [the] Sudan." Later, as the Anglo-American plan on incorporation ran into strong opposition at the United Nations, United States officials moved, for pragmatic reasons, to support a federal-type compromise that would link all of Eritrea as a unit to Ethiopia. At the time, the United States received the Emperor's warm appreciation for its efforts on his behalf; Ethiopia's head of state, in a gesture of reciprocity, made it clear to American representatives that he looked forward to a continuing

United States military presence in Eritrea after the federation was implemented. However, the long-term consequences of this tilt toward the Selassie regime have proved costly in years afterwards. Not only did it gain the enmity of the Eritreans who resented the leading role of the United States in championing the federal solution at the United Nations, but the support for Selassie linked the United States strategically with the old order in Addis Ababa, most particularly through the training and equipping of Ethiopia's armed forces. To be sure, United States expenditures on the Ethiopian military were modest by subsequent standards (between 1953 and 1970, total United States military aid to Ethiopia amounted to an estimated $305 million), but they were nonetheless important to the stability and performance of the Selassie regime. By the way that the United States-backed Ethiopian army suppressed nationalist movements in Eritrea and elsewhere, it came to symbolize the suppression of class and nationality interests in the country at large—until Selassie was overthrown and the new regime changed course, including the forging of new alliances with the East bloc countries.[6]

United States involvement is also evident in other African ethnic and nationality disputes, partly to promote territorial integrity and partly to pursue global strategic interests. For example, following the formal resumption of relations with the Sudan in July 1972, the United States did try, in an informal manner, to influence Gaafar Nimeiri to adopt a positive policy on Southern Sudanese issues. During the late 1970s and early 1980s, it not only opposed the redivision of the South and the application of the Sharia law, but it placed limits on the kind of military equipment that it provided to Sudanese forces. The restrictions on the use of military aid began to ease around the time that Colonel John Garang, the Sudan People's Liberation Army (SPLA) guerrilla leader, refused to negotiate in earnest with the Transitional Military Council in the spring of 1985. Later, as Garang's meeting with the prime minister, Sadiq al-Mahdi, proved unproductive and a civilian airliner was shot down by southern-based forces, a State Department spokesman in Washington pointedly denounced the airliner's destruction and called on both parties "to settle their differences peacefully." Clearly, a shift of mood had taken place in Washington, prompted partly by a feeling that the democratically elected al-Mahdi regime deserved support, and partly by its irritation with the SPLA for its willingness to rely increasingly upon Ethiopia and the Soviet Union for military backing. The consequences of this mood change were soon evident. As those elements within the State Department who identified with the Sudanese government's objectives on maintaining national unity, by military means if necessary, gained an upper hand, the former restrictions on providing Sudanese forces with critically-needed armored vehicles and other essential equipment eased. Strategic objectives again were accorded a higher priority than other competing goals, most notably the United States commitment to the self-determination of peoples.[7]

Whereas global considerations led the United States to buttress the power of the state and its institutions in the Ethiopian and Sudanese conflicts, they inclined American policymakers, under the recent Ford and Carter administrations, to identify themselves with the processes of political change in the former colony of Rhodesia (now Zimbabwe). Although it is important not to overstate the American role in facilitating change in Rhodesia, it is nonetheless significant that United States representatives were a part of the third party diplomatic effort at all three stages of the mediatory process—Secretary of State Henry Kissinger's attempts to spur on the dialogue among local political actors by calling, in his Lusaka speech of April 1976, for all-party negotiations leading to majority rule and independence, and his two dramatic meetings with Ian Smith in Pretoria, South Africa, in September 1976; the Anglo-American Consultative Group mediation initiative in the spring and summer of 1977, offering the whites security by means of constitutional guarantees while meeting the key African nationalist demand for political power, was followed by the issuance of a set of the Anglo-American proposals which became the basis for ongoing discussions for a year or so; and the important behind-the-scenes supportive role played by the United States in the British-orchestrated all-party conference at Lancaster House in the fall of 1979. Not only did the United States House of Representatives' refusal to terminate sanctions in the summer of 1979 prevent a lessening of external pressures on the Rhodesian regime, but the United States helped to overcome a deadlock on the land issue at Lancaster House by its timely offers of financial assistance and by its quiet lobbying of the Front Line states in favor of their bringing pressure to bear on Robert Mugabe and Joshua Nkomo to agree to the United Kingdom's Lancaster House proposals. From 1976 to 1980, the United States played a significant role in the arduous process leading to Zimbabwe's independence.

International political pressures for United States involvement in ethnic conflicts are also evident in the case of South Africa. Over the years, most articulate American opinion formers have rejected South African claims that the country's race relations policies were to be regarded as a domestic matter. Describing white minority domination as a threat to international peace, a variety of American interest groups have recently urged the imposition of a broad range of diplomatic and economic sanctions intended to make the continuation of current apartheid practices more painful; by raising the costs on present practices, they seek to induce political and economic change. Pressure has been placed upon United States business and commercial firms in South Africa to ensure equal treatment for all employees and, despairing of the impact of limited reforms, liberal interest groups have gone on to urge corporate divestment.

Clearly, then, in those situations where recurrent patterns of intergroup relations are irregular and unpredictable, and where the differences among élites become intense, the conflict seems likely to spread, affecting not only the countries and people in their region and continent but the international community as well. The United States, as a major world power and one that is uniquely diverse, cannot expect to remain insulated from such disputes where its public becomes aroused. Domestic pressures to intervene combined with a policy tradition of supporting the territorial integrity of existing states and perceived global security requirements are likely to make it difficult for American decisionmakers to remain on the sidelines as mere spectators. Moreover, the internationalization of ethnic conflicts affects regional tensions (the SPLA's use of support bases inside Ethiopia) which spill over into the global arena and cause the superpowers to be drawn in. But what are the implications for United States policy of these domestic and international imperatives to become involved?

The Implications for Policy

For the reasons stated above, the United States frequently lacks the luxury of remaining aloof from Africa's ethnic and nationality conflicts, even where no vital American interest would appear to be at stake. At this point, it seems essential that we look at the ways in which the United States has been drawn into these overseas conflicts and the potential costs and benefits of these actions. I move from the most general and low cost responses to such conflicts to those entailing specific policies and holding out the possibility of relatively high costs for an external actor.

1. *The Flow of Refugees.* Refugees are persons pushed from one locale to another by natural disasters, lack of economic opportunity, social privation, or political repression and instability. They may move voluntarily, or in response to directives from state officials, to another area within the state (i.e., Tigrayans in Ethiopia; Africans, Coloureds, and Indians in South Africa) or to another state in the region or beyond (Uganda's Acholi and Langi to Tanzania during Amin's period of rule; the Tutsi to Uganda; the Ogaden refugees to Somalia; the Eritreans and northern Ugandans to the Sudan; Southern Sudanese to Ethiopia; Namibians to Angola; South Africa's blacks to the Front Line countries; and so forth). Such internationalization can also be seen in the movement of East African Asians, South Africans, Biafrans, and others to the West as the conflicts in their homes of origin became intense, although the numbers and relatively high status of the refugees involved in these situations tended to be less broad and dramatic than the cases noted above. For Aristide Zolberg and his associates, refugee movements are transnational processes which are often triggered by internal social conflicts: i.e., regime changes, whether revolutionary or counter-revolutionary, and the formation of new political communities, especially the creation of a number of smaller states out of the former colonial empires. The violence and dislocation that accompanies these changes of regimes and boundaries creates insecurity for the dispossessed classes and newly exposed minority ethnic peoples, causing the old élite and the newly insecure ethnic minority peoples to make the difficult choice of whether or not to uproot themselves and to migrate abroad. This choice is likely to have a destabilizing impact on the region as a whole, something inimical to a "status quo" oriented country such as the United States. Not only do the new tensions created by these refugee flows make the development of regional resources very difficult (for example, the Nile River waters), but the displaced persons are likely to seek to avenge their perceived wrongs, participating in political activities aimed at bringing about regime changes or boundary alterations. This can prove a source of instability in the region; it can also complicate the foreign policies of receiving states overseas. Most often the means selected have been peaceful and have conformed to United States political norms. Biafrans in the United States collected substantial funds to aid the cause of their beleaguered kinsmen at home and contacted Congressmen and

other public officials in an attempt to influence them to support the cause of the secessionist movement. However, on a few other occasions, as in Sweden and Canada, there are suspicions that extreme separatists have resorted to violent deeds in an effort to even scores and to promote their objectives. The results are to place those United States policymakers seeking to reconcile regional and global interests with humanitarian concerns in a political dilemma that may be difficult at times for democracies to face.[8]

2. *Political and Military Alignment with African States.* As already noted with regard to Ethiopia and the Sudan, the imperatives of global strategy are likely to be perceived by a superpower as outweighing those of human rights considerations, especially during a Cold War period. United States officials have been quite explicit on such priorities. In his address to the United Nations General Assembly on October 16, 1952, for example, Secretary of State Acheson was frank in according a higher value to security objectives than to the "fulfillment of national and individual aspirations." This emphasis upon national security purposes leads policymakers to seek out alliance partners overseas who will promote stability in their countries and region and who can be counted upon to align themselves with the United States in critical conflict situations. It is not surprising therefore that Haile Selassie, who supported the United States on a number of issues at the United Nations and sent Ethiopian forces to Korea in the 1950s and to Zaire in the 1960s, received American military assistance as well as diplomatic support for his stance on the Eritrean question. The United States inclination to support African friends is, of course, much broader than the nationalities issue, but United States identification with the emperor's purposes on the Eritrean issue shows how this particular issue embroiled the United States in Ethiopian politics. Similarly as Sudan's President Nimieri called upon the United States for increased military backing in the face of a perceived military threat from the Soviet-supported Libyan forces of Colonel Mu'ammar al-Qaddafi, the Americans responded most generously, even though it involved the United States in difficult relations regarding the conflict in the Southern Sudan. The same point can be made regarding United States economic and military assistance for the regimes in Morocco, Zaire, Somalia, and South Africa.[9]

But assistance to these regimes, justified as it might seem on global security grounds, may entail a high political cost over time. Such aid brings the United States into close proximity with some governments disliked by large elements of their populations, majorities as well as minorities, for their repressive

tendencies, their ethnic and racial discrimination, or their tolerance of corruption. Should these regimes prove unable to repress political oppositions
or nationality and ethnic-based resistance groups, as happened in Haile
Selassie's Ethiopia, there is no guaranteeing that the new political rulers will
want to align themselves with the United States after they have assumed
power. Efforts to limit the use of American military aid to defensive purposes against external enemies rather than against the domestic opposition
elements in a country may soften the image of the United States as a patron
of authoritarian rulers. Such curbs may well have been a factor in stabiliz-
ing United States relations with the Sudan following Nimeiri's fall from
power, but it is certainly nothing that can be counted upon. What is likely
to prove critical is less what a patron power does in the way of legal restrictions or quiet behind-the-scenes pressures than what the African public
perceives, rightly or wrongly, for a power to have as its basic purpose. The
temptation to align the United States with "proven allies" is one that has
to be assessed in each situation in terms of regime practices and local power
configurations to determine whether short-run advantages appear to outweigh
long-term disadvantages.

   3. *Diplomatic Protest.* General support for a ruling coalition by no means
precludes protests by external governments of human rights violations. Hence
it is not surprising to see frequent resorts to this type of diplomatic activity
in both black and white-led Africa. Most significantly in this regard, the
United States has publicly criticized South Africa's abuse of civil liberties,
residential segregation, educational discrimination, homelands policy, and
destabilization programs in an effort to promote greater political moderation and fuller participation by ethnic groups in the economic, political, and
social life of their country. Such protests not only help to establish international standards of appropriate behavior toward ethnic and national
minorities, but they reassure the American public by giving the impression
of an active governmental involvement in correcting perceived wrongs. To
criticize the shooting down of a Sudanese airliner, the application of the South
African Group Areas Act, or the harassment of Ugandan Asians and others
by the Amin government is to show concern; however, while involving
relatively low costs, such protests tend to be of limited effectiveness. On April
20, 1987, Charles Redman, a State Department spokesman, issued a statement condemning violence in Sri Lanka and calling on all parties, especially
the militant Tamil minority, "to enter into meaningful negotiations without

delay." As in the African cases a preference for peaceful adjustment of issues was made manifest, but this criticism had little effect since it involved no apparent American commitment in the form of pressures, sanctions, or offers to mediate the dispute. Resisted as an unwarranted interference in the domestic affairs of other countries, these protests had a limited impact while creating suspicions in various quarters, at home and abroad, that the United States was not really committed to resolving the conflict.[10]

4. *External Non-Military Pressures.* A powerful country such as the United States can exert a wide array of pressures on a state seen to be abusing the civil and political rights of its disadvantaged ethnic and nationality groups. In fact, the United States, despite some reluctance on the part of various administrations, has invoked a number of measures intended to alter the behavior of such states as South Africa, Rhodesia, and (Amin's) Uganda toward their own citizens. United States pressures have included the closure of the American embassy (Uganda), the temporary cessation of bilateral aid projects (Uganda), inactivity on the part of such United States government programs as the Export-Import Bank and the Overseas Private Investment Corporation (Uganda, Rhodesia, South Africa), limitations on the use of military assistance (the Sudan), a ban on the export of military equipment (South Africa, Rhodesia, and Uganda), and embargoes on trade and investment (South Africa, Rhodesia and Uganda). In the case of Uganda, about which less is known generally, the 1978 trade embargo on coffee imports was a Congressional initiative intended to protest President Idi Amin's "savage abuses of the Uganda people." The United States had previously admitted a number of stateless Ugandan Asians into the country but was now broadening its protest of Amin's human rights violations to apply to politically disadvantaged African groups as well. By making such moves the United States was certainly refusing to subsidize ethnic discrimination and human rights violations. However, even if non-military protests weaken such regimes, they are not likely in themselves to prove decisive in changing them. Amin's regime fell before a combined invasion of Tanzanian forces and returning Ugandan troops; the Smith regime was forced to turn over power because of a military stalemate and because of unrelenting external pressures for majority rule. Over the long term, sanctions seem likely to cramp and isolate the South African regime, but it remains to be seen how critical a role they can play in bringing about political change.[11]

5. *Military Intervention.* No type of intervention in overseas conflicts having an ethnic or nationality dimension holds out the prospect of higher poten-

tial costs than an American military intervention. Not only do such interventions involve an intrusion by a powerful Western country in African affairs only decades after colonialism but they incur high financial and political costs for both the United States and its local allies. Looking back at the United States military intervention in Lebanon on the side of a pro-Western and Christian-led regime in 1958, former President Camille Chamoun, while remarking that it did halt the movement toward an intercommunal massacre, nonetheless expressed some misgivings over the dramatic nature of the United States response to the Lebanese call for United States military assistance (in all, some 2,500 troops) under the Eisenhower Doctrine. As President Eisenhower himself was reported to have said to Prime Minister Harold Macmillan the day before the landing of American forces: "he realized that it might open a Pandora's box, but the alternative course [to fail to stick by one's friends] was disastrous." In a complex and interdependent world, surely, the decision to employ military force ought to be no light matter; as subsequent events in Lebanon were to show during the Reagan period, interventions which lack clear and realizable political objectives can prove harmful to the public interest.[12]

Up to this point, the United States military role on such issues in Africa has been less significant and less direct. The United States has provided important military equipment to Jonas Savimbi's National Union for the Total Independence of Angola and in the past gave its full support to the UN mediatory effort in the Congo (Zaire) in 1962, even at the risk of hostilities which eventually led to the reintegration of Katanga province with the rest of the country. From a military standpoint, such full support included military assistance for the Congolese National Forces and a military air and sea lift in support of UN operations in the Congo. But thus far there has been no United States military action equivalent to those in Lebanon. This might change, however, should the United States decide to become more actively engaged in the affairs of southern Africa or the Horn. Moreover, in the case of South Africa, United States military intervention, whether singly or in collaboration with other powers, has been advocated should domestic deterioration (including possible acts of genocide) lead to a general threat to international peace. Certainly a continuance of government repression of the black majority appears likely to give rise to calls at home and abroad for more effective international sanctions.[13]

6. *External Mediation*. As the internal disputes of African countries become intense, threatening human lives and property as well as regional stability,

it seems logical for external powers to seek to facilitate agreements between the various conflicting parties. Often such an intermediary role represents high risk diplomacy, particularly where the mediatory power or powers have a perceived interest in the outcome. Despite their concern with the results of an agreement (to maintain a pro-Western regime in power in the Congo or to prevent Soviet expansionism and political instability in Zimbabwe), however, the United States and its allies did manage to promote integrative outcomes in such instances. In the case of South Africa, the mediatory effort has largely been a Commonwealth initiative up to this time, but the United States has been well informed as to the process and has assisted this attempt by its sanctions legislation and by its indirect pressure on the African National Congress to suspend its use of violence at the time of the 1986 Commonwealth Eminent Persons Group's attempt to set a framework for negotiations. Both the South African government and the main black nationalist leadership are in close touch with American officials, and a future role for the United States, alone or in conjunction with others, remains a real possibility.

Conclusion: Implications for United States Policy in the 1990s

As the foregoing discussion indicates, where Africa's ethnic conflicts become intense and ethnoregional units make non-negotiable demands upon the state, disputes are likely to spread across regional borders and to become broadly internationalized. In a world made increasingly interdependent by the flows of information and commerce, news of communal struggles for political and economic opportunity become common knowledge in a brief time. Quite often, the result is to link all major international actors to the particular ethnic issue of the moment. In this regard, the United States is affected as much as any major power. Its involvement follows from several overlapping factors: most particularly, the domestic pressures of its citizenry upon the United States government (especially those shocked by the terrible consequences of civil war (as in Biafra) or the ruthless denial of basic human rights to the majority African community (as in South Africa); a policy tradition of support for the territorial integrity of postcolonial states (a tradition that was given dramatic expression at the time of the Congo crisis, and then reaffirmed during the Biafran war and the crisis on the Horn); and the government's global strategic assumptions, particularly its determination to resist the alleged expansionist drives of the Soviet Union and its allies. In certain cases, where countries are remote and no East-

West dimension or territorial change is involved, the process of internationalization has not been pronounced and the United States and its general public have not felt compelled to intervene (Burundi and Zanzibar are cases in point). But in a variety of other major conflicts (Biafra, the Sudan, Ethiopia, South Africa, Rhodesia) the United States government has found itself drawn in, and in some instances, even pulled into the spreading conflict. In the current South African conflict, for example, whether the United States government votes sanctions against white minority dominance or attempts to pull back from the confrontation, it finds itself part of the conflict—both at home and abroad.

In determining its policies on ethnic and nationality conflicts, the United States government frequently prefers to play a subordinate or supporting role, allowing local actors to mediate disputes or giving the Organization of African Unity or European allies considerable scope to undertake the process of resolving a conflict. Where this is not possible and the United States government feels called upon to play a leading role, it obviously prefers to reconcile the objectives of global security, the prevention of territorial secession, and the securing of human rights and ethnic and racial self-determination. But what if a trade-off between these objectives cannot be denied? Then, as the Acheson quotation noted above indicates, security is accorded a higher value than human rights considerations. This helps to explain the continuity in United States policy choices, whether it involves a decision to support the regime currently in control, despite its handling of an ethnic or nationality issue within its own borders (Ethiopia, Morocco, the Sudan), or whether it involves a decision to work for political change, as in colonial Rhodesia or South Africa. Certainly, the decision to intervene actively in a state-society struggle has been no light matter and, from the standpoint of various administrations, has generally revealed the global security priority to be uppermost.

Yet globalist inclinations are no certain guidelines to the specific tactical decisions most appropriate in conflicts of this sort. On such questions as to whether or not to admit or assist refugees, to side with the ruling regime or its adversaries, to protest, or to invoke diplomatic, trade, or military sanctions, a global security orientation usually gives few rules of thumb to apply in particular situations. Are low-cost initiatives adequate to achieve the goals set out by the administration and to satisfy the legitimate demands of domestic and foreign publics? Or is the situation grave enough that a high cost intervention seems warranted? Clearly, there are dangers that powerful lobbies on the Washington scene (pro-Biafran, pro-African moderate in Rhodesia, pro-white

South African) will sway the United States government from a determination to assert national objectives. In light of such dangers, the most appropriate policy would normally seem to be staying above the conflict as far as possible, supporting the process and trying not to take sides. This would seem to be a major lesson of the Rhodesian settlement. In this instance, the United States played a secondary role, supporting a well orchestrated British initiative. It backed the mediation effort, not particular sets of actors within the process. The larger results have vindicated the prudence of such an approach.

But whether or not mediation is likely to be appropriate depends upon the situation at hand. An American-led mediatory initiative (as in Namibia) has been shown to be a high-risk type of diplomacy because of the way that the United States has been perceived to be drawn in and compromised by the process. The decision to lead a mediatory initiative, then, is a difficult one, and involves calculations on national interests, public reactions, the commitment of resources, the special strengths an outsider can bring to the conflict situation (i.e. whether it is in a position to influence one or more of the parties), particular weaknesses, and so forth. Perhaps, on reflection, other strategies, such as multilateral actions, indirect pressures, material and nonmaterial inducements, and so forth, will come to seem more appropriate.[14]

In this context, then, the point that must be stressed is the likelihood that the weakening of old connections within existing African states will in all likelihood lead to an increase in ethnic crises which are likely to spill over into the international arena and require a United States response. In order to make that response an appropriate one, it is necessary to determine strategies for dealing with each dispute in situational terms. Wherever possible, it seems desirable to stay above a conflict, supporting the process of conflict management taking place regionally or from the outside. What such an approach involves is a recognition that United States interests are far broader than security concerns, or the desire to pick winners, and that effective conflict management which results in a widely accepted agreement is an important value in and of itself. It is time to begin to think as systematically as possible in advance of the conflicts and crises of the 1990s about the kinds of situations in which the United States has interests and what kinds of actions, if any, are likely to be prudent.

Notes

1. These themes on the management of low intensity conflict are developed in Donald Rothchild, "Hegemonial Exchange: An Alternative Model for Managing Conflict in Middle Africa," in Dennis L. Thompson and Dov Ronen (eds.), *Ethnicity, Politics, and Development* (Boulder, 1986), 65-104; Donald Rothchild, "State and Ethnicity in Africa: A Policy Perspective," in Neil Nevitte and Charles H. Kennedy (eds.), *Ethnic Preference and Public Policy in Developing States* (Boulder, 1986), 15-61; Donald Rothchild, "Middle Africa: Hegemonial Exchange and Resource Allocation," in Alexander J. Groth and Larry L. Wade (eds.), *Comparative Resource Allocation: Politics, Performance, and Policy Priorities* (Beverly Hills, 1984), 151-80.

2. Naomi Chazan, "State and Society in Africa: Images and Challenges," in Donald Rothchild and Naomi Chazan (eds.), *The Precarious Balance: State and Society in Africa* (Boulder, 1988), 325-42.

3. Manfred Halpern, "Choosing Between Ways of Life and Death and Between Forms of Democracy: An Archetypal Analysis," *Alternatives* 12 (1987), 5.

4. Crawford Young, "Comparative Claims to Political Sovereignty: Biafra, Katanga, Eritrea," in Donald Rothchild and Victor A. Olorunsola (eds.), *State Versus Ethnic Claims: African Policy Dilemmas* (Boulder, 1983), 219; and Donald Rothchild, "Collective Demands for Improved Distributions," in Rothchild and Olorunsola, *ibid.*, 172-76.

5. Leo Kuper, *The Pity of It All* (Minneapolis, 1977); Onyeonoro S. Kamanu, "Secession and the Right of Self-Determination: An O.A.U. Dilemma," *Journal of Modern African Studies*, XII (September 1974), 355-76; United Republic of Tanzania, *Tanzania Government's Statement on the Recognition of Biafra* (Dar es Salaam, 1970). For South Africa, see also Chapter 10.

6. Acheson telegram to American Consul, Asmara, April 19, 1950, National Archives, RG 59, Box 1349; Acheson telegram to American Embassy, London, June 14, 1950, *ibid;* Peter Schwab, *Ethiopia: Politics, Economics and Society* (Boulder, 1985), 10.

7. Quoted in *New African* (London), 229 (October 1987), 22.

8. Aristide R. Zolberg, "L'influence des facteurs 'externes' sur l'ordre politique interne," in Madeleine Grawitz and Jean Leca (eds.), *Traité de Science Politique* (Paris, 1985), 567-98; Aristide R. Zolberg, Astri

Suhrke, and Sergio Aguayo, "International Factors in the Formation of Refugee Movements," *International Migration Review,* 20, 2 (1986): 151-169; Charles McC. Mathias, Jr., "Ethnic Groups and Foreign Policy," *Foreign Affairs,* LIX, 5 (1981), 996; *New York Times,* July 14, 1987, 1.

9. Letter from Warren R. Austin to Walter White, 18 December 1952, National Archives, No. 845A. 411/12-2252.
10. *New York Times,* 21 April 1987, 8.
11. *Standard* (Nairobi), September 30, 1978, 6.
12. John Foster Dulles Oral History Project, The Princeton University Library, Interview with Camille Chamoun, Beirut, 28 August 1964, 25, 46-48; Ann Whitman Diary Series, July 14, 1958, Dwight D. Eisenhower Library; and John Foster Dulles, Memorandum for President, July 15, 1958, 3 in Dulles Papers, White House Memoranda Series, Box 7, Eisenhower Library.
13. Memorandum from Joint Chiefs of Staff for Secretary of Defense, December 11, 1962, John F. Kennedy Library, National Security Files: Congo, Box No. 28A; C.C. O'Brien, "What Can Become of South Africa," *Atlantic Monthly,* 257, 3 (1986), 66.
14. Interview, Ambassador Donald F. McHenry, Washington, D.C., May 14, 1987.

The Authors

Lisa Anderson is Associate Professor of political science, and Assistant Director of the Middle East Institute, at Columbia University. She taught at Harvard University from 1981 to 1986. She received her Ph.D. in Political Science from Columbia University. She also holds an M.A. in development studies from the Fletcher School of Law and Diplomacy at Tufts University and a B.A. from Sarah Lawrence College. She has travelled widely in North Africa and the Middle East. She is the author of *The State and Social Transformation in Tunisia and Libya, 1830-1980,* (Princeton, 1986). She also writes for the *Washington Post* and the *New York Times*.

Mohamed T. El-Ashry is Vice President for Research and Policy Affairs of the World Resources Institute in Washington, D.C. A graduate of Cairo University and the University of Illinois, he previously taught at Cairo University (1966-1969), and was Professor and Chairman, Department of Environmental Sciences, Wilkes College, Pennsylvania, 1969-1975. Prior to his appointment with the World Resources Institute, he was Senior Scientist at the Environmental Defense Fund, 1975-1979, and the Director of Environmental Quality, Tennessee Valley Authority, 1979-1983. He is the editor of *Air Photography and Coastal Problems* (Stroudsburg, Pennsylvania, 1977); *Water and Arid Lands of Western United States* (New York, 1988).

Dorsey Berger is a research assistant at the World Resources Institute, and is presently an M.S. candidate at Clark University.

Michael Faber has been Director and Professorial Fellow at the Institute of Development Studies at the University of Sussex, following seven years as Director of the Technical Assistance Group of the Commonwealth Secretariat. He was educated at the University of Oxford and the University of Michigan before becoming a foreign correspondent for the *Sunday Times* (London). He is President of the United Kingdom chapter of the Society for International Development. His publications include: *Towards Economic Independence* (New York, 1971); (with Roland Brown), "Changing the Rules of the Game," *Third World Quarterly,* II, (1980), 99-119; *Sisyphus and the Mountain of Third World Debt* (New York, 1988).

Reginald Herbold Green is Professional Fellow at the Institute of Development Studies at the University of Sussex. He was educated at Whitman College and Harvard University. He has been a student of the political economy of Africa since 1960 and has spent about 13 years in Africa, while living, working, and travelling in over 30 African countries. He has served as advisor to several African governments and organizations including Tanzania, Zimbabwe, SWAPO, and SADCC, and to a number of international agencies. He has published more than 200 chapters, monographs, and books. He co-edited (with Philip Ndegwa and Leopold Mureithi) *Management for Development: Priority Themes in Africa Today* (Nairobi, 1987), 2 v.

Kenneth W. Grundy is Professor of political science at Case Western Reserve University. He was educated at Ursinus College and Pennsylvania State University. His books include *Guerrilla Struggle in Africa* (New York, 1972); *Confrontation and Accommodation in Southern Africa* (Berkeley, 1973); *Ideologies of Violence* (Columbus, 1974); *Evaluating Transnational Programs in Government and Business* (New York, 1980); *Soldiers Without Politics* (Berkeley, 1983); *The Militarization of South African Politics* (Bloomington, 1986).

Albert E. Henn is an Associate Director for Health Programs of the Harvard Institute for International Development. He directs the Institute's Health Programs. Henn is also on the faculty of the Harvard School of Public Health, where he lectures on health policy and management. A public health physician, he was educated at Michigan State, Wayne State, and Harvard

Universities and spent nine years with the United States Agency for International Development working in fifteen Francophone and eight Anglophone African countries, and in Washington, D.C. His background combines extensive experience in primary health care in Africa, familiarity with the United States Agency for International Development, experience designing rural maternal child and health and oral rehydration therapy programs, and an intimate knowledge of the international health arena. He is also the Cambridge co-ordinator for the HIID's health projects in Senegal, Chad, Djibouti, Zaire, and Cameroun.

Mark N. Katz is Assistant Professor of government and politics at George Mason University. He received a Ph.D in political science from M.I.T. He has previously held positions at the Department of State, the Brookings Institution, and the Woodrow Wilson International Center for Scholars. The main focus of his research is Soviet relations with the Third World. He is the author of *The Third World in Soviet Military Thought* (Baltimore, 1982); *Russia and Arabia: Soviet Foreign Policy toward the Arabian Peninsula* (Baltimore, 1986).

Helen Kitchen, Director of the African Studies Program at the Center for Strategic and International Studies, Washington, D.C., has been monitoring African political developments and United States policy toward Africa for three decades. Her many publications include *Some Guidelines on Africa for the Next President* (Washington, D.C., 1988); *South Africa: In Transition to What?* (New York, 1988); *Angola, Mozambique, and the West* (New York, 1987); *U.S. Interests in Africa* (New York, 1983); *The United States and South Africa: Realities and Red Herrings* (Washington, D.D., 1984); *Africa: From Mystery to Maze,* (Lexington, 1976); *Footnotes to the Congo Story* (New York, 1967). She served as the director of the Africa area study of the [Rockefeller] Commission on Critical Choices for Americans (1974-1976), and has been the editor of three widely read periodicals: *Africa Report* (1960-1968), *African Index* (1978-1982), and (since 1982) *CSIS Africa Notes.*

David Laitin is Professor of political science and Director of the Center for the Study of Industrial Societies at the University of Chicago. He was educated at Swarthmore College and University of California, Berkeley. He is the author of *Politics, Language and Thought: The Somali Experience*

(Chicago, 1977); *Hegemony and Culture: Politics and Religious Change Among the Yoruba* (Chicago, 1986); (with Said Samatar) *Somalia: Nation in Search of a State* (Boulder, 1987).

Charles N. Myers is Research Associate at the Harvard Institute for International Development, and Lecturer at the Harvard Graduate School of Education. He was educated at Dartmouth College, and at the Woodrow Wilson School of Princeton University. He spent five years as Visiting Professor on the Faculty of Public Health at Manidol University, Bangkok, Thailand. He is the author (with Dow Mongkolsmai and Nancyanne Causino) of *Financing of Health Services and Medical Care in Thailand* (Bangkok, 1985); (with Orathip Tanskul, Chanet Khumthong and Chayada Siripirom) *Community Finance of Primary Health Care in Thailand* (Bangkok, 1985); with Ricardo Galan and Daniel Luecke), *Analysis and Projection of Demand for Health Manpower in Colombia* (Bogota, 1978).

Robert I. Rotberg is Academic Vice President for Arts, Sciences and Technology at Tufts University. Prior to 1987 he was Professor of history and political science at the Massachusetts Institute of Technology and a Research Associate at the Center for International Affairs, Harvard University. A graduate of Oberlin College, Princeton University, and the University of Oxford, he previously taught at Harvard University. He is the author and editor of 30 books, including *South Africa and Its Neighbors: Regional Security and Self-Interest* (Lexington, 1985); *Namibia: Political and Economic Prospects* (Lexington, 1983); *Suffer the Future: Policy Choices in Southern Africa* (Cambridge, Mass; 1980); *Black Heart: Gore-Browne and the Politics of Multiracial Zambia* (Berkeley, 1978). He writes for the *Christian Science Monitor,* the *New York Times,* and the *Boston Globe.* He edits *The Journal of Interdisciplinary History.*

Donald Rothchild is Professor of political science at the University of California, Davis. He was educated at Kenyon College, the University of California, Berkeley, and Johns Hopkins University. He has been a visiting faculty member at universities in Uganda, Kenya, Zambia, and Ghana. In recent years, he has written or edited the following books: *Racial Bargaining in*

Independent Kenya (London, 1973); *Scarcity, Choice, and Public Policy in Middle Africa* (Berkeley, 1978); *Afro-Marxist Regimes* (Boulder, 1987); *The Precarious Balance: State and Society in Africa* (Boulder, 1988). A co-authored book, *Politics and Society in Contemporary Africa,* is forthcoming.

John Underwood is a senior economist with the International Finance Division of the World Bank. He is coordinator of the Policy and Analysis Unit in that division. He was educated at Iowa State University and the University of Minnesota. Prior to joining the World Bank in 1984, he was chief of the International Development Section of the Federal Reserve Board. He has co-authored "An Analysis of the External Debt Positions of Eight Developing Countries through 1990," *Journal of Development Economics,* XXI, (1986), 283-318; "Wage Contracting, Exchange Rate Volatility and Exchange Intervention Policy," in Jagdeep Bhandari (ed.), *Exchange Rate Management Under Uncertainty,* (Cambridge, Massachusetts, 1984); *Food Security and Food Policy in a World of Uncertainty,* (New York, 1979).

Index

BY PAT MARTIN

This index does not include: Reference matter from the footnotes, entries in the bibliography, or names cited only in the preface.

Not indexed separately: Sub-Saharan Africa, Washington, United States and Africa, U.S. Policy toward Africa except specific chapter section devoted to policy recommendations, names cited in endnotes, tables.

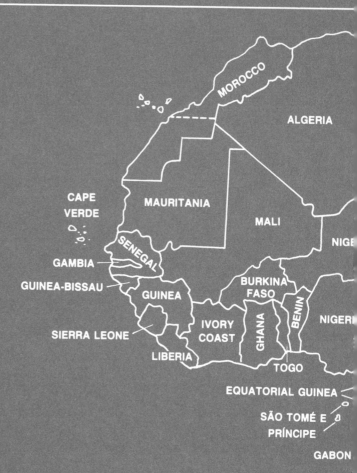

MOROCCO

ALGERIA

CAPE
VERDE

MAURITANIA

MALI

NIGE

SENEGAL

GAMBIA

GUINEA-BISSAU

GUINEA

BURKINA
FASO

BENIN

NIGERI

SIERRA LEONE

IVORY
COAST

GHANA

LIBERIA

TOGO

EQUATORIAL GUINEA

SÃO TOMÉ E
PRÍNCIPE

GABON

Africa